Ring of Hell

The Story of Chris Benoit
&
the Fall of the
Pro Wrestling Industry

By

Matthew Randazzo V

ISBN 10: 1-59777-579-7
ISBN-13: 978-1-59777-579-3
Library of Congress Cataloging-In-Publication Data Available

Book Design by: Sonia Fiore

Printed in the United States of America

Phoenix Books, Inc.
9465 Wilshire Boulevard, Suite 840
Beverly Hills, CA 90212

www.phoenixbooksandaudio.com

10 9 8 7 6 5 4 3 2 1

To Mom, Melissa, Stevie, and Cookie.

Contents

Preface

"It's a business you can't explain to anyone. They have to be in it. If you try to tell somebody what the business is like, they'll never understand. Just think if I said to you that you were going to be a wrestler:

'Well, what will I have to do?'
'You'll have to go where I send you.'
'Will I have any days off?'
'No, no.'
'Will I make a lot of money?'
'Probably not. ...And we'll want you to take these sharp pieces of razor and stick it into your face whenever we tell you to. And you're going to have to go out to the people and incite riots.'
'Will I get any hospitalization?'
'None at all, none at all.'
'Will I get a car to drive?'
'No, you'll have to drive your own car, pay your own gas.'
'What about the hotel rooms?'
'No. Stick nine of you in a room, I don't care.'
'GET ME THE JOB! I WANT TO DO THIS!'

Who would do that?"

BOBBY "THE BRAIN" HEENAN, 2005

Chapter I
The Mark

"The world [of wrestling] doesn't push you to the depths of darkness. *You* do. That drives me nuts.... It's not the world of wrestling that drove [troubled wrestlers] to alcohol, the world of wrestling that drove them to drugs. You do that to yourself."

CHRIS BENOIT IN 2004
At the time abusing steroids, painkillers, alcohol, amphetamines, and psychiatric drugs because, as he told his father, "If I want a job, I have to."

THE MOST SACRED, BEAUTIFUL THING IN THE WORLD TO CHRIS BENOIT WAS PROFESSIONAL WRESTLING. Among his admiring colleagues, it was considered an indisputable fact that no one in the world took "the art" of pro wrestling more seriously. Performing in a wrestling ring was the transcendent creative high that Benoit dedicated his life to chasing. Benoit was addicted to that in-ring euphoria, and his obsessive hunger for his fix warped his personality and his priorities. He made sacrifices to advance and later to sustain his career that most people would not make for country, creed, love, or wealth. By most accounts a thoughtful and compassionate man in his private life, Benoit within the confines of pro wrestling was a self-righteous fool who repeatedly jumped headfirst onto a hard canvas until all four lobes of his brain sported brown polka dots of dead, rotting tissue. Benoit was wrestling's tortured artist; he tortured himself and called it art.

Benoit dispatched his professional duties according to a medieval code of honor founded on sacrifice, humiliation, and the ritual self-infliction of pain as punishment for every flaw. Behind the scenes, this hysterical fanaticism motivated Benoit on one occasion to threaten to intentionally cripple himself on national TV if he was given a storyline he didn't like. While training in Japan, Benoit suffered physical abuse worthy of the Inquisition in order to be taken seriously as a wrestler. When it was his turn as a veteran to discipline the "Young Boys," Benoit beat, choked, ridiculed, and humiliated the rookies.

Somehow, this otherwise normal and kind family man believed that the most important thing in the world was his rank in pro wrestling's bizarre, militaristic backstage brotherhood. One pro wrestling legend and longtime coworker of Benoit's told me that Benoit "wanted to be the guy that all the other guys pointed to and said 'He's the best.' He wanted 'locker room respect' as being the 'best of the boys' more than anything else in life. He was possessed by the desire." The sacrifices Benoit made to achieve this nebulous goal cannot be defined as anything other than insane.

Known as an uncommonly doting and gentle father, Chris rarely saw his children so that he could make every date of his outlandish international touring schedule. Married to a woman with legendary sex appeal, Benoit left her at home to spend thousands of monotonous, lonely nights in dreary hotel rooms with stained carpets. A financially secure millionaire who lived in a mansion, Benoit left his luxurious home every week to pilot rental cars on interminable, transnational road trips with a junkie traveling partner who he dared not trust with any of the driving responsibilities. The friend of countless wrestlers who suffered fatal heart attacks due to steroid abuse, the naturally slight Benoit nonetheless knowingly poisoned his cardiovascular and endocrine system with the enormous amounts of bodybuilding drugs needed to sustain his wrestling career. Benoit sacrificed his relationship with his family and his quality of life so that he could perform in the wrestling ring, and, when Chris Benoit performed, he did his best to sacrifice what was left of his health and sanity.

In the words of former World Wrestling Entertainment[1] (WWE) writer Dan Madigan, "Benoit always left it *all* in the ring. He was never satisfied unless he left every drop of his soul in that ring every single goddamn night. He felt he owed it to the business he loved." Benoit demonstrated his love and respect for the business by performing to the absolute limits of his drug-enhanced physical endurance in every match he wrestled, no matter how irrelevant. Nicknamed "The Cyborg" backstage for the way he combined the ferociousness and energy of an animal with inhuman mechanical precision, Benoit's wrestling style was a relentless onslaught of authentic violence and reckless crash-test-dummy stunts. In a profession where even the lazy and cautious end up physically ravaged, Benoit worked far too hard; he put far too much of himself into every move, every strike, every fall. Chris Benoit crippled himself for a living.

By the time he was forty, Benoit's body was in constant blinding pain, and his profoundly damaged brain was further scrambled by years of heavy amphetamine, steroids, alcohol, painkiller, and psychiatric drug abuse. For most of his life, Chris Benoit was a study in irreconcilable contrasts. In the end, "Chris Benoit—the mentally disturbed, self-mutilating wrestling freakshow" and "Chris Benoit—the decent family man" became one: Benoit murdered his own son with a variation of his fictional character's signature wrestling hold.

It is blackly hilarious that, in a medium where lazy writing leads to idiotic plotlines in which the most saintly

---

[1] In 2002, McMahon lost the rights to the acronym "WWF" in a lawsuit and renamed his World Wrestling Federation promotion World Wrestling Entertainment. For the sake of simplicity and clarity, I will refer to Vince McMahon's promotion as World Wrestling Entertainment (or WWE) throughout the book.

good guys undergo unexplained split-second transformations into Satanic maniacs, it was "the best man in pro wrestling" who would commit the most gruesome, savage, and inconceivable real-life crime in wrestling history. None of Chris Benoit's unlikely achievements can compare with his last, miraculous feat: he united wrestlers and fans alike around a single episode which was the undisputed low point in pro wrestling history. Though it does not boast its own championship belt, the Bottom of the Barrel has arguably always been the most hotly contested title in the world of wrestling.

Conceived by carnival conmen and mobsters as a watertight method of scamming ignorant sports gamblers, pro wrestling from the beginning has been a cruel, lawless, and corrupt business. It attracts the same sort of mad, marginal misfits and street-smart predators commonly associated with touring rock bands, motorcycle gangs, or the porn business. Chris Benoit was considered too decent, too honest, and most of all *too small* to survive in pro wrestling. There he could expect to be humiliated and tortured by his gigantic circus-freak ex-con colleagues; worked to death by the shitbag promoters who make fortunes selling tickets to slapstick farces in which their ill-paid, uninsured employees kill themselves for applause. Yet the humble, shy, soft-spoken Canadian gentleman with a reputation as wrestling's most devoted father was the last man anyone would have ever expected to put all of wrestling's killers, crooks, and conmen to shame.

After all, how could polite, respectful Chris Benoit compare to people like WWE Chairman Vince McMahon, Jr., the jacked-up billionaire whose feudal business practices have guaranteed that the wrestling industry will be a gruesome, high-fatality meat grinder for decades to come?

This is how: on Friday, June 22, 2007, Chris Benoit bound and strangled his sedated wife Nancy with a TV cord. In the early morning of June 23, Benoit woke his sleeping seven-year-old son Daniel and fed him the anti-anxiety pill Xanax. Shortly afterwards, Benoit suffocated Daniel with his bare hands; Daniel's unusual wounds were consistent with Benoit's trademark wrestling submission hold, the Crippler Crossface. Finally, after a day of indecision over whether he should continue his pro wrestling career until his crimes were discovered, Benoit tied a noose around his own neck using a cord from his Lat Pulldown weight machine and lynched himself.

Not only does Benoit thus deserve a special pedestal in wrestling's gallery of ghouls, he deserves to be its spokesman. No wrestler more precisely embodied in his life, and continues to embody in his death, pro wrestling's dysfunctional culture than Benoit. Obsessed with wrestling from the age of eleven, Benoit was not only a product of the pro wrestling industry; he was the one wrestler that bosses, writers, wrestling veterans, and green rookies alike pointed to as the ideal pro wrestler, the paragon of pro wrestling values, a day-in-day-out tutorial on how a good and upright pro wrestler should live, think, and behave. "His whole life was wrestling beginning to end," says Benoit's mentor, Bret Hart. Chris Benoit was the ideal pro wrestler and the caricature of that ideal.

Chris Benoit was the ultimate *mark*—wrestling lingo for a fan, especially one who believes wrestling is real or treats it with exaggerated respect as if it were real. Originally a carnival term for gullible audience members or gamblers who could be easily defrauded, a mark is just a sucker to be exploited. Dozens of personalities who I have interviewed all repeated the same diagnosis: "Chris Benoit was a mark for the business."

Benoit was a mark every time he volunteered to harm himself unnecessarily for a thieving asshole promoter, and Benoit was a mark for allowing the audience's bloodlust to determine how much damage he inflicted on his own body. Benoit was a mark for performing his favorite move, the flying headbutt, every match for over a decade despite being told by the move's inventor, Harley Race, that it can lead to profound spinal damage. He observed its effects first-hand as his idol, the Dynamite Kid, became crippled and mad after performing it for his entire career. Benoit performed his headbutt even though it gave him frequent concussions; he even performed the move *while still recovering from the concussions it gave him*, volunteering to fall from great heights directly onto his head while already suffering from traumatic brain injuries.

But the move looked so *cool*! Occupationally insane, Benoit bought into the fundamental wrestling con that sacrificing your body and a normal life at home for a career in the business is somehow admirable or glamorous. Though most wrestlers admired Benoit's idealistic devotion to the business and his willingness to sacrifice everything to it, a smaller group of wrestlers— the pragmatic few who "were in it for the pocketbook, not the scrapbook"—thought marks like Benoit were pathetic dupes. The best wrestler was the wrestler who got paid the most for doing the least, not the grappling jihadi who treated *pro wrestling* as an artistic pursuit that justifies martyrdom. Pro wrestling is showbiz, not sport. Hulk Hogan can still walk around his many mansions; the Dynamite Kid can't get up from his wheelchair and walk to his mailbox to pick up his welfare check.

However, to many *workers* (old-school carnival lingo for wrestlers), Benoit's unabashed markdom was part of what made him such an iconic, inspiring figure. At heart, Chris Benoit was just a big fan, someone who had irrationally followed his childhood dream and continued to pursue it long after he knew better. In this, Benoit was certainly not unique; according to wrestling agent Bob Barnett, "Most wrestlers are big marks; they buy most of what they are told because they want to believe in the business so badly. They're straight-up, gullible marks. You have to be the biggest mark of all to stay in such a fucking horrible business."

After all, wrestlers knowingly tolerate a lifestyle that arguably entails a higher likelihood of premature death than membership in the Mafia or the Marines. Benoit was a millionaire who lost close friends and associates at a clip more appropriate to a crack cocaine dealer.

Shorn of its pretensions, pro wrestling is a form of popcorn entertainment in which the performers usually surrender the majority of their waking moments traveling to, training for, recuperating from, and performing in slapstick morality plays in which they voluntarily inflict profound physical damage on their bodies. The sacrifices required of a pro wrestling career dwarf even the ultimate payoff, a primetime television run with Vince McMahon's WWE monopoly.

Marvel at the ludicrous bargain even big name wrestlers accept with WWE: an independent contractor's job at a multibillion-dollar corporation in which global TV stars enjoy the benefits and job security of migrant laborers, pay their own travel and health expenses, rarely see their families, and are obliged to maintain a naturally impossible physique and perfect attendance record despite a demanding 150-plus-days-per-year travel schedule and an ever-accumulating inventory of bodily wear-and-tear. Worst of all, they must voluntarily sustain irreparable injury to their brains and bodies in the process of making what is usually laughably bad TV.

Substance abuse under these conditions is not only inevitable; it's obligatory for ninety-five percent of the wrestlers who wish to keep their jobs in the WWE. Pro wrestling is a fundamentally illicit business, one wholly predicated upon and powered by illegal drug use. Formerly jacked-up wrestling star Konnan admits, "Everybody—I can guarantee you, 100 percent from top to bottom—everybody's either on steroids, painkillers, they drink or they take recreational drugs, and in the case of half the guys, all four."

At his natural athletic peak of around 5'9" and 180 pounds, Chris Benoit was woefully unimpressive by wrestling standards: a pale, plain-faced Canadian with bad hair, short T-rex arms, an average build, and a quiet personality conspicuous only for its shyness, humility, and insecurity. In a wrestling industry often euphemistically referred to as "size conscious" in the same way that the Ku Klux Klan is "race conscious," Chris Benoit not only had no hope of fulfilling his dreams without massive chemical help; he had no hope of making a living. Even a grossly steroid-enhanced Chris Benoit was still publicly derided as a "vanilla midget" by Kevin Nash, his 6'10", 300-pound booker in World Championship Wrestling. Chris Benoit at his biggest was still smaller than Vince McMahon, his juiced-up sixty-something, 6'2", 240-pound boss, who briefly made it corporate policy in 2004 that any wrestler, no matter how talented, who wished to apply for a job at WWE be at least his own height and weight.

This ubiquitous and unquestioned size prejudice was constantly on Chris Benoit's mind during every second of his wrestling career. His friends describe him as being neurotically obsessed since childhood about his inadequate height and physique, which explains why he developed his steroid habit while still in puberty. Like most of his contemporaries, Benoit used steroids and human growth hormone not only to get the jacked-up physique that is a prerequisite to getting hired by a major American wrestling company but also to maximize the effect of his limited workout time on the road and recuperate from injuries more quickly. This drug habit made Chris Benoit's career possible by giving him the means to overcome his lack of size and charisma. Thanks to steroids, Benoit could burden his small frame with upwards of forty pounds of bulging artificial muscle and wrestle a more exciting, physically punishing, and dangerous style than even his insanely self-destructive competitors; a wrestling style so exciting that it forced his bosses to make him a star despite his sub-par height and interview skills.

This drug-fueled lifestyle made Chris Benoit a millionaire international TV star and wrestling legend. This lifestyle also killed a preposterous number of Benoit's friends, destroyed his body, and ravaged his forty-year-old brain to the point that it exhibited decay consistent with an eighty-five-year-old Alzheimer's patient. Child-killer Chris Benoit is no victim—the voluntary choice to pursue a pro wrestling career is fundamentally too stupid, irresponsible, and silly to ever allow for victimhood.

Even if Chris Benoit is responsible for accepting the toll of the pro wrestling lifestyle, that does not answer the question of whether the damage done to his psyche by the wrestling business was responsible for his homicidal meltdown. Benoit's friends who have spoken with me certainly believe it was. However, Benoit showed warning signs of mental instability and psychological distress from the early days of his wrestling career, long before it could be blamed on accumulated concussions or drug abuse. Friend Chris Jericho tells a story of how, after a minor show match in which a young Benoit made a bordering-on-invisible error, Benoit fled from the locker room and hid in a dark boiler room at the back of the arena, where he repeatedly chastised himself for making a mistake and performed 500 hack squat exercises as "punishment." Benoit extended this chillingly cruel behavior to other wrestlers who he felt had disrespected or let down "The Business," engaging in acts of appalling sadism to avenge minor breaches of etiquette.

Benoit had a longstanding reputation for burying his emotions in exercise and excruciatingly painful feats of physical endurance, to the point that some believed Benoit had lost all capability of dealing with emotional distress outside of inflicting pain and physical harm on himself. Some wrestlers called him "Houdini" due to his habit of mentally disappearing in the middle of conversations, staring blankly at nothing in an eerie goggled-eyed daze for shockingly long periods of time. WWE wrestler Ken Kennedy, the originator of the

"Cyborg" nickname, was in awe of Benoit's inhuman ability to sustain pain and his enthusiastic embrace of it in workouts. Though it is a safe bet that the damage done by the pro wrestling industry heavily contributed to Chris Benoit's psychotic end, the evidence that suggests Benoit had latent mental issues irrevocably muddies the picture.

Though the behavioral repercussions of the physical, emotional, and mental damage left by Chris Benoit's career may be in doubt, the damage itself certainly is not. The hundreds of hours of Benoit's wrestling career committed to film makes his one of the most lavishly documented acts of self-destruction in human history. Onscreen appears an excruciatingly slow-motion suicide as Benoit goes from babyfaced adolescence to balding, grizzled middle age to premature senility and physical collapse.

In the same way that Bret Hart kept up with the Benoit family almost exclusively by periodically seeing them at wrestler funerals, wrestling's mutilating toll can be traced on Chris Benoit from the death of one friend to the next. The difference between the stoic, businesslike, well-composed, physically maintained Chris Benoit who wrestled in the 1999 tribute match to his friend Owen Hart, and the brain-damaged, ogre-faced drug addict who suffered a televised emotional breakdown after a tribute match to his best friend Eddy Guerrero six years later is undeniable. This was an ill man whose agony over the loss of his best friend was being televised as the main event for *two* consecutive WWE television shows; whose incandescent pain was being used to distract wrestling fans from the complicity of WWE's policies in Eddy Guerrero's death.

This beloved father of three was also the family-murdering monster who shameless cable TV news ringmasters would make into an irresistible boogeyman, a "roid rage" Jekyll & Hyde whose crime gave them an excuse to rifle through wrestling's coffin-load of dysfunction. Thanks to Chris Benoit, the entire world was invited to gawk at an open casket view of the wrestling business: the death toll, the drugs, the steroids, the concussions, the schedule, the inhuman work conditions, the Mafia code of secrecy, the promoters' hush-hush complicity and encouragement of their wrestlers' illegal behavior. Across the media spectrum, the true nature of pro wrestling was discussed honestly and, at times, intelligently before a national audience. Millions of wrestling fans who had been living in willful denial were given compelling reasons to reconsider their support of such a demeaning, destructive racket. Insofar as it made everyone involved in wrestling for once honestly confront the truth about the business, the Benoit media frenzy was one of the healthiest developments in wrestling history.

"The ironic part is that Chris loved wrestling more than anyone," says Benoit's former colleague Chris Kanyon. "And he may end up being the one that saves it." There are few hypothetical events that are less conceivable by the human mind than the pro wrestling industry being "saved" in any meaningful fashion. The grisly example of Chris Benoit did not change WWE's business practices in the least, and Vince McMahon paid no price: 2007 was WWE's highest grossing year ever.

Under unprecedented pressure to close ranks and demonize Benoit so as to exonerate the wrestling industry of all responsibility, Benoit's colleagues and friends praised him as one of the best men they had ever met, a man whose final acts they could not accept as belonging to the same person. They stood by the integrity and decency of Chris Benoit's character and dismissed "roid rage" as a comically ill-informed red herring, endlessly frustrating the news hosts who wanted a simple, good-and-evil story that they could weave into Major League Baseball's never-ending steroid controversy. The praise of Benoit's character by almost every single wrestler who was interviewed in the month after his death gave Benoit more good press than most celebrities received cumulatively over their entire career.

Though only someone suffering from pro wrestling's version of Stockholm syndrome could look at Benoit's past and not see any cruel, sadistic, and psychologically twisted behavior, Benoit's friends were right, to a degree. There is no way to reduce the ghastliness and inherent absurdity of a man who was good in so many ways committing such a vile act. There is also no good explanation for why intelligent, decent people commit their lives to a farcical industry that they know destroys their body, devastates their soul, ravages their families, and kills their friends. This is not a story about rational, conventional people. This is a story about pro wrestlers in the pro wrestling industry. This is a story about unconventional people doing irrational things for inexplicable reasons. This is a surreal story, stranger than fiction.

The drug-addicted cretin who knowingly turned himself into a crippled junkie for pro wrestling fame is surreal in comparison to Chris Benoit, the friend and family man; and that loving father and doting husband is surreal in comparison to Chris Benoit, the wrestler. The only way to comprehend how this bisected personality came into being is to view Benoit's life in the context of his equally surreal environment. Chris Benoit worked in an industry that encouraged and rewarded him for cultivating his basest qualities until they consumed him whole. This is one man's journey through the world of pro wrestling.

Chapter II
A Small Man

> "You know, before I got in this business I
> was completely straight."
>
> CHRIS BENOIT
> *Drinking after the funeral of a fellow wrestler.*

AN OUNCE OF TROUBLE

BORN TO CATHOLIC FRENCH-CANADIAN PARENTS IN
MONTREAL ON MAY 21, 1967, CHRISTOPHER MICHAEL
BENOIT WAS A SMALL BABY WITH VIBRANT, GLOWING BLUE
EYES. His parents Michael and Margaret were a friendly,
modest, middle-class couple that doted on their only son.
Chris was an extremely obedient, shy, and diminutive
child, and his meek disposition and fragile build stirred
his parents' protective instincts. Well into puberty,
Benoit's sister Laurie could manhandle her brother in
their living room wrestling contests, once breaking a chair
in the process, the first of hundreds that would lose their
shape to Benoit's body.

"I always thought he would be an architect or a
man of the cloth because he was so quiet," Benoit's mother
told the *Edmonton Sun*. Alone in his room reading books
or daydreaming, Benoit was "an extremely quiet child, to
the point that you even worried about him," according to
his father. Benoit was no trouble in the classroom,
dutifully doing his work and earning decent grades.
Despite being woefully undersized, Benoit also was a

"tenacious" and gifted school athlete. Even at an age when sports are just an organized play date for most boys, Benoit impressed his gym teachers and coaches with his "tunnel vision" determination to succeed and passion for practice. All available sources portray Benoit as an average child who, according to his mother, was never "an ounce of trouble."

Benoit's first exposure to pro wrestling came at the age of three, when he first saw the young Andre the Giant on Quebecois TV. Though Benoit maintained a cursory interest in wrestling in Montreal, the usual wrestling extroverts and giants did not captivate the quiet, bookish, and insecure boy.

At the age of twelve, the Benoit family moved cross-country from Montreal to Edmonton, the icy capital of the western Canadian province of Alberta. Situated along the glacier-fed North Saskatchewan River, Edmonton was an oil boomtown that covered a huge expanse of the cheap, sparsely populated, fertile prairie land.

Soon after arriving in Edmonton, Benoit watched his first episode of Stampede Wrestling taped in nearby Calgary. Much like Montreal wrestling, Stampede had its share of cartoonish wrestling clichés: the giants, the villainous foreign menaces, the rampaging third-world savages, and the smiling blond-haired, blue-eyed heroes. Despite its smalltime provincial production quality, corny Canadian announcing, and at times ancient heavyweight stars, Stampede in 1979 was on the cutting edge of the global wrestling industry. Alone among wrestling promotions north of the Rio Grande, Stampede Wrestling showcased small, young, agile wrestlers—heroes that tiny Chris Benoit could relate to, whose boots he could fantasize about one day filling.

Though he admired Stampede owner Stu Hart's son Bret, then a curly-haired beanpole, Benoit was absolutely transfixed by a small English wrestler named the Dynamite Kid. With pale skin, a plain face with a slightly upturned pig nose and weak chin, and a short sinewy body with tightly-muscled abs, the twenty-one-year-old Dynamite Kid didn't *look* like a pro wrestler. In fact, he closely resembled Chris Benoit, which was not lost on the pubescent boy who identified with his new hero to the point of remodeling his body, hair, and mannerisms in his image.

Dynamite overcame his unimpressive looks and stature by feats of staggering athletic ability. The tiny Dynamite would not only throw far larger opponents with a suplex that would snap like a whip, but he would even climb to the top ring rope and suicidally perform his trademark suplex from there as well, tossing both himself and his opponent careening back to the mat. The fans gasped in awe when Dynamite leapt across the ring from the top rope and drilled his head into his prone opponent like a kamikaze fighter; eager to top himself, Dynamite began to perform his flying headbutt from the top of ladders and even from the top rope to the concrete floor below. While most Stampede wrestlers were happy to cut open their foreheads with razor blades and get hit with chairs during wild brawls, only Dynamite would ask an opponent to run him over with a car.

In addition to these unprecedented acrobatic stunts, the roughly 5'8", 170-pound Dynamite carried himself as the equal of any man in a brawl or street fight. Benoit watched with exhilarated disbelief as Dynamite stood nose-to-chest with huge football players and bodybuilders without displaying the slightest fear. From the moment Benoit discovered the Dynamite Kid, his sole ambition was to be a pro wrestler.

"Ever since I first laid my eyes on the Dynamite Kid I've tried to emulate him," Benoit wrote on his webpage in 1999. "I've tried to look like him, walk like him, and talk like him. I'd spend time in my bedroom throwing punches and kicks at the bed pretending to be him. I started lifting weights at 13 to try and clone myself after him. He definitely lit a fire inside me that still burns strong today."

The Dynamite Kid made a profound psychological impression on Benoit, the intensity of which remained undiminished long after his teenage years. As a thirty-three-year-old world champion, Benoit incessantly referenced Dynamite's name on his Web site like a religious fanatic invoking his prophet, even when answering questions wholly unrelated to him. As an adult, Benoit would still admit to being painfully awkward and awestruck in the presence of the Kid, who was hardly imposing by that point.

Discovering the Dynamite Kid empowered twelve-year-old Chris Benoit, who at the time was competing for playing time on the school sports teams against contemporaries nearly twice his size. Dynamite was his hero because, like Benoit, he overcame his larger competition through superior work ethic, skill, and athletic technique. When Benoit spoke about Dynamite's appeal it was usually in regards to his athletic grace and coordination, like a baseball trainer dissecting the mechanics of a prospect's swing. "I looked up to him so much. He was my Superman, my Batman, my Spiderman, my comic-book superhero," Benoit said years later. "His style was so aggressive, so technically sound. Everything he did looked so snug. There was no wasted movement."

Despite his slight build, Dynamite still possessed a lean, well-defined boxer's physique that dazzled Benoit. Immediately after his introduction to Dynamite, Benoit began to display the monomania that would define his later pro wrestling career. His parents were barraged with entreaties for a weight set; the quiet, docile boy who rarely had anything to say suddenly chattered endlessly about the Dynamite Kid and how badly he *needed* to start lifting weights so could be like him. Three or four years behind his classmates in physical development, Benoit looked to bodybuilding as a corrective treatment for his scrawny, childish body.

On Christmas Day of 1979, Michael Benoit gave his son the weight set he so desired—a day he would later regret and come to see as his son's undoing. In a room of the house cordoned off and covered with mirrors, Benoit began lifting every free moment, living in his "weight room." His home workout routine was supplemented by workouts at the school gym during lunch hour, which made the sweaty, exhausted seventh-grader regularly late for his next class. Benoit's school friends volunteered to be his training partner, but he broke them one after another; no one could or wanted to keep up with Benoit's obsessive training regimen. "When I have a goal, I try to have tunnel vision to that goal," Benoit would later say. Those friends who were not similarly fixated on wrestling drifted away from Benoit, who could talk of nothing but the Dynamite Kid.

With his head shaved in imitation of Dynamite, Benoit nagged his parents into bringing him to the regular Saturday Stampede wrestling shows in Edmonton. Among a crowd with a disproportionate number of hormonal teenage girls and mentally challenged children, the otherwise invisible Benoit quickly distinguished himself as the loudest, most unrestrained, and most emotionally invested fan in Edmonton. Soon, whenever a Stampede wrestler mentioned "that kid in Edmonton," they all knew it was Benoit he was speaking about.

When "that kid" began showing up early for shows, milling about for a chance to meet or catch a behind-the-scenes peek at Dynamite, some of the friendlier wrestlers let him help set up the arena and assemble the ring. Soon, before the doors were opened, Benoit was testing the ropes and jogging around the ring, taking very careful falls onto the hard mat. Most of the *babyface* (lingo for "good guy," sometimes shortened to "face") wrestlers, who were professionally expected to be nice to fans, soon became fond of the humble kid who was eager to carry bags, sweep the floor, or help put up the ring. The most friendly of the wrestlers, Bret Hart, was initially under the impression that the thirteen-year-old Benoit was only eight or nine.

After a year of arriving early and staying late at Stampede's shows in Edmonton, Benoit had become acquainted with every major wrestler on the roster *besides* the antisocial Dynamite Kid. The suspense of always coming so close to meeting his idol began to drive Benoit to the point of hysteria; he would later characterize his mindset at the time as a maniacal, "Gotta meet him, gotta meet him...." Benoit begged some of the Stampede crew members to introduce him to Dynamite, but they were reluctant to do so because it would jeopardize the storylines that portrayed the Kid as a dastardly loner. Finally, Benoit could take no more.

Benoit tiptoed backstage at the Edmonton Kinsmen Field House and, with reckless courage, knocked on the locker room door and insisted that the Dynamite Kid be produced so that he could meet his hero. According to Bret Hart, it was probably Stampede owner Stu who answered the door and took a grandfatherly shine to the ballsy little kid who wouldn't take no for answer. Stu escorted Benoit into the babyface dressing room. The boys looked around at each other and, seeing none of the other beat-up, exhausted workers adopt their in-ring character, decided just to forget about *kayfabe* (the Mafia-esque code of secrecy and etiquette that governed wrestling) in front of this little twerp who they all knew. Someone fetched Dynamite, who broke kayfabe by entering the babyface *locker room* (the "locker room" is also an insider term for wrestling's behind-the-scenes community and culture); he walked up to the young Benoit.

Bret Hart said that Dynamite "was playing the role of the nasty punk-rock kind of heel and...he [wouldn't normally] break character to be nice to any kids. But he knew this kid really loved him, and he saw something in him." To the surprise of some in the locker room, Dynamite was gentle and sweet to the boy, kneeling down and shaking Benoit's hand as he blushed, shuffled his feet, and nervously avoided eye contact. "He was a nice enough kid," Dynamite recounts in his memoir. "He told me he was working out—he showed me his muscles—and he said, 'When I'm older, I want to be a wrestler, exactly like you.'" Dynamite uncharacteristically smiled.

Lost in this heartwarming scene was any understanding of *why* this sweet, humble little kid idolized the Dynamite Kid, who in *and* out of character was the most unlikable and evil prick in the wrestling business. "It was unusual that a scoundrel such as Dynamite would have a fan who so obviously worshipped him," wrote Heath McCoy. "His job was to inspire hatred." Dynamite's uncharacteristic kindness to Benoit may have been an indirect act of cruelty, an attempt to get under the skin of his cousin, the babyface star Davey Boy Smith. Davey Boy loathed Benoit for booing him, the good guy, when he faced Dynamite, the bad guy. When he heard of the special treatment given to the little twit who embarrassed him with boos when he called for applause, Davey Boy was livid—which was likely Dynamite's intent. The Dynamite Kid was more often motivated by malice than kindness.

More so than his decision to become a pro wrestler, it was Benoit's choice of Tom "The Dynamite Kid" Billington as a role model and professional ideal that led to his self-destructive lifestyle. It is possible to be a pro wrestler who is also a well-adjusted adult, but it would be impossible to pattern yourself down to the tiniest detail after Tom Billington without doing yourself and others profound harm.

THE SUICIDE BOMBER

TOM BILLINGTON WAS A SMALL MAN, AN INDIGNITY HE WOULD AVENGE UPON THE ENTIRE WORLD. Raised to value toughness above all else, Billington was tormented to the point of insanity by insecurity over his girlish size. He compensated by terrorizing everyone he met until they all knew that, height and weight aside, Tom Billington was a hard, heartless bastard who presented a terminal menace to absolutely everyone he met. Billington could only feel secure in his manhood if everyone knew he was not only the toughest real fighter on the streets but also the best *fake* fighter to ever step into a wrestling ring.

Billington was born into a family whose trade was violence, on the outskirts of Wigan in Northwest England, a dismal industrial shithole known for its coal mining, high concentration of bars, and fine submission wrestlers. In this notoriously tough town, the Billington clan was so infamous for its viciousness that it had once held the office of local executioner by birthright. Tom's grandfather had been a legendary bare knuckles boxer whose psychotic temper was so feared that no one dared to set foot on the sidewalk outside of his home. Under the pitiless tutelage of his grandfather, Tom's father and uncle became professional boxers in their own right, and they expected Tom to carry on the family tradition.

The Billington family bred violent sociopaths. From birth, Tom was ridiculed and beaten whenever he showed weakness. His father's parenting method was summarized in Billington's own words as, "If I did something wrong and he caught me, he'd crack me one, straight in the face." Though spindly and short, Tom proved to be an athletic prodigy who instinctively mastered any sport he tried, including gymnastics. At the age of twelve, his father began Tom's full-time boxing training and, after a local wrestling coach saw his potential, the thirteen-year-old Tom took up wrestling as well. One year later, he dropped out of school to train as a wrestler six days a week. Part of his training was conducted at the infamous Snake Pit *shoot* (real) wrestling school in Wigan, where the adult martial artists tortured the frail, untrained Billington—who in contemporary photos seemed to barely weigh over 100 pounds—until he could no longer stand and his face and arms had been skinned red from mat burn.

At the age of sixteen in 1975, Tom Billington turned professional as "The Dynamite Kid," wrestling on the local English circuit for pay that topped out at twelve pounds per match. Traveling away from home, Dynamite behaved like a brainwashed child who'd been raised in a cult and was engaging the outside world for the first time.

He was silent and blank-eyed backstage, viscerally uncomfortable with normal social interactions, his face twisting with dread and repulsion if a stranger talked to him. Suspicious of everyone and paranoid that he was secretly being laughed at, Billington was a miserable teenager described as having "a chip on his shoulder." In the relaxed atmosphere of English shows, where many wrestlers spent their pay immediately afterwards drinking at pubs together, no one knew what to make of Tom Billington. Dynamite would arrive at the show with his gruff father at his side, quietly sulk in a corner of the dressing room until his match, run out and execute the most batshit-crazy stunts anyone had ever seen performed in a wrestling ring...and then leave without a word to anyone.

Dynamite wrestled like a suicide bomber. Unlike most English wrestlers, who wrestled a ginger, choreographed style, the small teenager with the slicked-over hair threw his slight body around as if he were intentionally trying to cripple himself. Seemingly oblivious to his lazy colleagues or half-drunk audience, Dynamite dispatched his in-ring duties with the lonely, fanatical determination of a monk. As far as his colleagues could tell, Dynamite received no joy or tangible benefits for putting on the most self-destructive and acrobatic performances at the poorly attended provincial wrestling shows. There was no way of analyzing Dynamite: he was just a silent, emotionless automaton that was programmed to self-destruct as flamboyantly as possible whenever he entered a wrestling ring.

After one particularly spectacular match, a young Canadian wrestler with a mop of blond Prince Valiant hair approached the nineteen-year-old Dynamite. Bruce Hart promised the standoffish Billington a free car, free apartment, and $400 a week if he wrestled for his father's territory in Western Canada. Dubious of Hart's claims, Dynamite asked his wrestling coach to make the arrangements for him and ensure that the Canadian was for real. Shortly afterwards, Dynamite heard back that his coach had confirmed the offer with the legendary Calgary wrestling promoter Stu Hart, one of the world's most respected grapplers and wrestling coaches. With twenty pounds cash in his pocket, Dynamite flew to Canada to become what he could only classify as rich.

After Billington introduced himself to Stu, the old man looked baffled. Realizing that this insect-limbed thing was apparently one of his new wrestlers, Stu recoiled and emitted a grizzled sigh. "Ehhh, you're a skinny little bastard," Stu said as he looked down in disbelief at the pale, misbegotten anorexic that his son had signed. Apparently, the "Stu Hart" his coach had talked to was really one of Bruce Hart's teenage brothers impersonating their father. Dynamite was told unapologetically that he wouldn't be getting his car, his apartment, or his $400 a week; he could accept the charity offer of $350 a week, or he could somehow find his way back to Europe.

Billington was furious and humiliated. In order to convince him to come all the way to Calgary, the Hart family had lied to him and now saw fit to compound the disrespect by mocking him to his face. Walking into the Stampede locker room, Billington was given looks of incredulous scorn by the snickering giants, tough guys, and seasoned predators that comprised the roster. Billington was fresh meat walking into a prison shower, a naïve foreign teenager with little social experience entering an unimaginably hostile and exploitative workplace 4,000 miles away from his home. Billington would have to prove himself if he was to survive.

Within days of his arrival, the tiny Englishman in his outdated mod clothes began to arbitrarily knock out strangers in bars with a punching power that even the toughest wrestlers had to admit was astounding. Bums and vagrants were also convenient punching bags for Billington to taunt and slap senseless.

When the Hart brothers began to *rib* (play pranks on) Billington, he retaliated by scalding one brother's head until it was covered in blisters and dropping a knee onto another Hart's head with such force that his teeth almost flew out. Going on the offense, Billington drove wrestlers away from the territory with *his* cruel and merciless ribs, which went from poisoning coffee with enormous dosages of laxatives, to destroying a wrestler's entire wardrobe with scissors, to drugging and abusing unconscious coworkers. Perhaps Dynamite's most infamous prank was to put lighter fluid in the toilet bowl of a manager who he knew smoked cigarettes while defecating, leading to an inexplicable explosion that burned the old man from asshole to dick.

If a wrestler *bladed* (cut his own forehead with a razor to bloody his face during a match), Dynamite might run up and kick his hand, driving the razor directly into his skull. Davey Boy Smith, Billington's cousin who followed him to Calgary, was uncomfortable the first time he was asked to blade, so he asked his cousin to safely cut him. When Davey had second thoughts, Tom grabbed his cousin in a shoot chokehold, jammed the scalpel down into his skull, and then yanked it halfway across his head as blood sprayed over both men. One firm tug would have left Davey's scalp flapping on one side of his skull like a bad toupee.

Instead of reprimanding Billington, the Hart family indulged his sadistic behavior. Anyone who could not accept the rigors of traveling on the road with a violent sociopath six days a week was mocked and ostracized for being weak. Even the sons of the promoter grudgingly accepted Billington's abuse.

Tom Billington was immune from punishment, because he was the best pro wrestler Calgary had ever seen. In a smalltime family promotion where the main event match was often a morbidly obese, immobile freakshow "monster" with little wrestling skills versus one of Stu Hart's gangly teenage sons, Dynamite Kid's superhuman stunts left the crowds speechless. Wrestling Billington was like "playing with a balloon" or a ping pong ball; all a wrestler had to do was barely tap him, and

Billington would launch himself flamboyantly through the air, taking reckless falls that would cripple the average man. The Dynamite Kid's opponents never looked more formidable than when they were playing rag doll with the suicidal English nutjob who seemed oblivious to pain or injury. With Dynamite portraying the merciless English punk-rock butcher who tortured the hometown Hart boys, the Stampede territory enjoyed an overnight boom in business. Stampede had always been a big man's territory, but Dynamite's popularity left Stu no choice but to refocus the entire promotion around the small man's Mid-Heavyweight title division.

Stampede was not the only promotion that Dynamite revolutionized. For a per-tour fee of $10,000 and a spot in the company for his son Bret, Stu leased Dynamite and his cousin Davey to New Japan Pro Wrestling, one of the world's great promotions. New Japan paired Billington in a feud with Satoru Sayama, another undersized acrobat wrestling as the child-friendly superhero Tiger Mask, which would spark a nationwide wrestling boom. Aided by their smaller size, Billington and Sayama wrestled a breathtaking style so quick and acrobatic that it made most heavyweights look like lumbering, cautious oafs. For the first time in history, Dynamite and Tiger Mask made smaller wrestlers the biggest stars in Japan. Soon, Dynamite was making $5,200 a week in New Japan and traveling with five-star accommodations.

As in Canada, Billington's greatness as a wrestler was mirrored by his despicability as a human being. He was arrested twice for assaulting adolescent fans. After "a kid" patted him on the back, Dynamite in his memoirs brags that he "turned 'round, grabbed him...and dragged him over the barrier. I ripped all his clothes off, knocked him to the floor, and kicked him in the mush. Then I left him lying there in his underpants and carried on walking to the ring...." In another incident, both Billington and his cousin were arrested for a tandem assault on a pubescent boy in which Davey Boy lifted the victim over his head and threw him against a concrete wall as Dynamite hurried over to kick him in the ribs. These two incidents were isolated only in that Billington was, for once, punished. Bret Hart recalls in his memoir an incident where Billington called over a Japanese vagrant only to "spit right in his face" and say: "Fuck you, you dirty yellow bastard." Dynamite later snickered as he told the story of how he set wrestler Gypsy Joe on fire in a Tokyo McDonald's.

Tom Billington could not claim total responsibility for either his in-ring glory or his aggressive extracurricular behavior. Soon after his arrival in Stampede, Tom Billington began to swell with muscle. Within a few years, the Dynamite Kid had added as much as forty or fifty pounds of chiseled, plump muscle onto his skeleton. The trapezius muscles on either side of his neck grew until he resembled a goateed cobra.

Though still a half-foot shorter and a hundred pounds lighter than a giant bodybuilder like Hulk Hogan, Dynamite's enhanced body gave him the visual credibility to compete against anyone thanks to his ultra-violent style. Steroids played a transformative role in Dynamite's career, rescuing him from wrestling's small man's ghetto. Without steroids, Dynamite would never have been given a chance in New Japan, where the appearance of legitimate toughness was paramount. With his doped-up heavyweight physique, Dynamite got a higher-paying job in New Japan's competition, All Japan, and soon afterwards in the bodybuilding-mad WWE. As one half of the British Bulldogs tag team with the even more jacked-up Davey Boy Smith, Billington became an international television star who appeared on the *A-Team,* walked to the ring with Ozzy Osbourne as his manager, and could earn as much as $25,000 for a single match.

In addition to enhancing physiques, quickening rehabilitation from injuries, and improving performance, steroids were also a mood-altering drug that, in Dynamite's case, were preying on an emotionally and psychologically disturbed sociopath. "Steroids didn't just affect you physically, they affected your mind as well," wrote Billington. "At times I became so aggressive, somebody only had to look at me the wrong way for me to turn really nasty. I couldn't control it." When Billington met a martial artist who was making a show of stretching like a ballerina in the men's room, he did not hesitate to punch him right in the face on principle.

Steroids in concert with mushrooming alcohol and amphetamine abuse evaporated what little self-control Billington had and encouraged his descent from an emotionally abused teenager who could be pitied into a nightmarish adult monster who could only be feared and loathed. Moments before marrying his naïve teenage bride, Billington had to be dragged away from fighting a bum to get to the ceremony. If he caught his young wife reading in their household, the jacked-up Billington showered her with abuse for making light of her uneducated husband and, if particularly incensed, began to injure himself until she groveled for him to stop.

Of course, steroid abuse was merely one of the many manifestations of the real cause for Dynamite's decline: his insecurity over being a small man in a giant's profession. Failure was an unacceptable validation of his own worst fears about himself, and the psychologically fragile Tom Billington was willing to do absolutely anything to succeed despite his size. Dynamite set the fatal precedent that a small man could make it in WWE if he literally crippled himself by taking exponentially greater risks and punishment in the ring than his competition, jacked his body up on life-threatening dosages of steroids, and consumed absolutely whatever drug was necessary to allow him to work every show, no matter how injured. Billington's lifestyle caused physical and psychological degeneration that would transform a millionaire WWE celebrity into a wheelchair-bound cripple living on the dole in public housing, ranting against "niggers" and his "brainwashed" children—all before the age of forty.

The story of the Dynamite Kid is a cautionary tale that—to aspiring wrestlers, desperate to succeed at any cost—became an inspirational underdog story. "I'd do it all again. I wouldn't change a thing," wrote the Dynamite Kid, whose professional and family life ended in his thirties. "I know it sounds strange coming from a guy whose wrestling career put him in a wheelchair, but it's true. Wrestling was my life, and I loved it."

This was the man whose career blueprint Benoit chose to follow like it was a treasure map; the man he idolized and mimicked to the day he died. This catastrophic failure of a man provided Benoit with a tutorial on how a small man can become a star in the wrestling business at the cost of his health, sanity, and family. Benoit followed his example until he was even more damaged and hopeless than Tom Billington himself. Benoit was not alone in retracing Dynamite's steps over the cliff: his two best friends, Brian Pillman and Eddy Guerrero, would do the same.

THE GAS

"I DO NOT THINK I HAVE THE RIGHT TO CALL ANYONE A MARK, beleive [sic] me," Chris Benoit wrote on his webpage in 2000. "I was the biggest. I remember going to see Stampede Wrestling every week, hoping to get the chance to talk to Dynamite. I was about 13 or 14, and I wanted to impress him so much, that I would wear three or four T-shirts over each other trying to look muscular. Sometimes I would just cut the sleeves off the t-shirts and wear them under a sweatshirt hoping he would notice or better yet say something about how big my arms were getting. I've got a picture of myself here at 14 years old beside Dynamite. If you notice I'm wearing three shirts and probably a number of cut off sleeves underneath."

Benoit's all-consuming ambition as a teenager was to improve his physique, both to impress Tom Billington and to prepare for his eventual wrestling career. Benoit chose time alone with his dumbbells over a normal teenage social life, turning his friends away because he didn't want to shorten his workout routine. In addition to his workouts at home, Benoit's acquaintances within Stampede introduced him to the local gym community, where the teenager could learn the nuances of weightlifting and bodybuilding.

It was inevitable that Benoit would be introduced to anabolic steroids; it was inevitable for anyone who took weightlifting seriously in North America in the early 1980s. Easily available and completely legal, steroids were widely and openly used, and it was impossible for a serious weightlifter to avoid witnessing countless examples of the superhuman results that came with their use. The most impressive juicers made a comfortable living preying on the incredulous gawkers at the gym, offering the most pathetic teenage pipsqueaks a personal supply of the miracle drug that would transform them into towering Schwarzeneggers.

Unsurprisingly for a self-conscious teenager so hell-bent on becoming muscular, Chris Benoit was using steroids by the age of fifteen or sixteen according to local wrestler Joe Zajko. There was no reason for Benoit *not* to use steroids: only in common usage for less than a decade, there was little evidence of any serious side effects. Like many newcomers to steroid use, Benoit was probably first given Dianabol pills, which were less intimidating than an injectable liquid steroid, possibly with a handful of anti-anxiety pills to calm the "rush" that followed. For the rest of his life Benoit was rarely, if ever, clean again. Always on muscle enhancers of one type or another, often in quantities that were huge even by pro wrestling's standards, Benoit would die with a testosterone level ten times higher than that of the average adult male.

"Benoit was into steroids big-time, we all were, but Benoit was into them more than anyone," said Tom Billington. "He wanted the perfect body and would do anything to get it. I think I was closer to him than anyone, and I warned him about overdoing things." By the age of eighteen, Benoit could bench press 400 pounds.

Steroids have many beneficial qualities for aspiring athletes and entertainers, especially when combined with an effective weightlifting and exercise regimen. Anabolic steroids are chemical derivatives of testosterone that increase the rate at which an athlete produces proteins, formulates new muscle, burns fat, and rehabilitates from injuries, leading to gains in muscle mass, strength, and cosmetic appearance that would be impossible without pharmaceutical assistance. An athlete in peak condition can obtain incredible improvements in his strength and physique simply through the addition of steroids to his normal training regimen. If laziness, injury, or a demanding schedule prevents an athlete from continuing his normal training program, steroids might allow him to maintain his physical status quo while doing less. An undersized athlete can gain the bulk muscle mass necessary to match larger athletes in strength, just as a scrawny actor or model or rock star or pro wrestler can artificially equip himself with the physique that cameras love.

Benoit turned to steroids to overcome nature. The side effects that he might have noticed on his own include testicular shrinkage, severe acne, the growth of breast tissue (very rarely accompanied by male lactation), increased body hair growth, mood swings, manic rushes of energy comparable to mild amphetamine use, and a shortened temper.

"I knew only too well the explosive rages you could get. The more you took, the angrier you became," Tom Billington said in reference to his counseling of Benoit on his steroid use. "The only answer was to take tranquilizers like Valium. I warned Benoit to be careful; the wrong combination could send you over the edge. ...But, like me, he was a bit puny at first and had to put on the weight if he was to survive. Steroids were the only answer."

The most serious side effects of steroids were invisible and unpublicized when Benoit began his habit. Though steroids promote unnatural levels of muscle growth, the body's connective tissue never grows and becomes overstretched, leading to a higher rate and increased severity of injuries. In addition to causing kidney disease, swallowing an oral steroid like Dianabol for a prolonged period of time weakens its ability to normally metabolize toxic substances and can cause damage severe enough to lead to liver cancer.

Since the heart is a muscular organ, it too becomes enlarged, leading to impaired function and a severe increase in the likelihood of cardiac problems, ranging from congestive heart failure to heart attacks to sudden cardiac death. The risk of these possibly fatal cardiac maladies is compounded by another common side effect: an increase in the level of bad cholesterol (LDL) and a decrease in the level of good cholesterol (HDL) in the user's bloodstream. This cholesterol imbalance causes plaque to clog the arteries at a quicker rate, leading to heart disease. These side effects, exacerbated by the rampant drug abuse in pro wrestling, have caused dozens of wrestlers to prematurely die from massive heart attacks over the past two decades.

All of these side effects decrease in likelihood if the steroid user cycles off regularly. Unfortunately, since wrestling has no off-season, professional wrestlers with an unemployably small natural build like Benoit can never afford to cycle off completely. By choosing a career where he could never work without the aid of steroids, Benoit was unwittingly ensuring that, by middle age, he would be suffering from a critically elevated risk of organ failure.

However, what Benoit would have considered the most severe side effect of anabolic steroids was comparatively immediate. Little did Benoit know that adolescent usage of steroids stunts skeletal growth. While attempting to bulk up in size to compensate for his short stature, the late-bloomer Benoit may have robbed himself of those precious few inches of height and reach that would have made him a viable wrestler *without* a lifelong addiction to poisonous pharmaceuticals.

Chapter III
Kayfabe

"Everything this industry has given me and
my family, I owe that to Stu. He's the one.
A good part of what I have in my life right
now and who I am, I owe to Stu."

CHRIS BENOIT

THE FAMILY BUSINESS

"THE WRESTLING BUSINESS WAS DESIGNED AND RUN
ON AN AMERICAN BLUEPRINT," WROTE WRESTLING LEGEND
DUSTY RHODES IN HIS MEMOIR. "That blueprint mimicked
the Mafia.... Professional wrestling was made up of more
than 20 regional promotions run by families under a code,
and that code was, 'Take care of your own territory, keep
your business within the family, and hold your ground.'
...Oh, and like the Mafia, there was another unwritten
rule...one rule that was never questioned by anybody.
'Business is business.'"

Originally a racketeering network which was
governing a fraudulent gambling racket that also
happened to be popcorn entertainment, the pro wrestling
industry—like the Mafia—developed its own governing
body in the mid-twentieth century. In 1948, the wrestling
dons coalesced under the banner of the National
Wrestling Alliance (NWA), an international coalition of

promotions that recognized the same rules, territorial borders, and world champions. With a few notable exceptions, NWA promoters were known for shorting the IRS and wrestlers alike on their cut of the profits and slave-driving their employees through a punishing touring schedule that broke the wrestler's ability to maintain a normal life outside of the industry. Wrestlers had their promotional preferences due to fluctuations in pay, workload, locale, and the promoter's personality, but overall, business was business.

Of the NWA's dozens of global affiliates, by the 1980s Stampede Wrestling was among the least powerful, wealthy, and glamorous. Unimpressed by the mediocre pay, blistering cold weather, abysmal travel conditions, low international profile, and Alberta's uninspiring social scene, most name wrestlers would never dream of joining Stampede's regular roster. Stampede was a territory manned by Stu Hart's immediate family, green local wrestlers looking to make a name en route to a better paying job elsewhere and broken has-beens and never-will-bes struggling to maintain a toehold in the business.

Stu Hart was the product of a biblically miserable and destitute childhood. The son of a poor farmhand in Saskatoon, Alberta, Stu was born in 1915 under Wild West frontier conditions. His father, Edward, had the personality of a wild-eyed medieval peasant, prone to hysterical bouts of religion, severe abuse of his family, and vigorous shaking of his pitchfork at government authority. Stu spent his early childhood as little more than a pack animal, drafted into his father's repeated failures to establish himself as a self-sufficient homesteader. For three years, Stu lived out of a canvas tent on the sub-Arctic prairie, surviving off gophers and squirrels, and spending subzero nights spooning the family dog for warmth as his father alternated between raving about his enemies and playing the harmonica.

After his father was imprisoned over a deranged blood feud with a dry-goods storeowner, the Hart family was committed to the care of the Salvation Army in

Edmonton. Briefly liberated from service in his father's crackpot crusades, Stu had little else to do besides hang around the YMCA, where he discovered that years of harsh physical labor and gulag living conditions had transformed him into an athletic dynamo. The teenage farmhand with the granite build, Herculean brute strength, and explosive bull-rush speed quickly mastered the local amateur wrestling ranks. Trained by the toughest *shooters* (master submission wrestlers) in Canada, Stu became one of the world's foremost experts at inflicting pain.

After World War II circumvented his dreams to be an Olympian amateur wrestler, Stu became a pro wrestler. With his broad chest, intricate musculature, authentic wrestling background, and Rock-Hudson-good looks, Stu Hart was an instant star. Mobbed by hormonal girls on the way to the ring, Stu stood down crooked old carny wrestlers who believed pretty boy wrestlers should be mangled and disfigured on principle. As a wrestler, Stu not only found stardom but also found himself a stunning Long Island socialite wife named Helen.

Stu founded Klondike Wrestling in Calgary in 1948, which underwent various name changes before becoming Stampede Wrestling. Servicing an audience of hardy ranchers, coal miners, oil drillers, and redneck shitkickers, Stampede in its 1950-1970's heyday specialized in hard-hitting, bloody, chaotic brawls. Stu trained new Stampede wrestlers in the traditional shooter's way: he taught them how to fight for real before he let them learn how to fake it. If Stampede ever offered up the type of cartoonish, phony action that typified pro wrestling elsewhere, the hardass bar-brawling audience would riot and heckle, yelling at Stu, "What is *this* shit?" Stampede earned the reputation as the North American promotion that most stressed authentic violence and shoot wrestling skills. Stampede wrestlers were hard men who earned an honest wage knocking the shit out of each other in front of rowdy honky-tonk crowds.

At first, business was robust enough for the former homeless farm boy to purchase a personal limousine, a fleet of Cadillacs, and a three-story, twenty-room, 8,000-square-foot gabled mansion planted like a fortress on a hill overlooking Calgary. The handsome Mr. and Mrs. Hart gamely tried to fill the grandiosely named Hart House with Harts, producing eight strapping sons and four comely daughters at a rate that made former debutante Helen feel like a broodmare. These human Harts were joined by a rapidly expanding jungle troupe of over a hundred cats, dogs, hens, goats, and cows that Stu, the softhearted farm boy, collected. The mangy menagerie would eventually welcome the addition of Terrible Ted the Wrestling Grizzly Bear, who in the summer lived under the porch.

The high-strung aristocratic matriarch of Hart House had no affinity for housework, which maybe should have forestalled the purchase of an aging imperial palace, let alone the addition of an indoor zoo and twelve children. Puppyish and doting with his wife, whom he happily pampered with homemade spa and nail treatments, Stu consented to handle all of the cooking, housework, and parenting while also making time to wrestle and train.

Even Martha Stewart might have been unequal to singlehandedly maintaining a hygienic and inviting environment in an 8,000-square-foot mansion populated by a dozen children, a dozen cats and dogs, and a *goddamn grizzly bear*! Having spent his formative years in a canvas tent and grimy wrestling gyms, Stu was a stranger to modern domesticity. Driving through the wee hours of the morning back to Calgary after a show, Stu rushed to milk the cows, feed the farm animals, and fix breakfast for his horde of Harts. Running to the basement refrigerator, Stu thoughtlessly pulled out ingredients that he had no idea were horribly rotted or moldy. While making breakfast, multi-tasking Stu scanned the floor for errant cat or dog turds, which, if spotted, he would flip into the trash with the same spatula he used to flip his flapjacks.

Maintained by Stu's rushed, improvised homemaking skills, the baroque mansion deteriorated into something of a post-apocalyptic madhouse. Visitors to the house lost their breath, felt their eyes water, and became lightheaded within seconds of being exposed to that *smell*: a rotting, musty, moldy house perfumed with decades worth of cat and dog feces. The stiff, crunchy carpets were piss-stained and painted with dog shit skidmarks; the curtains were shredded; the fixtures were cracked or broken; the splattered, peeling wallpaper resembled molted snakeskin; the yard was overrun with broken glass, Cadillacs that looked to have been car-bombed, and filthy, collapsing wrestling rings. Terrible Ted the Grizzly skulked around, licking ice cream off the toes of the Hart children and occasionally ambushing Helen in the basement when she tried to do the laundry. The house was often overrun with wrestling stars like Andre the Giant and Abdullah the Butcher, while aspiring wrestlers training with Stu in the basement filled the house with agonizing screams. Chris Benoit would one day live in the attic; he may not have been the most troubled person to ever live at Hart House.

It is hardly surprisingly that the twelve children reared in this decaying madhouse were psychologically fascinating specimens. "If you looked up dysfunctional in the dictionary, that's the Hart family," said long-suffering Stampede mainstay Bad News Allen. Raised with an exaggerated pride in their invincibly tough father, the twelve Hart children carried themselves like Canadian nobility, which was ironic considering their largely unsupervised Hart House upbringing led them to act like street urchins. Bossy, crude, foul-mouthed, violent, filthy, and completely oblivious to normal social etiquette, the Hart clan was a subculture unto itself.

Their bizarre behavior was accessorized by comedic bargain-bin wardrobes made necessary by Stu's prodigality. When Stampede was profitable, Stu splurged on Cadillacs, limousines, and decorations for the house; he once bought six chandeliers in one day. These spending sprees left Stu so unprepared for the cyclical downturns in business that, according to Bret Hart, the family was often "too poor for real pants" and toothbrushes. The Hart-family circus drove in a limousine from their 8,000-square-foot mansion with its six chandeliers and when the limo doors opened, they disgorged twelve humiliated children dressed in ratty gym shorts into the subzero Calgary snow flurries.

The Hart children were further warped by Stu's typical-for-the-era decision to respect kayfabe in the household. This led to twisted scenarios where the young Hart children watched in anguish as their father was given near-fatal beatings, all the while begging their inexplicably indifferent mother to call the police. Bret Hart once watched a Stampede TV episode in which heel monster Archie the Stomper promised to break into Hart House, abduct his mother, and *piledrive her headfirst into the highway*—only for Archie to show up at the door the next day! The young Bret, hiding under a table, shaking and praying, slowly emerged to see Archie jovially chatting with his mother. This story goes a long way in explaining why Bret had such trouble differentiating between wrestling and reality later in life.

The damage done to the Hart boys by Stu's pro wrestling career was not only psychological. As kind and nurturing as Stu could be as a father, "In the gym, it was a different world," remembers Ross Hart. Raised by his violent father and his shooter mentors to believe that pain was the only way to teach a man humility and toughness, Stu literally tortured his male children. Dragged down into "The Dungeon," the Hart House basement where Stu trained aspiring wrestlers how to shoot, Stu applied excruciating submission holds onto his small sons until the blood vessels in their eyes popped and their legs were unable to stand. The Hart sons hobbled to school with otherworldly crimson eyes, broken noses, fat lips, and skin decorated with Jackson-Pollack-like speckles of mat burn, scrapes, and deep grape bruises. Uncommonly nurturing and maternal under normal circumstances, Stu disciplined the Hart boys with bursts of violence that included lifting them by the hair and tossing them headfirst down stairways. Even the Hart family pastimes were violent: after Sunday dinner, Stu played with the boys by having them run around the basement as he threw heavy medicine balls at their legs.

Afterwards, the Hart boys were ushered into the locker room showers for a rare rinse, during which Bret Hart claims that his elder brothers made a habit of pissing into the smaller boys' eyeballs and mouths. Sadism in the father bred sadism in the sons. This dysfunctional fixation on pain and humility would be handed down to Benoit.

The intrusion of the eight Hart sons and their peculiar relationships with reality into the family business during the 70s and 80s caused pandemonium. All eight Hart boys were involved with Stampede as wrestlers, referees, or backstage talent, and all four Hart girls married wrestlers connected with Stampede. The twelve Harts brought their sibling rivalries into the promotion, creating a stressful political battle royale that elderly Stu was too softhearted and exhausted to contain. The backstage politics became maddening for outsiders, because some of the Harts were completely fucking mad. The conniving Harts included Smith Hart, a deranged pervert and multiple-time deadbeat father with a daughter named Satanic Ecstasy, and Dean Hart, a conman and weapons smuggler with a Samoan Mafia contract on his head.

The top Hart backstage was Bruce Hart, a tiny, unlikable megalomaniac with an unprincipled thirst for power that was worthy of Macbeth. Fueled by booze, drugs, and that special Hart-family brain chemistry, Bruce specialized in surreal, psychedelic wrestling gimmicks like Judas Roosenbloom, the jive-talking black pimp with a Jewish heritage, and Zodiak, an ax-wielding intergalactic masked witch doctor. Egged on by his brothers, Bruce ordered English manager J.R. Foley, doing a rich tycoon gimmick, to shave his mustache down to a Hitler smudge, dress up in fatigues, goosestep down to the ring, and deliver a ranting rendition of a Winston Churchill speech—without any explanation whatsoever to the TV audience. Bruce also made a point to push himself as a physical monster equivalent to the Terminator: heels regularly began to wield everything from swords to hatchets to bats in their futile battles against the mighty pansy-demigod Bruce Hart.

Unsurprisingly, Stampede under Bruce Hart began to stagnate. Outside talent was reluctant to get too involved in a promotion run by the bad-trip braintrust of Bruce and his right-hand man, Smith Hart. Stu became so disillusioned with his own promotion that he began to seriously consider his wife's entreaties to put the old nag out of its misery. Bad News Allen recalled Stu pulling him aside and telling him, "I wish somebody would take that little piss-asshole Bruce Hart off to their territory, and, uh, and put him in the first match every night and beat the crap out of him. And after they beat the crap out of him, then they'd piss on him. That little bastard."

Right as Bruce was supposedly on the cusp of his long-promised creative breakthrough, Stu received a message from Vince McMahon, Jr. Assuming control of his father's Northeastern Atlantic seaboard territory, the brash McMahon had turned rogue, launching a nationwide campaign of conquest against the lethargic, old-fashioned, defenseless promoters who didn't realize that national cable television made their NWA-enforced borders irrelevant. Using his deep New York City coffers and media connections, McMahon began to purchase the top stars of the competition and run opposition in their territory and television market. In 1984, Vince promised to invade Stampede's territory with his larger-than-life stars and expensive productions values and run Stu and Helen's smalltime mom-and-pop operation out of business.

Though kowtowing to McMahon would be recognizing that the old-school way of life and code of honor was dead, Stu Hart felt he had little choice. It's no surprise that Stu was unwilling to bet the family fortune on Bruce Hart's generalship in a war against the most ruthless, rich, and cold-blooded promoter in America. Stu accepted a buyout from McMahon that included jobs in WWE for his best wrestlers and a minor office job for Bruce.

Unsurprisingly, both Bruce and Vince backstabbed Stu Hart. Appalled that he wasn't given a job as a wrestler or booker, Bruce violated the agreement with WWE by promoting Stampede shows on his own. Once Vince had stolen Stampede's marketable stars and established his brand in the territory, he used Bruce's indiscretions as an excuse to claim that he could no longer afford to pay Stu the agreed-upon price. To the misery of Helen, Stu reopened Stampede Wrestling in 1985, with chronic fuckup Bruce once again pulling the strings.

Since most of Stampede's stars had fled the territory after its demise looking for work, Bruce desperately needed some new talent to fill the Stampede roster and make it viable once again. When word went out that Stampede Wrestling was recruiting talent, the co-promoter of Stampede's Edmonton shows, who happened to be the vice-principal of Benoit's high school, contacted Bruce and told him he had the perfect young prospect to replace Bret and Davey Boy as Stampede's handsome young babyface star. Chris Benoit was going to train with the Hart family.

THE DUNGEON

TRAINING WITH STU HART WAS ONE OF THE GREAT MYTHOLOGICAL RITES OF INITIATION IN PRO WRESTLING. Any alumnus of the Dungeon in the basement of the Hart House was accorded instant respect as a tough-guy shooter in locker rooms from Tokyo to London. Everyone in wrestling knew the stories of genial old Stu Hart's dark fetish for sadism, how he licked his lips and rubbed his hands together like a starving man at a buffet when some brash young athlete asked to train with him. Stampede wrestlers had told Benoit that Stu specialized in taking trainees "to the top of the mountain"—inducing pain as severe as possible without "separating life from body." When the trainees screamed and wept with pain, then Stu would sink in the holds even deeper, indifferently grunting, "Come on, be a man" or "Have some self-respect." Stu believed that a pro wrestler should above all else be tough and humble, and the only reliable solvent of a rookie's ego and fear was the merciless, concentrated application of pain. After a trainee experienced true pristine pain, there would be nothing left for him to fear, nothing that could ever faze him in the ring.

The stories of wrestlers who were physically and psychologically broken in the Dungeon were legion. A who's who of wrestling legends had begged for mercy, wept, vomited, pissed, and shit their tights, not to mention blacked out completely, in Stu's expert embrace. Those who knew how to defend themselves were not safe, either; Stu was notorious for fighting dirty with anyone who dared to give him a fight. One of his favorite maneuvers was to spur an uppity shooter in the testicles so hard that his nuts turned the color of an eggplant and swelled to the size of crystal ball. Others had their heads "accidentally" cracked through the wall or drilled into the exposed metal pipes on the low ceiling.

Benoit knew in gruesome detail what awaited him in the Hart-family Dungeon, and his enthusiastic embrace of the sacrifice is an indication of how seriously he wanted to be a wrestler. Through his last few years of high school, Benoit had been receiving informal training from Mike Hammer, a local wrestler remembered "for his hard-living ways and a kinky penchant for sadomasochism." Through Hammer, Benoit knew how to perform basic stretches, exercises, and *bumps* (when a wrestler falls to the mat as a result of a move or strike delivered by his opponent), but he had none of the shooting knowledge it would take for him to be able defend himself in the Dungeon. Benoit was volunteering his body up to known sadists against whom he was defenseless. This was what it took to be a pro wrestler.

Fresh out of high school, the eighteen-year-old Benoit arrived at the Hart House, the Graceland of Canadian wrestling, for his first day of training in the summer of 1985. He was led down to the basement, which contained a bedraggled gym shower that looked to have been dredged up from a sewer, a furnace room with a roaring rickety incinerator, a laundry area contained within a "concrete bunker," and the Dungeon gym itself. The Dungeon's heart was a never-washed seventeen-by-seventeen-foot wrestling mat dyed the mottled color of vomit, piss, and blood. The wood-paneled walls were dimpled, cracked, defaced, and stained with blood; some of the exposed ceiling pipes were ominously dented or crushed. Off to the side was weightlifting equipment that Stu, in one of his characteristic impulse buys, had custom-made with "HART" engraved into the iron.

Benoit stepped onto the hallowed Dungeon mat that smelled acridly of decades of sweat next to a row of monstrous bodybuilders that Bruce Hart had recruited to compete with WWE's jacked-up behemoths. Despite six solid years of weightlifting and a few years of ardent steroid use, Benoit was still probably the lightest applicant by thirty or forty pounds. Obviously, he was also the shortest and youngest man on the mat. Benoit surely felt self-conscious standing a full head shorter than the meatheads at his side, but he may have also taken solace in the well-known fact that the Hart family was especially hard on football players and bodybuilders to prove to them who the *real* tough guys were.

Bruce led the dojo class that day, slowly watching as the wall of *Playgirl*-ready beefcakes before him fled, one marketable hunk after another. "The first thing you had to do was to kick your feet out onto this carpet [mat]

over concrete," remembered Dungeon graduate Billy Jack
Haynes of his first day of training. "The carpet was *this*
[about half-an-inch] thin and you had to just tuck and roll.
Half the guys couldn't do it; the first time they did they'd
bite their tongue half off and they'd be bleeding and they
just dropped out." It was common for aspiring wrestlers,
no matter where they trained, to take only a single back
bump onto the shockingly hard mat and immediately quit,
realizing that there was no way to make that not hurt.
The vast majority of those who stayed past the first few
bumps quit over the next day or two as their legs stopped
working and they began to puke uncontrollably and piss
burning, red streams of blood. The random onset of
temporary blindness also dissuaded a good percentage
during the first week.

There is no "right way to fall"; everything a pro
wrestler does hurts. There is no way to make the
punishment a trainee takes in even the simplest training
session anything less than a profound shock to the body.
The body is not supposed to take 100 prat falls in a row
directly onto the spine, let alone every day for months in a
row. Though the brain can come to terms with the pain
with the help of drugs, the human body *never* acclimates
itself to such physical trauma—it simply degenerates.
Even a veteran wrestler taking a perfectly executed basic
bump risks death, temporary paralysis, or even
spontaneous ejaculation; future ECW world champion
Tazz was inexplicably gripped by an earthshaking orgasm
immediately after taking a routine suplex from
Kevin Sullivan.

One can imagine a group of narcissistic, tough-guy
bodybuilders instantly rethinking a career in pro
wrestling after the Harts induced them to shit, piss,
vomit, or even ejaculate all over themselves in public.
Within a few days of training, wee Chris Benoit was one of
the few students left. "[Benoit] was a natural," remembers
Ross Hart. "He learned everything so fast. He was always
patient and respectful, never a know-it-all. ...He was

willing to do whatever it took to break in." The Hart family was especially impressed by Benoit's eagerness to work out with seventy-year-old Stu, even after Stu had done his best to break his will. "He was very willing to work out with Stu," says Ross. "That was his stamp of approval. He thought, 'I'm going to learn from this. This is what it takes to be accepted.'" Benoit had also been told by previous Dungeon graduates the secret of surviving a Hart-family stretching: never scream, never beg, never sell it, and eventually Stu or Bruce or whoever would get bored. Contrary to legend, though Stu occasionally stretched Benoit, it was Bruce Hart and Mike Hammer that handled the bulk of Benoit's basic training.

Working for his father during the week, Benoit took a Greyhound bus from Edmonton to Calgary every weekend to train with the Harts, which he hid from his mother. When his mother found out, she was appalled at the punishment he was taking and thought, "When he's forty, he's going to be hurtin'."

Benoit's training progressed quickly from shooting and bumping basics into actual in-ring practice. Even the most basic wrestling maneuver has its nuances. For example, when wrestlers "run the ropes," there is a great deal of conditioning, training, and know-how involved. An untrained wrestler can run back-first into the stiff twine ropes and collapse as if he were shot, writhing and gasping for air on the mat; if he doesn't learn how to situate himself properly, a trainee can suffer liver damage or a cracked skull just from running the ropes. Even a basic flat back bump carries with it the risk of broken arms or a concussion if the timing or technique is not perfect.

After thousands of repetitions of simple solo maneuvers, Benoit began to train with other wrestlers, which carried with it greater risk and difficulty. The simplest pro wrestling moves require skill and know-how to be performed safely, and absolutely any wrestling move is potentially fatal if performed incorrectly. Any wrestling move is essentially a cooperative dance maneuver for two that both wrestlers must be able to perform on command with perfect timing. Since a traditional pro wrestling match is usually improvised outside of the finish and a few major spots, any wrestler must be able to seamlessly execute any move within a second of the move being "called" through body language or a whisper by the wrestler in charge, usually either the heel or the more seasoned wrestler.

The body had to be conditioned to fall in certain ways in certain situations as an unthinking reflex, so that an exhausted or concussed wrestler can naturally protect himself even if his mind is not clear. Benoit took thousands of textbook-perfect bodyslams, clotheslines, suplexes, and even punches in a supervised practice setting before ever being allowed to take one in the heat of a match. After taking thousands of repetitions with a partner just to get the mechanics down, Benoit impressed the Harts by finding other partners on which to practice *perfecting* the moves: making them snap with that one-of-a-kind force and speed that only Dynamite could manage.

As important as it was to learn the mechanics, the physical aspect of pro wrestling was the lesser half of the art. After all, the biggest star in pro wrestling was Hulk Hogan, not the Dynamite Kid; even in the allegedly traditional NWA territories, the most popular face star was the obese one-move-wonder Dusty Rhodes. Bret Hart in his memoir tells a poignant story of touring Japan with Dynamite that illustrates what really matters in pro wrestling. After their mundane undercard matches, Billington and Bret were watching the main event starring the 350-pound former janitor, Abdullah the Butcher. "Before they even touched each other," Bret writes, "Abdullah abruptly broke into a karate stance, yelling, 'Wooo!' and that was all it took to bring the house down. Some guys just had the look. Tom rolled his eyes, thinking of how he killed his body to get the same reaction." While the wheelchair-bound Dynamite lives on welfare, the elderly, immobile, enormously fat Abdullah the Butcher has been a headlining star in Japan getting paid as much as $20,000 a week for the past thirty years. As Benoit would never learn, the Dynamite Kid approach to wrestling was the absolute dumbest.

Learning how to perform a suplex that looked slightly more painful than anyone else's was great, but learning how to elicit a riotous crowd reaction while sitting in a harmless headlock was more important. The art of selling was the most pivotal aspect in a successful wresting match, the ability to make every move look credible and devastating even if it never made contact. After all, the first step in satisfying a wrestling crowd was to make them suspend their disbelief, and that could only happen if they were given a reason to believe in the pain, in the desperation, in the story. When wrestlers say that they "learned how to work," they're using the carny definition of "work"; a good wrestler learns how to *fake*.

As he learned how to work a match and work a crowd, Benoit also learned the all-important rules of working a wrestling locker room. No matter how great a young wrestler was, he would be hazed, assaulted, and even blackballed if he did not abide by the rules and etiquette of the secret brotherhood. To ignore or forget a single minor rule was seen as disrespecting the veterans, shitting on tradition, and belittling the entire industry. According to these rules, a good, respectful young wrestler must:

1. Always immediately introduce himself to everyone, no matter how hostile or intimidating, in the locker room individually by name.
2. Always shake hands *very softly* with every wrestler he introduces himself to.
3. Always remember every wrestler he's ever met, no matter how briefly or how long ago, so as not to offend them later when introducing himself.
4. Always shut up and mind his own business after introducing himself.
5. Always kiss a veteran's ass if they deign to talk to you.

6. Always blindly obey the veterans when they call the in-ring business.
7. Always thank your opponent after a good match, especially if he puts you over.
8. Always drink if the other Boys are drinking.
9. Always remove all contraband from the hotel room of a wrestler who overdoses and dies. (Yes, they actually needed to formalize a rule for this.)
10. Never question, criticize, or make an unsolicited suggestion to a veteran.
11. Never compare himself to a veteran.
12. Never perform another wrestler's signature move.
13. Never wear a color or article of clothing that another wrestler feels is integral to his image.
14. Never ask the promoter for a paycheck.
15. Never call the promoter and ask a question.
16. Never complain.
17. Never make suggestions to the promoter—just wait to be told what to do.
18. Never rat out another wrestler to the promoter, regardless of what he does to you, innocent bystanders, helpless maidens, or small children.
19. Never break kayfabe and tell an outsider anything at all about the Business.
20. Never put his own best interest ahead of the best interest of the Business.

After four or five months of keeping his mouth shut, working hard, and uncomplainingly "taking his lumps" from Bruce and Stu, Chris Benoit was told he was ready to debut with the resurrected Stampede Wrestling.

The eighteen-year-old Benoit made his debut on the weekly Friday television taping in Calgary on November 22, 1985. His first-ever professional wrestling match had the highly uncharacteristic honor of being televised. Billed at 210 pounds and dressed in long red tights modeled after Dynamite's, Benoit entered a tiny arena with visible empty seats sprinkled throughout the first few rows. With a pale, average athletic physique, Benoit was a handsome teenager with a Boy-Scout-next-door smile, perfect for Stampede's large audience of small boys and teenage girls. Tagging with clumsy heartthrob Rick Patterson, Benoit was facing the fearsome undercard heel team of Butch Moffat, a bearded two-year veteran with a pointy bald head and a normal workingman's physique, and Mike Hammer, his original trainer.

In what was aired of Benoit's first match, he understandably did little. The only offensive moves shown were a clothesline, a reversal of an Irish whip, some frail punches and kicks, and a well-executed sunset flip. Nonetheless, Benoit showed potential: his face sold the punishment he took, and when being dropped throat-first onto the Stampede ring's bouncy white ropes, for added realism Benoit took the blow directly onto his throat instead of using his hands as a cushion. In a sign of how much Stampede expected of him, Benoit was given the victory in his first match when Benoit's partner whipped Hammer into a sunset flip pin by Benoit.

For a first-match rookie, Benoit sold a beating like a professional and looked more polished than his three-year-veteran tag partner. By his fifth match, Whalen was comparing him to the Dynamite Kid, the best wrestler in the territory's history. Stu invited Benoit to move into Hart House until he found a place to stay in Calgary, an offer he accepted. Already, it was being said that Chris Benoit could become "Dynamite without the dark side"— if he survived the road there.

THE LOOP

STAMPEDE BROKE SPIRITS. Wrestlers did not work for Stu; they did tours of duty. Stampede was infamous for touring schedules that required their talent to travel hundreds of miles everyday in extreme weather conditions to put on shows for dangerously stupid redneck audiences. The Stampede crew that braved the Arctic weather, unimaginably squalid traveling conditions, awful pay, and the booking of Bruce Hart had to console themselves with the joy of wrestling in places like Saskatoon in front of what Bret Hart described as, "the usual crowd of about one hundred fans, which consisted mostly of busloads of mentally challenged kids, a handful of diehards and a few drunks." It was hardly a glamorous job: the mentally challenged fans at the Saskatoon shows, for once left unsupervised, were notorious for having sex during the matches and naming the resulting children after their favorite Stampede stars.

Stampede serviced a territory that covered the provinces of Alberta, Saskatchewan, and British Columbia, with occasional "garbage runs" through the Northwest Territories and Montana—an area of over a million square miles, larger than the combined nations of Mexico and Japan. This mammoth chunk of the earth was largely rural and sparsely populated, the major towns separated by mountains, vast stretches of pristine subarctic forest, and rivers and lakes serviced only by ferries. The country roads were muddy and unreliable in the warm months and covered by glacial expanses of deadly slick ice for the rest of the year. Even the most reliable highways were rendered dangerous by the herds of antelope, deer, moose, and buffalo that eyed oncoming cars with a look that Bruce Hart described as "Ahh, fuck you."

As often as six days a week, Stampede's ratty road show would traverse wild, all-terrain country in two ancient, dilapidated white vans. The eight or so babyfaces were packed into one van and the eight or so heels into the other, stuffed into tiny spaces with their bags on their lap like Calcutta bus passengers for road trips as long as fifteen hours. On an average year, they drove around 100,000 miles together.

In the summer, the un-air-conditioned vans became sweltering, pungent furnaces of wrestler BO. The heat also coaxed out the aroma of piss from the numerous stains on the carpet. In the winter, when temperatures dipped to thirty or fifty degrees below zero, some seriously tough men hugged each other close with numb limbs and frozen snot hanging from their faces, wondering why the Harts with their limousines and mansion couldn't have splurged for a heated car. While driving on winding mountains roads plated with ice, the van often narrowly avoided sliding clear off steep cliffs. During snow blizzards, the holes in the roof resembling the result of a Tyrannosaurus Rex attack and the gashes in the floor drained away the cumulative body heat in a tail of steam left in their wake like rocket exhaust.

With no airbags and barely any usable seats let alone seatbelts, the frequent accidents and breakdowns were always potentially fatal. Afterwards, when the casualty toll consisted of only *one* lost leg for Tokyo Joe Daigo or an only *mostly* ripped-off nose for Jim Neidhart, it was considered a miraculous deliverance. It was also common knowledge that, since only a pro wrestling company would actually travel on precarious rural roads during blizzards, a common automotive breakdown could likely result in death. If the vans puttered to a halt on a completely empty country road somewhere between such tour stops as Medicine Hat and Yellow Knife, it would take only a matter of hours for hypothermia to do the job.

If, due to mechanical malfunction or wrath of God, the vans could not arrive by show time, then no one got paid. Even if they arrived on time at whatever godforsaken Indian reservation or frontier outpost they were holding their show, Stampede's roster could look forward to riotous fans ready to take a swing at the wrestlers or nights spent at sleazy motels infested with the subhuman ogresses who made a living prostituting in places like Milk River, Alberta. The low quality of game never stopped the Stampede boys from maintaining a stable of groupies (known as *ring rats*) in each of these towns, though Benoit was notorious for *not* partaking in Western Canada's womanly bounty. "I never saw Chris try to pick up ring rats," recalled Ross Hart. "One girl he used to [date], you wouldn't see her at matches very often. She was very quiet and reserved, not too vocal or opinionated like some of the damsels who would come to the shows."

According to Ross, since Benoit woke up early every day to work out, he rarely drank and never partied to excess at night. He was "very straight," which made him unique. "I'm not proud to say it, but we were a bunch of junkies back then," admits Stampede manager Milad Elzein. Liberated from conventional adult responsibilities, the Stampede wrestlers lived in a state of perpetual frathouse adolescence, driven by the monotony of the road and macho peer pressure to perform outrageous feats of degenerate madness. Nonconformists by nature, they formed a feedback loop of eccentric, hedonistic, self-destructive behavior.

The 200 days a year of long, monotonous, cramped van rides naturally led to tension between the usually stir crazy, sore, drunk, and high wrestlers. The Stampede vans became long-form experiments in extreme psychological endurance. As a rookie, Benoit was one of the few wrestlers who actually enjoyed the rambling van rides. To him, these nightmare slogs were his fantasy road trips, the very essence of his longtime dream to be a Stampede wrestler. Listening to road stories and ribbing the boys made the teenage Benoit as giddy as an 80's heavy metal fan getting the opportunity to be a roadie on tour with Metallica.

"Every week ten or twelve of us would be packed into a van and driving from Calgary," remembered Benoit. "We had to entertain ourselves. Usually the weak one in the herd would get picked and the rest of the hyenas would jump on him, start ripping at him and tearing him apart until he snapped and cracked.... If you showed any weakness, they picked you apart.... Guys up there would rip the hell out of you and drive you out of town."

The stakes of these cross-country standoffs could be high. According to Bad News Allen, wrestler Corporal Kirchner once "completely cracked up" in the van, threatened to murder his tag partner Johnny Smith, and then jumped out onto the highway and made a mad dash for the American border. On another road trip, the giant Loch Ness finally snapped after years of torment and threatened to kick everyone's ass, which provoked the very wooly and very quiet Cuban Assassin to rebut this rash proposal by producing a knife from his boot and demanding satisfaction.

Benoit would later portray his Stampede years as an idyllic, local-kid-joins-the-circus adventure. In reality, he would suffer grave humiliation and abuse as the Hart brothers' favorite ribbing target. Ribs are a universally accepted part of the pro wrestling business, but Stampede was known as the home of the most merciless, cruel, and brutal ribs in the wresting world. Stampede's reputation for cracking psyches and ending careers was so bad that New Japan Pro Wrestling made Stu Hart promise to go easy on their big name prospect, Allen "Bad News Allen" Coage, before letting him work in Calgary. The 6'1", 260-pound Coage was an African-American Olympic bronze medalist in judo and all-round badass who intimidated even the toughest wrestlers. "Ever notice that most serial killers have three names? John Wayne Gacy, Clifford Robert Olson...Bad News Allen?" joked Benoit's first wrestling coach, Mike Hammer. What sort of prank could be so bad as to run a monster like Bad News Allen out of town?

A typical Stampede rib went something like this: a new wrestler who didn't know to always keep his thumb over his beer would have it covertly spiked with a heavy dosage of GHB, LSD, and some other incapacitating narcotic. Afterwards, he would be stripped naked, shaved of all of his body hair, given a drawn-on Hitler mustache, spray painted with lewd phrases and scenes of stick figure sodomy, have his hands superglued to his face, and then dumped nude and defiled into the frigid outdoors. Other Stampede favorites included spiking a young wrestler's beer with laxatives in addition to GHB and hiding all the nearby toilet paper, supergluing his ass cheeks shut, jerking off on his toothbrush, pissing and shitting into a wrestler's food or clothes, padlocking his bags and throwing away the key, mangling his wardrobe with scissors, leaving him on the side of the road during a blizzard, or intentionally humiliating him in front of his hometown fans.

Benoit suffered more than a few of these ribs in the process of "paying his dues." If he at any point had complained, the entire roster would have mocked him and driven him out of the territory. "What? You can't take a rib, you pussy?"

Even elderly Stu Hart liked a good rib. Some of his were harmless. Ole Anderson tells the story of how, after his first workout in the Dungeon, Stu joined him in the shower dressed in a suit. Slowly ambling more and more under the showerhead, the formally attired Stu began to massage Ole's shoulder while sighing, grunting, and endlessly repeating, "Ehhh, big shoulders, ehhh, big guy, ehhh, nice and stout, ehhh, big shoulders," in his grizzled countrified Canuck accent. Stu also liked more mean spirited ribs, such as the infamous "Mabel Parties," in which Stu would convince a new wrestler that there was a naughty housewife who liked to host hedonistic parties for the boys, only for her shotgun-wielding "husband" to show up during the introductions, shoot one of the Stampede veterans in the chest with blanks, and chase the rookie at gunpoint out of the house and down the highway.

Benoit's personal Torquemada was not kindly, stay-at-home Stu Hart, but rather his would-be heir, Bruce. Undersized and hopelessly awkward in the ring, Bruce's failure to get a job with McMahon had made him twisted and bitter, especially since his own brother Bret and a host of other Stampede veterans were currently making six figures in New York. Within months of Benoit's debut, it was clear to Bruce that, given enough steroids, the "Edmonton Kid" would follow Billington to the global stardom that had and would always elude Bruce. Bruce's response was to try to run the talented little shithead right out of the business, Stampede's best interests be damned.

"[Benoit] was a young kid coming along, and they [Bruce Hart's crew] were jealous of him," Bad News Allen recalled in an interview. "They could see this kid was gonna be good. They could actually see another Dynamite Kid.... He was just oozing talent." A proud, intelligent, and fiercely judgmental man, Bad News loathed most pro wrestlers for being phonies and degenerates. The only men Bad News respected were legitimate, no-bullshit tough guys like the Dynamite Kid—and, to the shock of the Stampede regulars who never saw Bad News approve of anyone, teenage Chris Benoit. Bad News developed such a liking for Benoit that he had his sister bake him a birthday cake, which Bad News brought backstage at a hometown Edmonton show. When Bruce heard that the cake was for Benoit, he muttered, "Well, he ain't eating that cake tonight," and told Benoit's opponent to destroy it.

"Chris was a dedicated kid; he worked hard. I hated the way they treated him," Bad News explained. "I'm one of these kinda guys who don't like to see people get abused." Bad News had a solution that would save Benoit from the Harts' arbitrary bullying and drive Bruce mad with envy at the same time. A main event star in New Japan Pro Wrestling (NJPW), where Dynamite Kid had made his global reputation, Bad News asked owner Antonio Inoki to do him a favor and bring in this hot young talent to train in the dojo en route to becoming a NJPW star, just like he had in the 70s. Trusting that anyone who could impress Bad News Allen must have potential, Inoki agreed to let the "next Dynamite Kid" live in the NJPW dojo and wrestle with the company for a year. As an afterthought, Inoki said he'd also pay the kid $1,000 a week as a gesture of his respect for Bad News.

Seven months into his career, Benoit was accepted into the most elite pro wrestling academy in the world. At the age of nineteen, Benoit would be touring with arguably the most prestigious promotion in the world, the legendary home of Tiger Mask. After years of watching bootlegged Japanese tapes of the Dynamite Kid, Chris Benoit would be following in his footsteps, just like he had always planned.

Chapter IV
This is New Japan.
It is like Soldier.

"My happiest time [in the New Japan dojo]
was when I was in the shower or on the
toilet. Because I was alone. This is New
Japan. It is like soldier."

OSAMU NISHIMURA[2]

THE GODFATHER OF SPORTS

AS RECENTLY AS 2004, YOU COULD STILL GAMBLE
ON THE OUTCOME OF PRO WRESTLING MATCHES. Wrestling
matches are still written about as authentic contests in
the sports section of the national newspapers, and it is
common to meet successful adults in Tokyo who speak
confidently of which matches they perceive to be merely
show and which ones were "too important" to be anything
but "real." Though the fixed nature of pro wrestling has
been exposed many times over the years, among fans it
still maintains a veneer of authenticity due to the grueling
dojo training that Japanese wrestlers endure and the fact
that their pro wrestlers are marketed as expertly trained

---

[2] My interviews with Mr. Nishimura were conducted via e-mail correspondence. Due to
his irregular grasp of the English language, in quoting him I have at times chosen to
regularize his English and correct various spelling, punctuation, and grammatical errors,
for the sake of clarity and to present Mr. Nishimura in a respectful light. I have in no way
altered or misrepresented his responses.

martial artists. Nowhere are wrestling fans more
fanatical, educated, and disproportionately wealthy than
in Japan, where until very recently pro wrestlers were
treated with slavish deference and adulation worthy of
courageous modern gladiators.

The pro wrestling industry came to Japan during
the American occupation after World War II. For
centuries, Japanese society had been predicated on a
racially supremacist, theocratic, warrior philosophy that
claimed that the Emperor was an invincible god, and
Japan's armies were destined to conquer Asia. The
apocalyptic shock of Japan's defeat in World War II left a
culture racked by an all-pervasive shame, disillusionment,
and insecurity before the conquering American invaders
and their manifestly superior civilization. Japan needed
an avenging hero to restore the nation's belief in
its strength.

As it has always been in America, pro wrestling
was the perfect medium for delivering crassly xenophobic
and jingoistic popcorn entertainment. A retired sumo
wrestler and budding pro wrestler in Hawaii called
Rikidozan was brought home to portray the defender of
Japan's honor. Rikidozan became one of the greatest
sports heroes in Japanese history, the karate-chopping
avenger, destroying the cartoonish American villains who
symbolized the much-resented continued presence of
occupying U.S. soldiers. His nationalist appeal was
improved by the decision to bill Rikidozan as a native of
Nagasaki, one of the two cities annihilated by American
atomic bombs.

Like everywhere else in the world, pro wrestling in
Japan was born of massive fraud. Rikidozan, the paragon
of Japanese racial might, was actually an ethnic Korean
born during Imperial Japan's occupation of the peninsula.
Korean immigrants are to this day treated with contempt
and revulsion as "dog people" by huge swathes of the
ethnic Japanese populace. Despite being incredibly rich
and famous, Rikidozan was still a Korean in a nation

where that made him less than human, and he carried himself like a misfit with something to prove. When drinking with some *yakuza* (Japanese Mafia) friends at a bar in 1963, Rikidozan was stabbed in the gut. In a stunt to prove how tough he was, he supposedly refused to seek medical help, and died from the wound.

Pro wrestling's appeal had been largely built around a cult of personality based around Rikidozan as the all-conquering hero. When Rikidozan was discredited and disgraced by his organized crime ties and sordid death, wrestling's reputation and popularity was threatened. Stories began to appear in the newspapers detailing wrestling's intimate relationship with the yakuza, which was an anathema to a populace trained to shun and ignore anything that was considered improper. Business would collapse for a few years until the stink of Mob-ties dissipated. In reality, the Japanese wrestling business had always been, and always would be, dominated by the yakuza.

Much of post-war Japanese society operated at the mercy and discretion of the yakuza. They exerted influence in Japan that rivaled the Mafia's power in Sicily, and their power was not predicated on secrecy. With as many as 100,000 official members, the yakuza distinctively tattooed their bodies and openly cavorted in bars and clubs with "yakuza" on the signs.

The yakuza owned or exerted influence over nearly all the major talent agencies, production companies, nightclubs, concert halls, and arenas in Japan; Japanese entertainers without a yakuza patron would have no chance to audition, no one to produce their material, and no venues at which to perform. Every Japanese prime minister over the past half-century has needed the implicit support of the yakuza, which subsidizes a handful of ultranationalist political parties that they use to harass, protest, and slander any politician who opposes their interests.

The yakuza at the highest levels were deeply invested in the pro wrestling business. It was a cash racket convenient for laundering money, and being a wrestling promoter provided a glamorous, testosterone-heavy hobby for star-fucking mobsters with huge stockpiles of dirty cash to spend. Japan Pro-Wrestling Entertainment, a major promotional company for wrestling events, was openly controlled by yakuza godfathers Kazuo "The Bear" Taoka and Hisayuki Machii in concert with war criminal Yoshio Kodama—arguably the top three gangsters in Asia.

"If we attempt to stop the yakuza from taking a piece of any show, they make it so that we can't perform in their cities," one native NJPW star told me. Scarcely has a major pro wrestling event occurred in the past few decades without an assortment of ritually tattooed yakuza, some with ceremonially amputated pinky fingers, sitting in the front row, ostentatiously wearing expensive *Goodfellas*-style suits or overcompensatingly docile Bill Cosby sweaters. The location of the yakuza section is sometimes passed around backstage to ensure that no one acts up or provokes that part of the crowd; the wrestling bosses and bookers usually make a point to perform some particularly painful, stiff strikes and moves directly in front of the yakuza to impress their benefactors with the "Fighting Spirit" of their promotion.

While the big city yakuza bosses involved themselves in the behind-the-scenes operations of the Tokyo-based promotions, the small town yakuza were deputized to handle the tours throughout the countryside. In my interview with Simon Inoki, the former President of New Japan, he explained how the business is set up while omitting the incriminating details. "The house shows are simply bought out by local promoters, not really gate and percentage system," Simon told me. "They pay a set fee to NJPW and they keep what they make. Most of them are arranged like this."

According to dozens of published sources and interviews I've conducted, the local promotional rights to shows conducted outside of Tokyo are either sold at a fixed rate to local yakuza, or the local promoter sells upwards of eighty percent of the available tickets to the yakuza at a bulk discount. After handing out free tickets to friends, the yakuza adopt a Girls-Scouts-with-guns sales and distribution method. After divvying the tickets to be sold, the yakuza travel to all the local businesses where they collect tribute or exert influence, compelling the owners to purchase tickets, the number increasing proportionate to the size of the company. When business was good, the business of selling tickets changed from violent extortion to the more profitable racket of ticket scalping and price-gouging.

The wrestlers who resurrected the pro wrestling industry in the aftermath of Rikidozan's death were his disciples Shohei "Giant" Baba and Kanji "Antonio" Inoki (the father-in-law of the previously mentioned Simon Inoki). Baba started All Japan Pro Wrestling, which became a NWA affiliate and generally pursued a traditional, theatrical American style.

New Japan Pro Wrestling, founded by Inoki, was more distinctly Japanese, influenced heavily by the Japanese martial arts tradition. "New Japan's theme is 'King of Sports,' that pro wrestling is the ultimate form of martial arts and that pro wrestlers are the strongest," Simon Inoki has said. "So all wrestlers are required to train not only pro-wrestling but ground wrestling and other MMA [mixed martial arts]." In NJPW, wrestlers gained just as much by showing *toukon* (fighting spirit) while taking serious, authentic beatings as they did by winning matches. Toughness, legitimate fighting skills, and a decorated athletic background were all-important in NJPW because it was sold to the audience as a 100 percent undiluted sport and therefore needed to look credible. Pro wrestling was just a fighting style like karate or jiu jitsu, with its own peculiar rules, conventions, and maneuvers, and Inoki was its master.

Though it took at least a decade to fully succeed, the booking plan behind Antonio Inoki was to replicate the personality cult of Rikidozan. Inoki became the world's master martial artist, the technician whose skill in pro wrestling was fused with expertise in traditional carny wrestling, amateur wrestling, judo, and jiu jitsu. Huge amounts of money were spent importing authentic fighting athletes such as heavyweight boxing champion Leon Spinks and judo gold medalist Willem Ruska to lose to Antonio Inoki in fixed "martial arts" matches that usually ended with pro wrestling maneuvers like backdrop suplexes or octopus holds that were thereby "validated" as being real to fans. Inoki even hyped a martial arts battle with Ugandan dictator Idi Amin, which was postponed soon after by a coup.

Buoyed by the development of a second generation of younger, faster stars like Riki Choshu, Tatsumi Fujinami, and Satoru "Tiger Mask" Sayama, by the early 1980s NJPW could make a strong claim to be the biggest promotion and Antonio Inoki the biggest star in wrestling. A celebrity on par with Muhammad Ali himself (who he fought to a draw in a notoriously crooked fight), Inoki was so worshiped by the Japanese fans that they'd rush to his side and beg to receive the honor of being slapped in face by the great Inoki. After receiving their "fighting spirit slap," some fans would collapse into hysterical fits as they bowed compulsively and thanked Inoki for the gift he had bestowed upon them.

Inoki knew the feeling—he allegedly acted in the exact manner to his yakuza overlords. According to the Dynamite Kid's memoir, Billington watched backstage at a show as Inoki was chewed out and slapped in the face by a yakuza boss. With all of his employees looking on, the mightiest fighter in the world responded by humbly bowing and thanking the yakuza.

Nearly two decades later, in 1999, years after Inoki had retired from active wrestling to become a Japanese senator and diplomat, National Wrestling Alliance

President Howard Brody encountered a similarly corrupt scene. He was accompanying NWA champion Dan Severn to a title match in Yokohama, for which the NWA had been promised a $10,000 bond. When Inoki failed to produce the money, Brody declared that the fight was off and was promptly escorted to a meeting with Inoki, who was sitting with a row of angry yakuza behind his back.

"Inoki was *sweating*," Brody told me with a laugh. "I wouldn't say he looked like a hostage, but he looked like his back was up against the wall, and he wasn't exactly comfortable with the position he was in." Inoki promised Brody that he would receive the $10,000 bond before he left Japan. When Brody asked Inoki's son-in-law, Simon, if the men he had just met with were yakuza, Simon responded, "Yeah," before thinking better of it, then hedging, "I *think* so." The next day, Brody was met at the airport by a yakuza who simply said, "No bond!" and handed him an envelope stuffed with $10,000 in crisp bills. "It was like something out of *The Sopranos*. I had been promised a bond made out to the NWA, not an envelope of possibly dirty cash at the airport. I guess that's just how they do business over there—that same group of guys pays everyone."

And when foreign wrestlers worked in Japan, the same group of guys paid them, as well. Though a NJPW gig was considered one of the two or three best jobs in the wrestling business, working in Japan created an odd disconnect for foreign wrestlers. While staying in five-star accommodations in one of the wealthiest, most technologically advanced, most sophisticated nations on earth, NJPW wrestlers were still nonetheless working for the Mafia in return for an envelope of dirty cash at the end of the tour. Those wrestlers that misbehaved, no matter how famous they were, would pay greatly for it. After Cowboy Bob Orton, Jr. kicked the local Kyushu promoter in the balls for trying to break up one of his bar fights, he had to be secretly smuggled out of the country to save his life. Yakuza troops flooded the hotel in Kyushu, ransacking it in search of Orton; yakuza hitmen were seen surveilling the lobby of Orton's hotel in Tokyo in case he tried to pick up his bags. When former NJPW champion Leon "Vader" White made a similar mistake, the 400-pound monster was less elusive. According to the story told to me by multiple sources, including another Japanese world champion, a large group of yakuza tied Vader down like a circus elephant and slowly tortured him with razor blades, slicing him with many small, strategically targeted cuts before expelling him from the country. A less famous wrestler might have disappeared.

THE BARRACKS

CHRIS BENOIT WAS NINETEEN YEARS OLD WHEN HE ARRIVED IN LOS ANGELES EN ROUTE TO TOKYO. Waiting for him was Darryl Peterson, an American rookie who would be joining him as one of the first non-Japanese talents to be trained in the NJPW dojo. Peterson fit the stereotype for a NJPW foreign prospect: a former NCAA All-American amateur wrestler who stood 6'6" tall and weighed over 300 pounds. Like their predecessor Bad News Allen, Peterson was an oversized heavyweight with legitimate fighting credentials and a distinctive look. Benoit was small, bland, and had no fighting credentials. Even with Bad News' recommendation, there is little doubt that Peterson was the more attractive prospect to management. Nonetheless, business was so good in NJPW that Benoit would make $50,000 cash in the coming year just to be a rookie trainee.

Despite his size, the tenty-five-year-old Peterson was friendly, an aspiring filmmaker and guitarist with little devotion to the business. Benoit may have wondered how anyone who wasn't completely obsessed and devoted to pro wrestling could survive the NJPW dojo. With his long rock star black hair and beard, Darryl Peterson aspired to become the pro wrestling character Lucifer Payne: a gigantic heavy metal demon in a black trench coat who carried his electric guitar to the ring.

Having been schooled in grisly detail about what to expect by Bad News and the Harts, it would have been clear to Benoit that Peterson with his cartoonish ideas had absolutely no inkling of the abuse and degradation he was about to endure. Even Benoit had little idea—Bad News' experience had been misleading. The Japanese had taken it easy on the terrifying judo bronze medalist. They would have no similar hesitation when dealing with the unassuming Benoit and the even-tempered Peterson. Thrown together by circumstance, the two would suffer immensely by each other's side and become friends.

The dojo was a sadistic boot camp that made Stu Hart's Dungeon look laid-back in comparison. Its usually teenage pupils endured merciless emotional abuse, constant and arbitrary corporal punishment of the most extreme sort, sexual humiliation, and cult-like indoctrination. Used with few variations by pro wrestling, sumo wrestling, and martial arts systems alike, the Japanese dojo system was a method of training that produced a body count. The NJPW dojo is a place where some kids actually *died*—many sources have alluded to a great multitude of training-related deaths that have been covered up by the yakuza. One in particular would make the press during Benoit's career with NJPW: the dojo murder of trainee Hiromitsu Gompei in 1995, when, according to my sources, the dojo regime had actually become more lenient than in Benoit's day nine years before.

Gompei's murder may be one of the most appalling episodes in pro wrestling history, especially since the alleged murderer became a huge star without ever facing punishment. Considering the involvement of the yakuza, it's not surprising that most NJPW wrestlers refuse to go on the record about the incident. The story I've been told by multiple reputable NJPW sources is that wrestler Kensuke Sasaki allegedly lost his temper with the young trainee who was not performing up to NJPW's athletic standard.

"What happened, the guy [Gompei] wasn't cuttin' it," claims one NJPW veteran. "And Sasaki lost his temper and, the way I heard it, suplexed him a couple million times pretty bad. I don't know if it was supposed to just hurt him, or worse, but he went way overboard. He made an example of the kid. The kid just died right in the ring. He was beat to death for not being good."

Another NJPW wrestler who spoke to me on the condition of anonymity asserted that the physically exhausted Gompei had just finished his workout for the day when NJPW booker Riki Choshu arrived at the dojo. Seeking to impress the disciplinarian Choshu, the trainers made Gompei start his four-hour workout from the beginning. Physically drained and suffering from repeated bumps to the head during his first workout, Gompei embarrassed everyone in front of the boss by being unable to keep up, leading to Sasaki's gratuitous response.

"No one took it personally that I could see besides [NJPW star, Japanese senator, and former Sasaki tag partner] Hiroshi Hase, who left the company. I mean, you didn't ever see him tag with Sasaki again, did you? [Author's Note: After nearly a decade, Hase would tag with Sasaki again on the fitting date of Halloween of 2004.] They just viewed it as, you know, '*Shit happens.*' It was just something that happened at the dojo and was, like, acceptable collateral damage. It was different around the office for a month or so, like quiet and tense. They were worried as hell that it would become a big news story. It didn't; Sasaki became champion a couple hundred times after that."

To this day, asking anyone involved with the Japanese wrestling scene about Hiromitsu Gompei is the quickest way to lose a source. As of February of 2008, Kensuke Sasaki was the world heavyweight champion of All Japan Pro Wrestling. Sasaki's top wrestling protégé, Kenzo Suzuki, fled Japan in 2003 after being involved in a dojo death scandal of his own, when Takayuki "Giant Ochiai" Okada allegedly died under his supervision. Suzuki thereafter became a WWE star.

Upon arriving in Tokyo, Benoit was met by a trainer who immediately established that he expected absolute silence, obedience, and discipline. Outside of exercise and drill directions, Benoit and Peterson would not be spoken to in English for months after their arrival. Transported to the NJPW dojo, Benoit walked through a large, barren gym with concrete floors, free weights, a worn ring, and tour posters on the wall. Escorted to a painfully small room stuffed with narrow bunk beds and sleeping bags on the floor, Benoit realized that privacy would exist only in the toilet stall containing a hole in the ground that he would have to squat over. The Japanese veterans walked past in a manner that told Benoit they were making a point not to acknowledge him. It was strictly enforced company policy that the veterans should be as mean as possible to the Young Boys to scare the weak away.

At the approach of the foreigners and the trainer, the Japanese trainees dropped their eyes and shuffled out of the way, busying themselves with menial chores in a desperate bid not to be noticed. They scurried meekly about like beaten children. Like Marines who exhale and grow balls as soon as their drill sergeant retires to his quarters, as soon as the trainers left, the native trainees gave the young *gaijin* (a mildly racist, ubiquitous term for foreigners) contemptuous looks that let them know exactly how small their chance of survival was. The average aspiring Japanese wrestler lasted less than one practice at the NJPW dojo; even the toughest amateur wrestlers and martial artists often became "dojo runaways" who fled in the middle of the night. The rate of graduation from the initial tryouts to debut in a NJPW ring was exceptionally small; according to some estimates, around one percent of prospective students in the 1980s graduated from the dojo, making becoming a NJPW wrestler nearly as prestigious as becoming an Olympic athlete. This was a mark of pride for the dojo—only the strongest survived, and, to your average, racist, old-school Japanese wrestler, there were no white boys tough enough to withstand Japanese training. "They did just everything they could to physically break us," Peterson said in a 2002 interview.

Benoit later claimed that he suffered a particularly brutal initiation to the dojo: he was ordered to stand in front of a gauntlet of native wrestlers who proceeded to punch him directly in each ear as hard as they could, one after the other, until both of his ears were mangled and bloody. For the rest of his time at the dojo, his trainers fixed tight headlocks across Benoit's busted ears until all of the cartilage was destroyed. Misshapen and engorged with hardened blood, Benoit's "cauliflower ears" were considered a badge of honor.

The average day at the NJPW dojo began at 8 a.m. when a trainer loudly trampled into the trainees' communal quarters and woke them up "military style." As they silently made their beds and cleaned up their quarters, the trainer barked in Japanese and punched them in the head if they were sloppy, slow, or made the slightest noise. After the trainees dressed in their identical NJPW tracksuit uniform, the entire class of shaven-headed grunts would be marched out for a long three-to-five-mile run. This was followed by a large communal Japanese breakfast of rice, miso soup, and an assortment of salted fish, fermented soybeans, seaweed, plums, pickles, and tea—a meal that left a starving Peterson and Benoit nauseous. They had no choice but to eat it with a smile; a decade later, a foreign trainee who complained was allegedly sodomized with a banana for his finicky taste in food.

Afterwards, there was an hour break for the chores assigned to the trainees. The Japanese dojo system operated according to a *kohai/sempai* system. In addition to his trainers, the Young Boy, or *kohai*, becomes an indentured servant to a veteran wrestler, the *sempai*, who in return for complete obedience will teach the Young Boy about the business. The Young Boy was expected to run errands for his sempai, from going to the grocery store to picking up his mail, in addition to doing his laundry, carrying his bags, polishing his boots, spotting him during workouts, and washing his back in the shower. One American wrestler told me stories of a referee in training who was kept up every night well past 2:00 a.m. doing all the all the laundry he had been given. When the American wrestler felt pity for the young referee and took him out for a beer, NJPW's management team of Riki Choshu and Masa Saito chastised him. "This is Japanese way. Don't be nice to Young Boy!" he was told.

A Young Boy's absolute obedience to his sempai naturally lent itself to abuse. Bad News Allen forced his Young Boy, Hiro Saito, to repeatedly gorge himself on food until he vomited, over and over and over, so that onlookers could be entertained by the scene. According to multiple sources, trainees in the Japanese promotion FMW were forced to masturbate into a refrigerated jar until it was full and then finally drink it upon their sempai's orders. Even Giant Baba, a superstar second only to Antonio Inoki, would obediently let his far smaller, less successful, and less talented sempai publicly berate and beat him well into his career. When wrestler Freddie Blassie asked Baba's sempai why he treated his megastar pupil so cruelly, he responded, "This is how I teach him. Otherwise, he'd be an idiot his whole life."

It's common for Young Boys to be asked to get into the shower with their sempai to wash his back, but there are many stories of Young Boys being instructed to do far more demeaning acts in the shower. The tamest story I've been told is of a large American wrestler in Japan who was in the locker room showers with NJPW superstar Shinya Hashimoto. "Hashimoto calls over his Young Boy and tells him something in Japanese. I go about washing myself, and suddenly I feel a washcloth very lovingly caressing me from behind. I turn around, and Hashimoto is smiling this wicked smile as he watches his poor Young Boy suffer the humiliation of washing me. I said, 'No, thank you,' but Hashimoto just egged him on, 'Go very slow. He big man, *very big* man. Take your time; get *all* the spots.' I felt bad for the poor kid because, if he had said no to Hashimoto, they would have whupped his ass so bad." Routinely compared to a "prison bitch" due to the shower duties, the Young Boy had to rely on his sempai for protection. If his sempai didn't step in and stand up for him, a Young Boy would be compelled to obey the orders of *any* NJPW veteran, no matter how inhumane or cruel.

After doing their assigned chores, at around 10:00 a.m. the trainees gathered in the main gym and began their workout. They would start, according to 1991 NJPW dojo graduate Osamu Nishimura, with "at least" 1,000 Hindu squats (a few hundred Hindu squats are enough to debilitate the legs of an average professional wrestler for a day or two) and 500 pushups. The trainers would beat their thighs with bamboo swords as they squatted and kick their ribs or sit on their backs as they did their pushups. If any of the trainees showed that they were in pain during an exercise, then they would be told to do the exercise again and again. "Your legs hurt? Okay, just give 200 more.... Good, good, now just 500 more and you are done." Afterwards, the trainees would be led through an arduous series of calisthenics, amateur wrestling exercises, and jump rope drills. Any wrestler who performed an exercise imperfectly could be spit on, punched in the face, kicked in the groin, or have his legs suddenly swept from under him.

The verbal assault was worse, coupling homophobic and racist insults with threats of public disgrace, torture, or even murder. "Screw up again, and I'll kill you!" was a common refrain. At every opportunity, the trainers were instructed to abuse the trainees so that only the most desperate and determined would stay. On a daily basis, the wrestlers were ritually sent home: "Call Mommy and Daddy and tell them you're coming home. I have no use for you!" They were only allowed to stay if they groveled and begged. The trainers attempted to provoke abject panic and desperation in their students, driving them to the edge of a psychological breakdown. Only when the trainers had provoked a primal, maddened, hell-bent fury did they let up—a wrestler pushed to his breaking point is a wrestler who looks like he's really fighting for his life in the ring.

After a brisk sprint, it was time for the trainees to enter the ring—only they wouldn't be wrestling. One of the established shooters on the roster stretched each trainee one after the other, torturing each by applying hold after hold until he screamed and begged for mercy. Though these lessons at times developed into informative, cooperative martial arts training sessions, they were just as often used as an excuse for a trained fighter to assault an opponent who could only fight back with permission. Benoit would later tell WCW announcer Chad Damiani that the Japanese trainers beat him so badly that "he wet himself" in the ring in front of his classmates.

After the shoot workout, each of the trainees would have a "pro" workout in the ring, which for the first two months consisted of nothing but taking bumps over and over and over until they pissed blood and were woozy from concussions. If one of the veterans had a new, dangerous maneuver he needed to perfect, it would be the trainees who took it dozens of times in a row while he worked out the kinks.

After a few months of training, the Young Boys were slowly allowed to practice basic moves with the veterans and trainers. It was the veterans' job to teach the Young Boys to look real by shrugging off the Young Boys' moves if they were anything less than full force. This wasn't WWE; this was New Japan, and it was *real* fighting, even if the matches were fixed. Each time the Young Boys threw a weak blow, the veterans would hit back for real, busting open their eyebrows and lips, insulting them, calling them women and "faggots," telling them that they'd never be tough enough to stand in a NJPW ring. This learning process would take months before the Young Boys learned to convincingly work

NJPW's "Strong Style"—pro wrestling that looks like it hurts because it does.

Even after their work looked good, the "sparring" practices continued, and the intensity of the physical and emotional abuse only escalated. The trainers need to make sure that any weakness that lies in the depths of their student's souls comes out during practice instead of in the ring on a live show where it can expose the business. The idea is to put wrestlers through such superhuman duress in training that they will be prepared for absolutely anything in the ring.

After the in-ring training ended at 2:00 p.m., the wrestlers adjourned to their own individual pursuits for a few hours. When I asked Osamu Nishimura what he did in his free time, he responded, "Young Boys have no free time. Always washing [veteran's] car, shopping [for a veteran], cooking, and training with an elder wrestler." Benoit suffered such intense homesickness that it's doubtful he wanted free time at the dojo; there was nothing to do but think. In those long, afternoon hours, the dojo was as quiet and lonely as a high school gym after school has been let out. Most trainees used the afternoon to take a nap, but if a trainer saw a Young Boy moping around or looking bored, there was *always* cleaning to be done. There was also always exercise: Benoit and Peterson were taken to Buddhist and Shinto temples and forced to run up and down the steps until they collapsed. They'd flip a coin afterwards to see who would have to get up and fetch some water so they wouldn't die from dehydration there.

Late in the afternoon, the Young Boys would convene once more in the gym to lift weights and do individual exercises. Afterwards, it would be time for dinner, which in many ways was the worst punishment of the day. *Chanko* was on the menu every night, a mucky chicken and vegetable stew consumed by sumo wrestlers to gain weight. Benoit found it revolting, and, as a new recruit, he was last to be served and thus got the dregs.

With a strict curfew in effect, Benoit had little to do after dinner besides rest his ailing body and wait for the midnight bedtime. On occasion, the trainers would smash through the door at 2 a.m. for a surprise workout.

Benoit loathed training in New Japan. He hated the food, the trainers, the culture, the loneliness, the homesickness, and the absence of conversation. Even for a graduate of the Dungeon, the pain was hellish and, unlike Stu's family atmosphere, there was never a point at which camaraderie and revelry intruded. On a brief trip home, Benoit talked with his mentors in Stampede, who reminded him of the Ivy League prestige associated with graduating from the NJPW dojo. He decided it was a sacrifice that a real pro wrestler should be ecstatic to make.

Returning to Japan, Benoit began to accompany the regular roster on NJPW's tours. Since he was being treated as a native Young Boy instead of a VIP gaijin talent, Benoit slept on the floors of tiny budget hotel rooms without in-room bathrooms or any sort of heating or air-conditioning. Benoit put up the rings before shows, did chores backstage, helped "injured" wrestlers walk from the ring, and stood in as the convenient victim when the villains went nuts. From his ringside post, Benoit was studying world-class wrestlers like Tatsumi Fujinami, Akira Maeda, and Nobuhiko Takada up close.

On January 2, 1987, "Dynamite" Chris Benoit made his New Japan debut after five months of training at the dojo. His opponent was Masakatsu Funaki, a member of Benoit's dojo class whom Benoit considered by far the most athletically gifted of any of the NJPW's Young Lions (NJPW-trained rookies). The handsome Funaki with his impeccable timing and strong shooting skills was considered a future NJPW superstar, but he did not defeat Chris Benoit that night. In a highly uncharacteristic show of the wrestling organization's esteem for Benoit, he did not lose his first match; it went to a draw. Wrestlers debuting from the dojo usually lost every match for months or even years. Benoit avoided defeat in his debut against the top athlete in his class; Funaki would leave pro wrestling to become one of the first great mixed martial arts superstars in Japanese history.

Benoit toured with NJPW as a Young Lion for six months, working early on the card, usually losing but showing great fighting spirit in the process. He was told to keep his offense simple and concentrate on looking authentic. Though the Young Lion matches were quite basic, they were fought with more intensity and viciousness than most main event matches on the cards. The Japanese Young Lions were desperate to get noticed, and, unlike cooperative American wrestlers, they would "eat you alive" if you didn't forcefully *take* your portion of the offense.

Though Benoit would win few matches in his first run with NJPW, he would garner two victories over future world champion Kensuke Sasaki, himself just a rookie. In August of 1987, a year after his arrival in Japan, Benoit was sent home to Stampede; they no longer needed his services as a Young Lion. Instead, in November of the same year, Benoit returned for his first full tour as a full-fledged gaijin roster member.

The change in accommodations and treatment was breathtaking. Instead of sleeping on floors, Benoit was booked in five-star American-style hotels with king-sized beds, air-conditioning/heating, and Western toilets. Instead of traveling in the back of the cramped Japanese bus with no one to talk to, he traveled in luxury on the foreign bus with other gaijin stars who were making $5,000-$20,000 a week, many of whom he knew from Stampede. When the gaijins arrived at arenas, a Beatlemania crush of fans surrounded the bus, waiting for monster stars like Bad News to charge out and toss them around. Benoit watched in wonder as Bad News belted teenagers and old men in the face and was thanked profusely for it. Instead of washing the balls of some old Japanese wrestler, suddenly it was Benoit who was being catered to, given expensive gifts by rich fans and taken out to $1,000 dinners by the yakuza. At the end of the tour, Benoit was given a deferential bow and an envelope with bank-fresh bills, easily hidden from taxes. On his first tour as a regular gaijin, Benoit wrestled his earliest unheralded singles matches against Keiichi Yamada, the young man who would become Jushin Thunder Liger, his greatest rival.

After establishing Benoit as a full-fledged gaijin roster member, NJPW told their promising Canadian prospect to return home and pay his dues for a few more years. All Young Lions needed a foreign "learning excursion" to perfect their craft before the crowd would take them seriously as threats to the established roster. Wrestlers who went on learning excursions were also expected to return with greatly improved bodies, utilizing improved access to bodybuilding drugs overseas to bulk up away from fans so their drastic overnight muscle gain would not be as obvious. Benoit would be no different than those before him.

When he had fully mastered the art of pro wrestling and remodeled his body, Benoit was promised that he could return to NJPW as a star. He would be the new Dynamite Kid to their new version of Tiger Mask.

Chapter V
The Boots of the Dynamite Kid

"Tom was scaring us. He now kept three huge Bullmastiffs and had amassed an arsenal of shotguns and pistols. When we took the kids to visit him and [his wife] Michelle, he sat on his back porch shooting at anything that moved, even though the kids were playing nearby in the sandbox. He seemed to take some sick pleasure in blowing the back legs off jackrabbits while he washed down pain pills with vodka and orange juice."

BRET HART

A CORNERED ANIMAL

IT TOOK THE MAFIA TO FINALLY PUT THE DYNAMITE KID DOWN. While Benoit was training in Japan in 1986, the Dynamite Kid was making over $300,000 a year as one half of the WWE tag champions, the British Bulldogs—until his suicidal in-ring style resulted in spinal damage so severe that he suffered temporary paralysis. His doctors insisted in the strongest terms possible that he must immediately retire. Only twenty-eight years old, Dynamite doubled his steroid intake, which was already at astronomical levels, to quicken his rehabilitation. After thousands of injections, Tom's ass became so scarred that it could bend a normal syringe without breaking the skin. No matter how muscular he got, the maddening back pain never subsided, so he loaded up on "drugstore-sized jars of Placidyl and Percocet" and drank "forty ounces of vodka every night before bed."

Dynamite's wrestling career had peaked. His body was too debilitated, drugged, and over-developed to match the young Dynamite's speed and skill, and his mind was too addled to carry its portion of the matches. Racked with pain, existentially terrified that his degenerating physical state would prevent him from wrestling, eviscerated with jealousy and constantly drunk, high, or roid-raging, Billington aged a decade in the two years after his injury.

Physically and professionally vulnerable, Billington compensated by abusing his colleagues. Always a locker room bully, he became the nightmare of WWE, the ribber who would stomp the joy out of his target's life. If Billington sensed a weak personality in the locker room, he made example of them to let everyone know that he was still dangerous. Dynamite became so desperate for validation as a man that he even bragged about reducing bird-armed Wayne "Honky Tonk Man" Farris, a feeble alcoholic and Elvis impersonator, to tears—a feat that hardly required the courage of a lion. More pathetic was Billington's abuse of Jake "The Snake" Roberts' pet python, which waited backstage in a tightly secured sack for Jake's matches. Billington poured scalding coffee onto the confined snake and stabbed it with steroid needles, sniggering to himself.

Jacques Rougeau was a sheepish French-Canadian lightweight whose tough brother Raymond had been his bodyguard and babysitter in the industry. Once Raymond was incapacitated by injury, Dynamite recognized in Jacques a defenseless target with no experience standing up for himself. Without any justification, Dynamite launched a concerted campaign to completely emasculate Rougeau to the point that Rougeau's own friends no longer respected him enough to greet him in public. How could anyone respect a man who meekly slunk away after Billington walked up and slapped the food out of his mouth at mealtime for no particular reason?

Though Jacques was the first to admit he was no tough guy—he preferred to quietly read in the locker room rather than talk shit—he hated Billington enough to grow balls. One day Billington made a point to sneer at Jacques while passing him in the hallway and, as he strolled slowly by, he crept extra close just to belittle Jacques, who had his eyes on his shoes. Suddenly, the meek French-Canadian looked up and belted Dynamite in the face with a fist loaded with a roll of quarters. Knocked senseless, Billington's jaw fell slack, and his mouth disgorged a goopy mess of teeth, shredded gums, and blood. Stunned, spinning, and blind with pain, Billington could not defend himself, braving an onslaught of loaded jabs to the face, which didn't end until Bad News Allen rushed in and separated them. The Dynamite Kid, the ultimate hard man, had just suffered a public ass-kicking in front of the entire WWE at the hands of one of the wimpiest men in wrestling.

Though the boys respected Jacques for standing up to Billington, the smart money was that he would soon be visiting a mortician. But Jacques was smarter than Dynamite: he took on the toughest psychopath in wrestling with a safety net. Dynamite's schoolyard bullying had limits to its efficacy.

A Montreal resident and local celebrity, Jacques had close friends within the notoriously bloodthirsty and trigger-happy Montreal Mafia. Taking a sheet of paper with the Billington family's residence in Alberta to one of his friends, Jacques told him that, if he did not call every night at midnight, to assume the worst and put a bullet in Billington's head. The next step in Jacques' plan was brilliant: he whispered what he had done to fellow Quebecois WWE wrestler, Adolfo "Dino Bravo" Bresciano, who just happened to be a real-life Montreal wiseguy who could confirm the story.

Naturally, Bresciano didn't want the murder of two WWE stars traced back to his neighborhood, so he informed Vince, who rather casually let Billington know that he would be murdered if he touched Jacques. Unable to avenge his humiliation, Billington coerced Davey Boy Smith into resigning from WWE with him. At the same time, Bad News Allen was tirelessly lobbying Vince McMahon to hire Chris Benoit as Dynamite's replacement.

Despite openly taking out a Mafia contract on a WWE wrestler, Jacques Rougeau would be a WWE mainstay for many years to come. Dino Bravo would be a WWE star until his retirement in the early 90s; within a year of his last match he was executed in a gangland murder. McMahon's nonchalance about the Mafia is not surprising; his family's exclusive rights to promote wrestling in New York City dated back to the days of Lucky Luciano, when every major sports venue was at least partially controlled by the Mob. Wrestling agent Bob Barnett's father was a NYC Mob attorney whose office was adjacent to the Mob-controlled athletic commission, and he regularly saw Vince McMahon's father personally dropping off envelopes of cash. Bob himself was introduced to the special ushers at McMahon's events that let in the "connected" for free.

Whatever sanity and emotional stability Billington had retained through his years of self-abuse was completely shattered by his exit from WWE. Billington's sick psyche had been held together by his ability to expend his aggression in the ring and in the locker room. This gave him a reputation as a wrestler and a hard man to salve his insecurities and constant opportunities for sadistic release. With a crippled body that no longer could perform in the ring, the only reputation Billington now had was as a has-been wrestler and Jacques Rougeau's bitch. Irreparable harm had been done to Billington's ego, and no matter how cruelly he ribbed the boys, there was now always plenty of aggression and hatred left over for himself. Billington was a snake feeding off its own tail.

Billington returned to his home in Alberta, purchased an arsenal of firearms, and offered to return with Davey Boy if Stu ousted Bruce and made him a booker.

Since Stu was convinced there wasn't a shittier booker in the Milky Way Galaxy than Bruce Hart, he accepted without hesitation. Happy to have an excuse to shitcan his son under any circumstances, Stu hoped that the return of two WWE wrestling superstars and Stampede legends would be the credibility boost needed to return the family business to chandelier-shopping-spree levels of profitability.

TWO TAILSPINS MERGE

CHRIS BENOIT WAS A WORLD-CLASS PROFESSIONAL WITH A BLOSSOMING INTERNATIONAL REPUTATION. As the only graduate of both the Hart Dungeon and the New Japan dojo, the two toughest schools in the world, Benoit had untouchable backstage credibility. Three years of harsh training, hazing, and ribbing had aged the boyish *Howdy Doody* shine from his face, and his lean, natural-looking teenage physique had been transformed into a painfully swollen steroid build. Benoit looked tough.

His in-ring style had developed into a robust reinterpretation of the Dynamite Kid's act. Dedicated Stampede fans began to speculate that Benoit's snap suplexes actually seemed more powerful than Dynamite's, and it was undeniable that Benoit's flying headbutts were higher and more graceful than Dynamite's. Benoit's headbutts even bested Dynamite's on the basis of their self-destructiveness: while Billington clearly cushioned his fall with his hands, Benoit held his arms up high like he was on a roller coaster and took the unprotected fall directly on his forehead. By the age of twenty, Benoit was collecting title belts and accumulating brain damage.

It can be assumed that Benoit was ecstatic when his hero replaced his primary tormentor Bruce Hart as his boss. Billington had always liked the terse and humble Benoit as a person, and he respected him professionally for graduating from the NJPW dojo. As far as his toughness, anyone who could earn the respect and praise of the harshest critic in the world, Bad News Allen, had to be one tough bastard. Billington was happy to hear that his biggest admirer had earned international acclaim, and Benoit's genuine reverence for him was a rare balm for his insecurities. Benoit was always there to listen sympathetically to his idol's tough-guy bluster and deranged shit talk.

Stamped fans eagerly awaited the all-time classic feud where Billington would pass the baton to his protégé. "In fact, if it wasn't for the difference in age," Billington wrote, "I would definitely have had Chris Benoit as a tag partner; that's how high I rated him." Dynamite practiced with Benoit in the ring and taught him exactly how to duplicate his moves, which was an indescribable high for Benoit.

Dynamite could use the political support that his wide-eyed lackey was sure to provide. It only took a few months of Dynamite's booking to wear out the goodwill and support of the Stampede roster. Though attendance initially spiked with the return of the British Bulldogs from the big time, it was immediately clear that Dynamite could no longer perform in the ring as he once had. Unlike wrestlers who rely on their gimmick and their charisma, Dynamite's popularity largely rested on his rapidly evaporating ability as a stuntman and acrobat. As soon as the casual fans attracted by the novelty of the Bulldogs left, Billington panicked, rightly realizing that Bruce would poison Stu and Helen against him if he were anything but a huge success.

With his job in jeopardy, Billington began to rush through money programs in an amphetamine-fueled fury to regain the huge crowds of the early 80s. Billington's seat-of-the-pants booking wreaked havoc on Stampede's storyline continuity. The new Stampede alienated the longtime fans by replacing Bruce's colorful characters and far-out storylines with Billington's austere, violent aesthetic. The desperation booking of elaborate stipulation matches drained these reliable draws of their meaning, and the countless cage/ladder matches with blood-drenched combatants drove away families and squeamish teenage girls. Both Stampede and Dynamite had entered a tailspin.

These few months on the road with Billington were the ultimate fulfillment of Benoit's dream to be a pro wrestler. Benoit was touring, not only as a peer of the Dynamite Kid, but as his friend and protégé. Benoit was also the booker's pet, scripted to hold both the Mid-Heavyweight and tag titles at once. Being in such close proximity to Billington, Benoit had plenty of time to study the downfall of his hero. Every morning, Billington needed speed to wake him up and painkillers to let him move, and he could not sleep without being heavily tranquilized by a cocktail of booze, pain pills, and potent downers. Sweating and slurring through his hate-filled rants, Billington couldn't hide that he was a pathetic old junkie. The only time anyone ever saw him smile was when he shot something, especially during the hotly competitive gopher hunts he held for his clique.

There's no reason to believe Benoit derived any insight into the dangers of the self-destructive lifestyle he shared with Billington. During his time with Dynamite, in fact, Benoit's tag-team with Biff Wellington was given the locker room nickname of the Mega-Doses for their steroid consumption, which must have been truly immense to stand out as excessive on a roster that boasted abusers like Dynamite, Davey Boy Smith, and Brian Pillman. Benoit watched Smith, Pillman, and Wellington all die from steroid abuse and nonetheless never curbed his habit. If Benoit learned anything from Billington's example, it was something destructive.

How much of Benoit's later sadistic behavior was learned at the foot of the master? Benoit already romanticized the wrestling businesses, its traditions, and its code of honor to the point that he would become enraged by any criticism or perceived disrespect to the business. The Harts, Billington, and his teachers at the New Japan dojo all enforced respect for the business through violence and humiliation, through "stretching" and ribs. All of Benoit's formative influences in the Business were merciless and cruel, so it should come as no surprise that a naïve young man who believed in wrestling like Jesuits believe in Christ would unquestioningly follow the sadistic example of his teachers. Ross Hart tells a story of watching Benoit lose his mind with rage and choke another young wrestler on the Stampede van for daring to violate etiquette by claiming he was as tough as the veterans. "He was a quiet kid, but when the steroids kicked in, I saw a different side to him, the anger and the sudden rages," Billington said of Benoit.

When Billington left to tour Japan for a few weeks in April of 1989, Bruce Hart secretly resumed his booking duties. Billington returned to see that his job had been stolen behind his back, which played directly into his paranoia and insecurity. The addled Billington concocted a plan for vengeance that almost killed half of the Stampede crew. As Bruce was driving one of the two Stampede vans, Billington handed him a heavily spiked drink, which Bruce smartly declined.

After this kamikaze plan failed, Billington insisted that half the roster get shitfaced before the next event to show disrespect to Bruce as boss. To explain away their late arrival, Billington kicked in the front window of their van so they could claim they were in an accident. Bruce reprimanded the drunk and seething Billington as soon as he arrived, which gave Dynamite the excuse he needed to break Bruce's jaw. Fleeing the building in mortal terror, Bruce ran to lock himself in the other Stampede van as a drunken lynch mob of Billington's supporters gave chase. As Bruce begged for mercy, Billington's crew rattled the van and tried to kick in the windows until the police arrived, which only provoked the maddened Billington to attempt to lead a riot against *them*.

Humiliated by Bruce, a pansy compared to rival Jacques Rougeau, the inconsolabe Billington became consumed by his addictions to the point that he was barely sentient, a mumbling lobotomy patient with clenched fists shuffling about backstage, lost in booze and bitterness. At home, he had taken to shoving a shotgun under his wife's chin when she talked back, traumatizing her so badly that she seriously considered murdering their two kids before killing herself to escape from Billington's abuse.

"When that wrestling ability diminished, so too did his self-esteem, his self-worth," said Billington's wife in an interview. "I remember him watching especially the Japanese tapes, his Tiger Mask matches, just over and over. It was an obsession with him, just regretting that he couldn't do that anymore." Behind the scenes, Billington was engulfed in a hateful feud with Davey Boy, which would eventually devolve into a breakup so acrimonious that Billington promised to murder his cousin if they ever met face-to-face.

The only person to whom Billington showed the slightest kindness was Benoit. In a moment that was easily the proudest of his life to that point, Benoit wrestled a match so good that it inspired the Dynamite Kid to come to the ring and bestow a pair of his boots around Benoit's neck. To a wrestler who would never be secure in his talents, it meant a great deal that his peers saw Billington, one of the best wrestlers in the world, deem Benoit worthy of wearing his boots. Nearly two decades later, those boots still sat in the "place of honor" in Benoit's home office. "I value them so much," said Benoit. It hardly mattered to him that Billington was so drunk when he offered his boots that he could barely stand.

On July 4, 1989, Stampede's babyface van was driving en route to the tiny mountain hamlet of Jasper when Ross Hart, the driver, lost control on an icy mountain road. For a few moments the van skidded to the ledge of a cliff, only for Ross to swerve instead into a station wagon. The impact launched Benoit from the back of the van like a rocket, a trajectory interrupted by Ross

Hart's instinctual lunge to grab him in mid-air. Instead, Davey Boy Smith soared headfirst through the windshield. Stampede's top babyface star and the anchor of its main feud suffered two herniated discs at the top of his spine and 135 stitches-worth of surface damage to his body.

With Davey Boy sidelined for the rest of 1989, the already languishing Stampede had no main event draws and thus no hope at all for survival. At the end of the year, Stu Hart closed Stampede to save what was left of the family fortune.

Though Benoit suffered a knee injury in the crash that should have kept him from wrestling for at least a month, he insisted on returning to the ring within three days. Business came first, as always. Despite bounced checks and a lucrative standing offer from New Japan, Benoit stuck with Stampede to the very end. In his last match in the territory, he lost to a wrestler named The Angel of Death.

Both Benoit and Billington left for Japan in the wake of Stampede's fall: Benoit to follow in his idol's footsteps, Billington to retire in what would be the highest rated wrestling program in the history of its timeslot. While Benoit would go on to greater fame than Billington ever attained, the Dynamite Kid would be abandoned by his tag partner and his family. After being beaten by civilians in a bar fight and given a one-way ticket to England by his wife, Billington returned home a broken man. Billington actually died twice during a subsequent overdose, only to be unmercifully resuscitated by paramedics. After a few years of competing in human cockfights held in the garages of gamblers, Billington lost the use of his legs. One of the greatest athletes in wrestling history is confined to a wheelchair for the rest of his life.

For years afterward, Bret Hart and Benoit would offer to fly Billington back to Canada to visit his children, but Billington was always too proud to accept. He would rather never see his kids than show his withered body in public.

The death of territories like Stampede Wrestling would turn out to be a tragedy for reasons other than nostalgia for wrestling's bygone NWA days. Most wrestlers would suffer greatly due to the industry's transformation from numerous regional, locally owned, mom-and-pop promotions into a marketplace completely dominated by two multinational conglomerates. The NWA business model provided regular paychecks and TV exposure for hundreds of wrestlers of all shapes and sizes, all of whom had leverage with their employers because there were so many other promoters who also needed talent to fill *their* cards. Careers were longer because the lack of head-to-head competition meant the wrestlers could work a safer style without worrying about being shown up. More wrestlers got a chance, and those who did perform could do so without surrendering their dignity wholesale to a promoter they found cruel or exploitative. They could always leave and still make a living.

When all the territories were absorbed or run out of business by WWE and WCW, the plight of most wrestlers became hopeless. The job market shrunk by over ninety percent, and while the handful of top guys enjoyed colossal salary increases, the average wrestler became completely disenfranchised. With so few spots available, competition became deadly; wrestling's notoriously high mortality rate is a phenomenon that arose as a direct result of the 1980s consolidation of the industry.

Suddenly, a wrestler had to passively accept awful treatment by management if he wanted one of the precious few jobs in WWE or WCW. Even giants were powerless in the face of overwhelming supply and minuscule demand.

"You know, when I joined WWF or WWE back in 1993," remembered the 6'10" Kevin Nash, "I signed a contract that said the only thing I was guaranteed was ten dates and 150 bucks. I was guaranteed $1,500. I was a 1099 [IRS code for independent contractors]. I had no health insurance. No dental insurance. Nothing for my family. When I signed that contract, I read that contract as a man at 29 or 30 years old." Though Nash was a physical freak with national television exposure, he signed the contract, which likely included a clause that stated that, even if WWE were criminally negligent to the point of *killing* Nash, his family would be owed no damages.

To earn the opportunity to sign such a shitty deal, a young wrestler had to abuse steroids, wrestle a more dangerous style, and work through all of his injuries. If a wrestler didn't make these sacrifices, he could never compete with the hundreds of out-of-work wannabes who were willing to do so. Unlike the NWA territories which kept a wrestler within driving distance of his family at most times, these international brands sent their wrestlers from one end of the continent to the other, leaving them very little time to scramble for the few available jobs. This in effect put an end to the camaraderie that had existed in the territories. No longer were wrestlers members of a freewheeling carny brotherhood, a traveling biker gang; now they were interchangeable cogs within a heavily bureaucratic corporate behemoth, cowering in their cubicles in fear of the next downsizing.

"We're all dying off to be a guinea pig for McMahon," said former WWE star Billy Jack Haynes. "I hear people ask, 'Well, why is McMahon responsible? You put it in your own system, you put it in your own mouth?' I'll tell you why. You could be making $300,000 in one year, but in one day you could be fired by McMahon. He had complete control. ...If [McMahon] fired you, *you couldn't work for another territory for one year* in the deal we had to sign. Everyone signed it to go to work. He was on a real powertrip."

"I remember the merchandising contract [WWE] gave us," said Bad News Allen. "It said, not only can you not work for Japan, you cannot work for anybody [else] in the universe. *The universe*? You mean this guy controls Mars and everything? It was unbelievable."

For anyone but the biggest stars, taking time off to spend time at home or recuperate from injuries put their careers in jeopardy, so most wrestlers self-medicated and neglected their families. The subsequent increase in emotional and physical strain led to the exponential increase in steroids, street narcotics, pharmaceuticals, and painkillers use. This pervasive drug culture transformed wrestling into the notorious death trap we know today. Instead of being an oddball blue-collar job for hammy showmen with athletic skill, wrestling became a dreary, desperate, Hollywood-style fame trap preying on the misguided dreamers willing to do *absolutely anything* for a chance at stardom.

Today, thanks to the fall of the territories, wrestling has less in common with its carnival and vaudeville roots than it does with the big money porn business, where a huge corporate infrastructure profits from the exploitation of drug-addled wannabe celebrities with grotesquely "enhanced" bodies. At least in porn, the talent works an easy schedule, and the damage the talent inflicts on itself in exchange for a cut-rate version of fame is usually not fatal. Even the most vigorous porn star would have a hard time fucking himself into a wheelchair for the rest of his life.

Chapter VI
The Silent Assassin

"Chris Benoit was the silent assassin. He
was the worst ribber in the business. He
ribbed hard. Those Calgary boys are fuckin'
nuts, and he was the most nuts."

SCOTT NORTON

THE WINGED HORSEMAN

KEIICHI YAMADA WAS CHRIS BENOIT'S DOPPELGANGER:
A SMALL, SERIOUS MAN POSSESSED BY THE PRO WRESTLING
DEMON. Ever since he was a small child, Yamada dreamt
only of a career in New Japan Pro Wrestling, and,
knowing that amateur wrestling credentials were the
surest way of overcoming his small stature, Yamada
practiced until he reached the Japanese national
championships. Even with an elite amateur wrestling
resume, however, New Japan refused to let Yamada try
out—he was just too short, only 5'4" or 5'5." Yamada's
stubby legs and arms hardly looked convincingly lethal for
a promotion that billed itself on its authenticity.

Yamada could not bring himself to accept NJPW's
rejection. Using his life savings, Yamada fled to Mexico,
where smaller wrestlers were more accepted, determined
to make such a name there that NJPW would have no
choice but to train him. Alone in a foreign country,
Yamada lived almost as a street urchin so he could train;
to the point that NJPW's Mexican liaisons contacted the

Tokyo office worried about the welfare of this tiny, pathologically determined Japanese boy. Impressed by his obstinacy, NJPW sent word to Mexico that Yamada would be given a chance if he returned to Japan immediately.

Once inside the dojo, Yamada flabbergasted his trainers with his work ethic; they had never seen a young man so single-minded, so hardworking. No matter how badly they treated Yamada, he only thanked them for taking the time to discipline him. Dynamite Kid took a liking to the "very polite and very respectful, very serious" young man, nicknaming him "Frankie Stein" in honor of his bad haircut. So did Bad News, who took notice of Yamada's toughness and determination as he watched the Young Boy silently carry Inoki's luggage on a tour of Pakistan while so grievously ill with a stomach virus that he looked like he would drop dead at any moment. Bad News and Dynamite were extremely stingy with their approval, and the only other young wrestler who so fulsomely earned their respect was Chris Benoit.

Unlike most Young Boys, who treat their graduation from the dojo like parole from prison, Yamada was reluctant to leave. When finally convinced, Yamada moved into a small apartment one block away. The new dojo class got used to the 2 a.m. visits from Yamada, who was too full of ideas to sleep and needed the entire dojo to wake up immediately so they could practice the innovative spots he came up with in bed. The tiny Yamada with curly black hair and a face like a plain Ricky Steamboat, worked out and used steroids until he was as wide as he was tall and could convincingly execute power moves typically used by much bigger men. Despite being built like a little tank, Yamada also retained his speed and acrobatic ability.

With his versatility and incredible brain for the business, Yamada was the perfect centerpiece for NJPW's junior heavyweight division, which had never recovered its Tiger Mask-era popularity. The juiced-up Yamada could give the fans the solid and believable Strong Style wrestling that NJPW's heavyweights worked in addition to the fast-paced, highflying style that Tiger Mask and Dynamite Kid had popularized. Like Tiger Mask, Yamada was given a mask and a persona from a popular TV cartoon to compensate for his bland image. After a learning excursion to Stampede, Keiichi Yamada became Jushin Thunder Liger, a superhero in a red and white full body costume complete with cape, glittery shoulder pads, and a horned mask. The Liger character entered to a bombastic, rip-roaring theme song with a wailing hair-metal guitar solo that drew an excited crowd response all on its own. The combination of the Jushin Liger character's pageantry and Yamada's incredible skills made Junior Heavyweight wrestling hot for the first time since the days of Tiger Mask.

With the demise of Stampede and the junior heavyweight renaissance in Japan, 1990 was the perfect year for Benoit's return to New Japan. Like Tiger Mask, Liger needed a gaijin rival intimidating enough to convince his young fans that their invincible hero was in jeopardy. More jacked-up than ever, Benoit was a monster for a junior heavyweight, and his training in the dojo meant that he knew how to work a brutal and believable Japanese style. Like Yamada, however, Benoit's personality and look was bland, at least too bland to play a superhero's archenemy; Benoit needed a mask and a new character. Consulting with Benoit in Calgary, NJPW agent Tokyo Joe came up with a meaningless name: the Pegasus Kid. For the indefinite future, Chris Benoit would be the masked Pegasus Kid, clad in a shiny blue mask with the profile of a horse on the forehead and wings spreading out around the eyes.

Benoit was horrified when he first practiced under the tight Pegasus Kid mask, comparing it to wearing a straitjacket around his head. Wrestling under a mask for New Japan later in the decade, Chris Jericho in his memoir described his first impressions as, "I couldn't see ...I couldn't breathe...I would've been okay at an S&M convention but how in the hell was I going to wrestle?" Benoit had to learn how to wrestle with limited peripheral vision and what felt like a starfish stuck to his face. And he would have to get it perfect on the first try; masked characters rarely can overcome a weak debut, because the inherent cheesiness of the gimmick demands an exceptionally strong introductory performance to be taken seriously.

Benoit debuted as the Pegasus Kid on the most lucrative pro wrestling event to that point in history. On February 11, 1990, Mike Tyson drew around 30,000 paying fans to the Tokyo Dome to watch his world heavyweight title fight with Buster Douglas. One night before, a co-promotional event held by New Japan and All Japan drew a sellout of 63,900 and around $4 million in revenue. On the second match of the show, the Pegasus Kid tagged with the villainous Naoki Sano to defeat Jushin Liger and Akira Nogami. The response was incredible. In Dave Meltzer's contemporary account in the *Wrestling Observer*, Pegasus Kid was "a blond-haired North American who got over tremendously working a Tiger Mask-type style," who Dave had a feeling "may be Chris Benoit." Four days later, the Tokyo Dome show would air in primetime on national TV, receiving an astronomic 23.2 percent rating. That meant millions more people had watched the Pegasus Kid's debut than had ever watched Hulk Hogan in America. Benoit's match was praised as the best match on the card, and one of the show's highlights was Pegasus' awe-inspiring flying dropkick from the top rope that launched Liger off Nogami's shoulders. Chris Benoit was not a star, but the Pegasus Kid definitely was.

A half-year later, before a sold-out crowd in the legendary Ryogoku Kokugikan, the sumo hall that was NJPW's "holy place," Pegasus Kid won the IWGP Junior Heavyweight Title, the most prestigious in the world for smaller wrestlers, from its most celebrated and popular champion, Jushin Liger. Chris Benoit was only the second foreigner ever to hold the IWGP Jr. title. More meaningful than simply being booked to win the title, the Pegasus Kid was *accepted* by the most discerning and knowledgeable wrestling fans in the world as a worthy champion. When Japanese fans feel a victory is undeserved, the arena will eagerly count along with the referee's first two counts and then recoil in shock after the unexpected third count, emitting a groan as if someone had exposed themselves in the ring. When the masked foreigner Pegasus Kid pinned the most beloved junior heavyweight native in Japan, however, the fans *cheered*, rising to their feet and applauding as Benoit stood on the turnbuckle and raised his finger in the air to tell them he was the Number One junior in the world. "Good guy or bad guy, in Japan, as long as you wrestled as hard as you could, the people didn't care," wrote Tom Billington.

THE GILDED PATH

A FOREIGNER WORKING IN NEW JAPAN IN THE 1990'S ENJOYED MAYBE THE MOST LUXURIOUS AND COMFORTABLE TOURING EXPERIENCE IN THE HISTORY OF THE WRESTLING BUSINESS. The pay was absurdly generous: even Bam Bam Bigelow's *manager* received $3,200 a week, and the biggest stars could make $300,000-$400,000 working only twenty weeks a year, all paid at the end of each tour in envelopes full of cash that would never be reported to the IRS. Unlike in America, travel expenses were also completely covered, from bullet train and first-class jet rides to suites in Western style hotel rooms. With the help of the fans and the yakuza, a wrestler could tour for years without having to buy a drink or a meal or a whore, dining in five-star establishments and partying in elite clubs and brothels. The female groupies were unusually stylish, wealthy, and generous with gifts.

Wrestlers were treated as legitimate, A-list sports stars and celebrities; an NJPW star could walk into a convenience store anywhere in Japan and see his name on the front page of the local newspaper and the cover of three or four magazines. The top film and music superstars in the country were eager to be your friend, pose in front of the paparazzi with their fists clenched next to yours, and buy you $300 cocktails at the hottest nightclubs in Tokyo. When you performed, you uniformly appeared in front of sold out arenas, including multiple dome shows each year that drew crowds upwards of 40,000 or 50,000 affluent, sophisticated fans.

NJPW's three-weeks-on, three-weeks-off touring schedule was unbeatable since, unlike any American company, the workers were always given time to heal their injuries, rest their bodies, and spend quality time with their families. North American wrestlers who made their career in Japan had a much better opportunity to maintain normal, well-adjusted family lives. Since Japanese culture stressed "employment for life" business practices and respect for one's elders, a gaijin star could wrestle for top pay for decades after their physique and athletic skills began to decline. If Chris Benoit had chosen to stay in Japan for his entire career, he would have made a reliable six-figure salary on a comparatively easy schedule for the rest of his life.

Benoit was the top gaijin in NJPW's junior heavyweight division during its most prolonged boom period. As the foreign powerhouse with the vicious technical skill, Benoit was the base for NJPW's high-flying natives. Benoit's success in the junior division encouraged NJPW to import the top young junior talent from North America, including the gifted second-generation wrestlers Eddy Guerrero and Dean Malenko. Together with heavyweight star Scott Norton, a 6'3" 350-pound world champion arm wrestler, Benoit, Guerrero, and Malenko formed an inseparable clique on the road.

With his small 5'6" physique, homely flat-nosed face, a stringy dyed-blond mullet, and nervous body language, Guerrero hardly looked like a star, but he was an uncanny talent in the ring. If Benoit was a great in-ring worker with little charisma, Eddy was a master of

every facet of the game. "He outclassed Benoit, because
there were so many speeds to Eddy," one of the great
bookers in wrestling history told me. "He also knew how to
make you *care* about him and his opponent. Benoit's
strength was to make people care about a *match*. With
Eddy, people cared about the character in the match." A
rising superstar in Mexico, Guerrero quickly mastered the
Japanese style and began to provide Benoit with competition
as the masked Black Tiger.

However, much like Benoit, who always was harder
on his own matches than anyone else, Guerrero was too
humble to realize his own talent. When he met Benoit, he
met him not as an equal but as an intimidated fan. "I liked
Chris from the moment we first shook hands," wrote Eddy
in his memoir. "But when the time came to get into the
ring with him, I was nervous as shit, even a bit intimidated.
The bottom line is, nobody can touch Chris Benoit.... He is
the gold standard."

Benoit quickly recognized how great Guerrero was,
and that, like him, the undersized Guerrero was only
great because he worked harder than anyone else, making
his size irrelevant. The business was the love of Benoit
and Guerrero's lives, and it was easy for them to relate to
each other because they shared the same psychosis. These
two humble, insecure, undersized, compulsive workaholics
forged a bond as outsiders in an industry full of egotistical
giants. Sensitive and gushing with emotional warmth,
Guerrero was a perfect confidante for the uptight,
emotionally cold, and occasionally sadistic Benoit, in
addition to being his ideal weightlifting and dieting partner.
(Guerrero's first name was Anglicized to "Eddie" by the
WWE later in his career. Eddy, however, short for Eduardo,
was what he considered his "real" name: how he signed it
himself, how his friends knew him, how fans first knew him,
and how the wrestling press has always referred to him.)

Dean Malenko was smaller than even Eddy and
Benoit, and his size issues were compounded by a bland
Steve Carell look and methodical submission-based style

that put casual fans into a coma. Though Malenko appeared dull and colorless to strangers, among friends he was known for his dry wit and laidback attitude.

These three unassuming junior heavyweights formed an unlikely brotherhood with mammoth tough guy Scott Norton, a barrel-chested powerhouse with long hair and a badass biker look. Secure in his job thanks to his size, Norton was an easygoing and friendly presence whose reputation for toughness left nothing for him to prove.

While in Japan, one of Benoit's closest friendships was with Norton. "We were best friends," Norton told me. "We were as close as can be. We got along great; some of my best years in the business were spent as Chris Benoit's buddy."

Since New Japan handled the transportation and accommodations from show to show, gaijin had no responsibilities whatsoever afterwards besides having a good time. Benoit's time in New Japan would be the wildest and most socially active of his years in wrestling. "It was draining on both ends," Guerrero said because the heavy partying at night was followed by even heavier workouts in the early morning. Eddy was known to become ten feet tall and a thousand pounds when he drank; as in the Stampede days, Benoit was more often than not the babysitter who made sure his nasty drunk friend did not wake up from his blackout in a hospital bed. Even Norton made sure to stay far away from Guerrero whenever he found his Jekyll in the bottom of a Sapporo beer bottle.

Eddy's booze-fueled transformation into a spiteful little bastard was especially dangerous because, more often than not, the gaijin was partying at the grace of the yakuza. It was a status symbol for the yakuza to be seen spending thousands of dollars on foreign stars at bars, nightclubs, strip clubs, and brothels. The yakuza would introduce the foreign wrestlers to their friends and underlings and have them sign autographs for everyone. In return for pretending to be friends, the yakuza bought the foreigners bottomless plates of Korean barbecue, nights of entertainments at bizarre live sex shows where the audience jumped on stage to participate, and thousand-dollar Japanese delicacies like turtle penis cocktails. At the end of the night, the yakuza shook their guests' hands with $1,000 rolled in their palm.

But the yakuza's hospitality was not unconditional, and the men who were happy to slap around Senator Antonio Inoki clearly were not reluctant to push anyone else around either. Chris Jericho was robbed by the yakuza for breaking a flowerpot, and a breach of etiquette by Tiger Jeet Singh caused the entire local mafia family to barricade a New Japan show with bats and chains. "I remember one time on the way down to the ring, some kid grabbed me and pinched my nipple," one New Japan wrestler told me. "I just backhanded him, not even thinking. Later that night, I got a knock at my door, and it was these two yakuza in black suits holding the kid by the collar. 'Did you hit this kid?' 'Yeah, I think so.' 'Why?' 'He pinched my nipple.' And then they beat the ever-living shit out of him right in front of me. When I told the office about it, they just told me that was how business was done in New Japan."

The civilian Japanese fans were just as eager to squander their hard-earned paychecks as the yakuza were to spend their illicit profits. Japanese culture attaches no social stigma to paying for social company, whether it be with the opposite sex or with celebrities, and "sponsors" spent thousands of dollars every tour to convince foreign wrestlers to spend time with them. "One of the foreigner's goals, I'd have to say, would be to find as many sponsors as possible, obviously, because you know if you have sponsors you will be taken care of," modern Japanese star Eddie Edwards told me. The behavior of the most deferential sponsors could resemble that of a slave, and their wrestlers often responded with treatment befitting a slavemaster. When Vader's elderly female sponsor was late picking him up at the Tokyo airport, the 400-pounder walked up and belted her across the face.

Despite an entire class of fans eager to pay them to party, ribbing still formed a large part of the gaijin crew's recreation. The most fun was had at the expense of wrestlers on their first tour in Japan who, for example, were told the phrase for "Please get me a taxi!" was the Japanese slang for "Suck my dick!" The Japanese boys also embraced this type of harmless rib, even with the largest and most intimidating American wrestlers. When Scott Norton first debuted with the company, referee Tiger Hattori walked up to him in the locker room and began to flatter him in front of all the boys. "Ohh, Scott, you have big legs. And, ohh, you have very big arms. And, ohh, you have big chest. But one thing—face look like faggot." Top star Shinya Hashimoto also specialized in ribbing the foreigners, once cornering a young wrestler at a show and seriously asking him to dismantle a rifle and smuggle it into Japan for him one piece at a time.

Among the gaijin, one ribber stood apart from the others. "I called Benoit the Silent Assassin," Norton said. "He'd act like this little choir boy who never gets into trouble when he was really the guy that was orchestrating all the ribs. Tiger Jeet Singh—he ribbed the hell out of him. He'd superglue his zippers on his bag, put padlocks on his boots and bags, all sorts of things. They'd do all that spike-a-drink-and-shave-off-the-eyebrows type of bullshit. The Nasty Boys [a tag team on the tour at the time] and him got into something, and, back in America, Benoit went out one night and poked holes in the radiator hose of their rental car the night before they were set to drive through the desert. They got stranded in the desert the next day."

"Chris always seemed to find it hilarious to watch me throw up," Chris Jericho recalls in his memoir. Jericho had always wanted to follow in Benoit's footsteps and wrestle for New Japan, and he finally got the opportunity to wrestle in front of NJPW management at a multi-promotion supershow. Though Jericho put on a good match, his drug use made him sick backstage. Benoit "ribbed" Jericho by escorting a member of NJPW management to the scene of Jericho's violent purging. "Look at this.... This guy's got no class," Benoit told the NJPW official while "laughing uncontrollably." Jericho was sure he'd never fulfill his dream of wrestling for NJPW after that first impression. More than one source has told me this story typified Benoit's sense of humor: mean-spirited and fixated on the humiliation of others.

Several people remember the time when Benoit encountered a New Japan referee who was crying uncontrollably backstage over a personal matter. Deeply amused by the spectacle, a cackling Benoit pointed at him like Nelson Muntz from *The Simpsons* and shouted "Haha! What a gay bitch!" When I asked a close friend of Benoit's to confirm the story, he said, "The story may or may not be true, but that sounds like him, unmistakably."

The Silent Assassin wasn't the only nickname Norton gave Benoit overseas. "When the boys would be out drinking and eating, we'd be laughing, having fun. And then you'd look at Benoit, and he'd just not be there. His eyes would be blank; he'd be on some other planet, just staring out to space like a zombie. He did this all the time, and we'd talk about him without him noticing. So I started calling him Houdini, because he would just disappear into thin air. Other than that he seemed to be having a good time; he was a happy guy."

Company morale in general was very high during Benoit's stay in New Japan, despite the deranged leadership of NJPW boss Antonio Inoki. The pelican-jawed wrestler's political success inflated his ego to James Bond-villain proportions. Convinced that one of his many investments in speculative pseudoscience would pan out and, in the words of one wrestler, "fulfill his destiny as the greatest inventor since Thomas Edison," Inoki blew NJPW's profits on a series of increasingly insane projects. For years, Inoki has promised to release a perpetual motion machine that would disprove the Second Law of Thermodynamics, and he assured Fidel Castro that he had devised a method for recycling crushed sugarcane stalks that would revolutionize Cuban socialism.

According to one source, Inoki lobbied for investors to fund a massive treasure hunt on Inoki Friendship Island, a speck of sand off the coast of Cuba that he purchased from Castro—along with a treasure map leading to buried pirate gold.

Inoki's social circle included other likeminded megalomaniacs as well: Saddam Hussein, who gave Inoki two golden swords that he promptly lost at the airport, and rogue North Korean dictator Kim Jong-Il. The friendship with North Korea's government would lead to a two-day NJPW supershow in the hermit kingdom's capital of Pyongyang, held in honor of international brotherhood and world peace. Produced during a manmade famine that killed millions, the North Korean special police herded 300,000 emaciated locals into May Day Stadium over two nights to watch an alien brand of combat sport known as pro wrestling. Brainwashed to blame North Korea's poverty on Westerners, the Korean fans were certainly the most hostile and bloodthirsty audience Benoit ever wrestled for; like most of the foreigners, he felt lucky to leave the stadium intact.

Young star Shinjiro Ohtani was not as lucky; when a botched stunt shattered multiple bones in his face, the North Koreans gave him two Tylenol and some athletic tape. They could not spare a doctor for a foreign capitalist. When Scott Norton spoke unflatteringly of the country on a bugged telephone, he was detained by the local KGB and interrogated for hours at gunpoint. Even ambassador of universal brotherhood Muhammad Ali, attending the festivities thanks to a paycheck from his formal rival Inoki, could not help but observe, "No wonder we hate these motherfuckers," as he watched the behavior of their North Korean hosts.

"As bad as the North Korean thing was, some of those Japanese boys wanted to kill Inoki," one American at the shows told me. "That wasn't the angriest I ever saw them, though. The funniest thing I remember was watching the Japanese guys the day they heard Inoki bought an island in the Pacific with their money. Oh *god*, they were pissed. They hated the idea that Inoki was spending *their* money on these wild schemes and on printing personalized, leather-bound menus for *each dinner guest at each meal* he hosted. If it wasn't for Riki Choshu and Masa Saito, New Japan wrestlers would have left in droves. They cleaned up his messes."

Distracted by his extracurricular activities, Inoki delegated control of the company to Riki Choshu, his "scary figurehead" who according to Simon Inoki was entrusted to run the plantation in the master's absence. Born to Korean parents, Choshu overcame the prejudice of his virulently racist and abusive trainers at the New Japan dojo by working himself so hard that he dumbfounded and eventually intimidated his own tormentors. Dubbed by Bad News Allen as the toughest shooter in New Japan, the squat, longhaired Choshu became one of the biggest stars in Japanese history during the 80s thanks to his extremely stiff and fast-paced heavyweight style. By the early 90s, Inoki had chosen him to be the site foreman who kept the employees in line through intimidation. Though privately very shy and sensitive, according to those who know him, Choshu was gruff and merciless when dealing with New Japan employees. "He took absolutely no shit and gave a lot of it," one New Japan wrestler told me.

"Riki Choshu is a very, very selfish man. If he doesn't like you, he will never push you [as a top star in the company]...and he will tell you so to your face," explains another New Japan native who left the company to spite Choshu. The corollary is that "Choshu's Boys" were always well-pushed, well-paid, and well-protected in the ring. "Benoit loved Choshu because Choshu was just like him: a tough underdog who worked his ass off," one Choshu favorite and Benoit friend said.

"Choshu was a *man*, I mean real fucking *man's man*, and it's so rare for the boys to get to work for someone like that in the business. It meant so much for Benoit to have a wrestler like Choshu's respect. Benoit was one of Choshu's boys, and when you're one of his boys, you *don't* let him down, it's not even an option. One day I walked up to Choshu with a completely torn bicep—I couldn't even move my arm—and he just said, 'Tape it up, or we'll get someone else to fill your spot,' and walked away without giving me a chance to respond.

"I remember working with Benoit on a tour of Japan," the wrestler continued. "And his ankle was the size of a ham hock. I mean, it was just broke, all fucked up. But he didn't say anything, and the office expected that of him. If you were a top guy over there, that office expected you to work hurt, real hurt. The ankle was just *broke*, but Benoit didn't say anything. He wanted that respect from Choshu as a guy who would work through anything."

Just as important to Benoit was the approval of Masa Saito, another extremely tough, grizzled veteran chosen by Inoki to watch over New Japan. With his wild black hair and potbelly, Saito looked like an aboriginal warrior prowling around backstage looking for a fight. Like Choshu, Saito took no shit; when the far younger and larger Vader overruled an idea Saito had for their match together and informed him that Vader "calls the matches, motherfucker," Saito nodded, went out to the ring, and promptly knocked Vader out for real. As the entire New Japan locker room stood watching at the curtain, referee Tiger Hattori began to count Vader out while mocking him under his breath. "One! (*Why you sleeping, you fat asshole?*) Two! (*Why your fat ass laying down, faggot?*) Three! (*Why not get the fuck up, you fat piece of shit?*)...."

By the mid-90s, another Benoit booster became New Japan management: Keiichi "Jushin Liger" Yamada, who was given control of the junior heavyweight division. Though Yamada's unforgiving professionalism could be hard for other wrestlers to take, he was Benoit's wrestling soulmate, both in the ring and backstage. To Benoit, Yamada may have been the only boss more philosophically attuned to himself than Choshu. "Liger is just the ultimate humble workhorse sort of guy. No ego, very self-deprecating, similar to Eddy Guerrero. Wrestling was what he wanted to do with his life, and he was very businesslike about it," one wrestling promoter who has dealt with Liger explained. As long as Benoit took pride in his wrestling and worked hard, he would always have the sympathy and support of New Japan's bosses.

Benoit's favorite member of the New Japan office would become one of his closest personal friends. Victor Mar was a Mexican wrestler who worked as Black Cat in New Japan in the early 80s and, after marrying a Japanese woman, became Inoki's talent liaison for touring foreign wrestlers. Known to foreigners as Black Cat, Mar was their lifeline, translator, tour guide, fixer, psychiatrist, nurse, and babysitter in a strange country where they did not speak a word of the language. Many wrestlers retained a strong affection for Black Cat after touring with New Japan, but Benoit and Norton became his especially close friends.

"Everyone loved Black Cat," says Norton. "Always happy, always kind—he was a real positive guy. He was everyone's support system and pick-me-up. For American and Canadian guys, Cat was our everything. He did everything for the guys. He was a great unconditional friend and fixer for every American guy over there. He ran the locker room. He spoke several different languages, and he'd go out to dinner with you and make sure you got everything you wanted. He would be on the ringside at some of the biggest matches I ever had—he'd tell you in sign language what to do, what came next, what the bookers wanted. It wasn't just a job to him, he truly gave a shit about you as a person.

"There's one story I always tell about Black Cat," Norton continues. "I was on a trip to Hong Kong for a show that Cat was promoting, and some sushi parasite I ate paralyzed me from the waist up. Though he hired medical care for me, Cat took personal care of me at my bedside for four straight days since I couldn't move my arms, my hands, my head. I thought I was going to die. He spoke some Chinese, and they sent a Chinese psychiatrist in to tell me I was crazy, that the problem was all in my head. I knew I was paralyzed for real then, because if I could have moved I would have ripped his head off. But Black Cat wouldn't give up until he found out what was wrong. He kept spending money and got Inoki to send a Japanese doctor over to Hong Kong who took one look at me and diagnosed me immediately. Cat wasn't going to leave my bedside until I got fixed. That was the kind of guy Black Cat was—just an incredibly devoted and selfless friend."

Cat assured Benoit of his job security and his place within the business and helped him work out matches with unfamiliar talent backstage. When Benoit experienced severe homesickness during his first wife Martina's pregnancy and the subsequent birth of their first child, David, in 1992, it was Cat who supported him and encouraged the quiet, pent-up Benoit to share his feelings. If Benoit's aberrant psychological behavior from the mid-90s on is any indication, then Cat likely played an important role in keeping Benoit healthy and stable during what would turn out to be his best time in the wrestling business.

Cat would also do anything he could to advance Benoit's career. "An obsessive wrestling nut who, on his day off, would be watching wrestling tapes," according to Scott Norton, Black Cat shared Benoit's passion for the business and understood that a wrestler like him most likely felt wasted instead of relieved during New Japan's breaks every three weeks. Since he maintained his connections in Mexico, Cat made Benoit an offer: when New Japan was not touring, Cat would arrange for one of the top Mexican promotions to fly him in as a top foreign heel. The money would be good, and Benoit would get to add a new facet to his wrestling skills and resume. This new schedule would never give Benoit's body time to recuperate from injury or allow him to see his family. Benoit enthusiastically accepted Cat's offer.

LUCHADOR

WRESTLING AGENT BOB BARNETT'S FIRST EXPOSURE TO LUCHA LIBRE CAME CIRCA 1970, WHEN HE SPOTTED A MAN IN STYLISH SUIT DRIVING HIS SPARKLING NEW BLACK CADILLAC EL DORADO CONVERTIBLE DOWN HOLLYWOOD BOULEVARD—WITH A COLORFUL WRESTLING MASK ON. "It was Mil Masacaras, who was then the hottest lucha star," says Barnett. Barnett would learn that Mascaras rarely took the mask off; he actually showered with the mask on backstage. Mascaras, like others before him, reportedly plans to be buried in the mask.

Lucha Libre, as wrestling is known in Mexico, was the creation of a minor Mexican government bureaucrat named Salvador Lutteroth Gonzalez, who in 1929 took a detour from official business in Ciudad Juarez to cross the Rio Grande and watch a wrestling card in El Paso. Stunned by the huge crowd he was told attended wrestling matches every week in the frontier outpost of El Paso, Lutteroth marveled at the business a promoter could do in Mexico City, one of great metropolises in the world.

Using the profits from his furniture side business, Lutteroth ran the first indigenous wrestling card in Mexican history on September 21, 1933. With a tiny budget that could barely pay the rent on the most dilapidated venue in Mexico City, Lutteroth struggled on the verge of bankruptcy for his first year in business. On the first anniversary of wrestling's debut in Mexico City, Lutteroth's luck skyrocketed: he won the national Mexican lottery and introduced La Maravilla Enmascarada, the first in a long tradition of masked wrestling sensations that would form the backbone of lucha libre. Using his lottery winnings, Lutteroth purchased La Arena Mexico exclusively for his La Empresa Mexicana de Lucha Libre (EMLL) wrestling shows and began to market a wildly successful product based around his larger-than-life masked superheroes and villains. For the next half century, the Lutteroth family would attempt to enforce an EMLL monopoly over pro wrestling in Mexico against furious opposition.

Lucha libre entered its modern era in 1952 as a direct result of one promoter's challenge to the Lutteroth monopoly. The opposition's television deal motivated Lutteroth to seek a movie deal for his own two top masked stars, the saintly Black Shadow and the ironically named villain El Santo. Producers in Mexico City liked Lutteroth's idea to promote EMLL's top masked luchadors in low-budget superhero features, but they had one condition: El Santo and Black Shadow would have to change roles.

Desperate to crush his competition, Lutteroth booked El Santo to decisively beat Black Shadow in a match in which the loser would lose his mask. The event was a spectacular success, transforming mask-versus-mask matches into cultural events far more important than any title match. To make these matches seem as important as possible, a wrestler's mask was marketed as the embodiment of his manhood, pride, and professional accomplishment. A luchador who lost his mask was emasculated, a superhero brought down to earth, forced to reveal and live under his piddling human identity.

Known for the entirety of his two-decade career as a *rudo* (heel), during which he set an informal record by kicking an opponent in the nuts *eight* times in a row, El Santo proved the producers right: he was born to play the hero. El Santo's movie career as Mexico's most virtuous and courageous hero would span over fifty titles, created an entire subgenre of luchador films, and made the silver-masked gentleman one of the four or five biggest cinema stars in Mexican history. Lucha libre became a fixture of Mexican culture, with lucha flicks in every movie theater and dozens of shows taking place across the country every weekend.

When Salvador Lutteroth retired and was replaced by his incompetent son in 1974, a number of outlaw promoters and disgruntled luchadors under the leadership of regional promoter Francisco Flores Mexico consolidated their resources and formed the Lucha Libre International. With competitive pay, responsive management, unprecedented opportunities for career advancement, and the best venues in Mexico, LLI quickly stole many of the hottest stars in the business, including El Santo and former NWA champion Lou Thesz. Known outside of Mexico as the "UWA" due to the licensing body used for its titles, LLI became the top promotion in Mexico. Flores' willingness to push the younger, smaller luchadors popularized the highflying, wall-to-wall action style that came to define lucha libre for American fans.

By the mid-80s, LLI had settled into its own reliable formula: booking the top natives, especially the Hulk Hogan-esque Canek, against the biggest wrestling stars from around the world. With promotional deals with WWE and NJPW, LLI became known for its supershows, where fans could see the international superstars they knew from their wrestling magazines compete against their hometown heroes. According to American luchador Kurt "Vandal Drummond" Brown, in the 80s, LLI "took out full page ads each week.... When I looked at these ads, it was astounding, like every week was a *Wrestlemania*. The shows were loaded with foreign talent, from Hogan to Stan Hansen to Inoki's crew." LLI attracted these big name foreign stars with generous pay, complimentary five-star resort accommodations, and free meals at the best gourmet restaurants. Outside of "a golden ticket" to Japan, a tour with LLI "was a welcome second place prize," according to Brown.

The success of the Canek-versus-the-world formula would also be the undoing of LLI. When Francisco Flores died suddenly in 1987, control of the company was inherited by his naïve, inexperienced daughter, Esperanza, and his nephew, Carlos Maynes. Without any idea what they were doing, Esperanza and Maynes artlessly repeated Francisco's booking formula ad nauseum. "The philosophy of Carlos and Esperanza was to keep things the way they were—heavyweights on top, protect Canek, invite foreign stars wherever they could be found," says lucha libre historian Jose Fernandez.

Although the novelty of importing foreign wrestlers to lose to Canek had worn off, Esperanza and Carlos had no idea what else to do. They stuck with Francisco's longtime foreign stars long past the peak of their marketability and, in some cases, past the point they could work. Mainstay Andre the Giant, debilitated by acromegaly and lifelong alcohol abuse, wrestled for LLI in a state of such physical decay that he could barely walk. In an LLI match with Bad News Allen, Andre sat on Bad News in the corner and promptly unleashed a torrent of tequila-scented diarrhea. The feeble Andre tried to lift himself to his feet, but each straining attempt triggered another burst of rancid feces all over Bad News.

Stale to the point of self-parody, LLI gradually lost talent and fans until, by the early 90s, the company had fallen to a distant second behind the Lutteroths' EMLL. With no idea what they were doing, Carlos and Esperanza turned to New Japan to send them yet more foreign stars to feed to Canek, and, when New Japan was only willing to send them junior heavyweights, they decided to repeat the Canek formula with their smaller wrestlers. Former LLI wrestler Black Cat assured his contacts at the LLI office that Chris Benoit as the Pegasus Kid, despite his lack of lucha experience, could hold up his end of a main event program and put on the type of exciting performances that had put LLI on the map.

The Pegasus Kid debuted at LLI's weekly supershow at El Toreo De Cuatro Caminos in Naucalpan, Mexico City, on February 17, 1991. Benoit had never performed at any venue remotely like El Toreo, which was a large bullfighting stadium with a circular mud bullring in the center and a bizarre netted ceiling of steel rafters with retracting steel slats. The surrounding areas were rough even for a Mexico City slum, which meant that every few weeks it bested the combined annual violent-crime tallies of Japan and Canada. This bloody corner of Naucalpan was undoubtedly the most dangerous and impoverished neighborhood Benoit had ever visited, and the locals took wrestling very seriously: it was the best distraction from their desolate lives that a few pesos could buy. The cathartic rush of a wrestling show drove them wild: a babyface could expect to be brazenly fondled and groped by dozens of girls as he left the arena, and a rudo could expect to be sucker punched, maced, bombarded with cups of piss and dirty diapers, and occasionally stabbed.

Black Cat likely told Benoit what to expect backstage at lucha shows: a relaxed, chaotic locker room filled with bare-assed Mexicans, some in masks, openly drinking, doing drugs, and defecating on toilets without stalls, toilet seats, or the capability to flush toilet paper. Used toilet paper was simply piled up on the floor like muddy snow banks. The wrestlers would be cold to Benoit as an outsider, especially on his first night, and since most spoke no English there'd be little social interaction. The rings would be as hard as pavement, and the conditions at the smaller shows were Third-World abysmal. Some shows would be held in filthy boxing rings, cockfighting pits, or in "rings" consisting of concrete platforms covered in sawdust. "The shower" meant a garden hose out back with a bucket, and sometimes the only lighting available was a rope strung over the ring that held a garbage can with a hobo fire lit inside of it.

Black Cat also schooled Benoit on how the in-ring action would differ from Japan and Calgary. The greatest superficial difference was simply that most matches were three-on-three tags decided on a two-out-of-three-fall basis, but that condition paled in comparison to the difficulties presented by the differences in wrestling styles. Even with a gifted luchador opponent, Benoit would be hard-pressed not to look hopelessly awkward and clueless in the ring. Unlike American- and Japanese-style wrestling, where every move, hold, and attack is performed on the left side of the body for the sake of synchronization, lucha libre is wrestled strictly on the right side of the body. Every single thing Benoit did in a

Mexican ring would have to be backwards, in the exact opposite fashion from how he had learned, practiced, and perfected it.

The action itself would have little in common with the Calgary/New Japan style that emphasized stiff strikes, painstaking authenticity, and hard "flat back" bumping. The backbreaking lucha rings and mindboggling thirteen- or fourteen-shows-a-week schedule forced luchadors to generally work a softer, lower contact, cooperative style to avoid injury that seemed patently choreographed and fake to outsiders. By necessity, luchadors replaced stiff strikes and bumping with a great deal of posing, comedy spots, histrionic selling, and elaborate Cirque du Soleil contortionist matwork. When luchadors did bump, they preferred low-impact gymnastic tumbles that gradually distributed the blow across a wide area of the body.

To compensate for this limited style, luchadors generally worked longer and more fast-paced matches, with few restholds or breaks. To give the fans *some* visceral excitement, many otherwise cautious matches would be punctuated by interludes of breathtaking recklessness. After a suitable buildup, luchadors would take to the air, performing death-defying acrobatic dives from the ring to the floor that left most Japanese junior heavyweights awestruck.

The dizzyingly fast pace of the matches and the luchadors' poor English skills meant that Benoit would have to wordlessly improvise at high speed with strangers who shared little if any common training and experiences. It should come as no surprise that, in his initial run with LLI, the Pegasus Kid with his winged mask and blue tights made an underwhelming impression. Intent on mastering the lucha style as he had the New Japan and Calgary styles, the heavily 'roided Benoit gamely attempted to mimic the gymnast-sized luchadors' dives, cartwheels, intricate ballet chain wrestling, and graceful tumbling bumps. He failed, looking like a clumsy bodybuilder. "On my first tour I kept trying to wrestle their style, trying to find that medium, and it just didn't work," Benoit recalled. "By the last week I started wrestling my style, but working within their brand of wrestling, and it just clicked." By the end of his first tour, the LLI promoters were impressed enough with the Pegasus Kid's potential to give him a victory over top junior star Villano III for the WWF Light Heavyweight Title.

While working with masters like Negro Casas and Gran Hamada, who had been successful in multiple styles for years, Benoit learned that the secret to versatility in the pro wrestling industry was not the chameleon-like ability to remake oneself but, instead, the ability to integrate your distinct character into the local environment. Instead of trying to remodel himself as a luchador, Benoit concentrated on being himself within lucha's conventions, working his normal style at a lucha pace and with lucha psychology.

"[Benoit] wrestled a technical style and was mostly matched with very versatile technicians, so all of his matches came out very good, but you would not say that they were a pure lucha libre style," says Jose Fernandez. "But, he brought a pacing and tough style that really impressed everybody—fans, wrestlers, and press. The magazines absolutely loved him and called him the best foreign wrestler to wrestle in Mexico since the days of Lou Thesz."

Benoit would take the lessons he learned with LLI and apply them in his other side job from New Japan. Catch Wrestling Association in Germany and Austria brought in Benoit to work their multi-week tournaments. Benoit wrestled in a huge CWA circus tent on the Danube in Vienna that held as many as 5,000 people every day for weeks. As the fans ate bratwurst and drank beer, Benoit wrestled the round-based, idiosyncratic European style with incredible self-assurance. Wrestling without his mask, he felt secure just being Chris Benoit from

Edmonton, the bloodthirsty student of the Dynamite Kid. Wrestling Irish toughman and New Japan regular David "Fit" Finlay night after night in brutal brawls with scientific wrestling interludes, Benoit built a reputation as the most gifted performer to wrestle in Europe since Dynamite a decade before.

Benoit's rapidly burgeoning wrestling talent and worldwide reputation convinced New Japan in July of 1991 that he no longer needed the crutch of the Pegasus Kid persona to get over. They informed him that they planned to have him lose his mask to Jushin Liger in Japan, which initially disappointed Benoit, who had become accustomed to wrestling under a mask. Black Cat consoled him with the information that he could make a big payday in Mexico by offering to lose his mask to one of LLI's top stars in a mask vs. mask match, which came with a monetary bonus that could reach into the six figures for the biggest stars. Benoit likely made somewhere between $1,000 and $5,000 extra to lose his mask (for the second time) in a fantastic match to top lightweight draw Villano III in November of 1991.

While Benoit would wrestle without his mask in Japan as Wild Pegasus, he would remain the Pegasus Kid in Mexico for the next four years. When LLI lost the ability to pay him in 1993, the Pegasus Kid began to occasionally work for the Lutteroths' EMLL at Arena Mexico. Though the Lutteroths were cheap and condescending bosses, Benoit made a point to visit whenever he could, despite the wife and small child at home whom he rarely saw. "I have so many good memories of working down in Mexico," Benoit said. "Not only from in the ring but outside, and camaraderie with the guys. Some of the guys...barely were able to speak English and I couldn't speak Spanish, and having that bond and forging relationships was really neat."

LAURELS

OUTSIDE OF JUSHIN LIGER HIMSELF, THERE WAS NO
MORE FAMOUS OR DECORATED JUNIOR HEAVYWEIGHT STAR
IN JAPAN THAN CHRIS "WILD PEGASUS" BENOIT. As
booked by his friend and wrestling soulmate Liger, Benoit
was the dominating foreign powerhouse of the junior
division. Used as the measuring stick against which the
smaller and weaker native stars would be judged, Benoit
harnessed a heavyweight's brute strength in executing a
devastating repertoire of technical wrestling moves. No
move in Japan looked more deadly than Chris Benoit's
powerbomb, which snapped the back of his opponent's
head and neck against the canvas with whiplash speed
and concussive force. If Benoit's opponent kicked out, he
would drop them on their head again, this time with a full-
nelson suplex that pinned them upside down to the mat.

Benoit established his dominance not through title
reigns (New Japan rarely let foreigners hold on to their
title belts for long) but through tournament victories.
Thanks to the preeminence of sumo tournaments in
Japanese sporting culture, NJPW has always placed a
strong emphasis on multi-day, round-robin tournaments.
With the popularity of the Liger-led junior division, it
became a New Japan tradition to give the smaller stars
their own showcase tournament every May/June. Filled
with diverse international talent, the annual Top (later,
Best) of the Super Junior Tournament was the biggest
event of the year for junior heavyweights. Japanese fans
believed that only phenomenal athletes with superior
durability, versatility, and cardiovascular health could
win these grueling multi-week tournaments, and thus a
tournament victory carried more prestige than any
title reign.

In 1993, Benoit became the first foreign wrestler
ever to win the TOSJ tournament, defeating the masked
El Samurai. Osamu "El Samurai" Matsuda was a
slovenly, homely, laidback guy with an infamously heavy
smoking habit and no particular interest in training who

somehow, to the confusion of the boys, became a physical dynamo in the ring. Benoit defeated El Samurai in the 1993 tournament finals in a fashion that elevated both men; after Samurai shocked the crowd by kicking out of Benoit's most feared offensive maneuvers, Benoit took desperate measures, drilling Samurai with a diving "avalanche" powerbomb from the top rope for the victory. "This one is sure to put some stress on your VCR's rewind and slow-motion buttons," declared the *Pro Wrestling Torch* of what was doubtless one of the most mind-blowing stunts of 1993. If Benoit's execution had been slow or botched, he could have landed directly on the top of his skull from eleven or twelve feet in the air. That Liger and Samurai trusted Benoit to safely execute such a complicated, potentially fatal move showed how highly he was esteemed.

In the 1995 Best of the Super Junior Tournament finals, Benoit would try to top even this stunt. His opponent was Shinjiro Ohtani, a twenty-two-year-old wrestling prodigy with unmatched toughness and physical gifts. Ohtani became a cult favorite in the United States for his unique character, which somehow combined the roles of the plucky underdog and the arrogant, insufferable dickhead; in a typical match, Ohtani would cockily wipe his boots across his opponent's face only to later collapse into tears and beg for the crowd's support in his David-versus-Goliath quest. In 1994, the rookie Ohtani had teamed with Benoit as his student and won the Super Grade Junior Tag League when Ohtani pinned Eddy Guerrero with a Benoit-style dragon suplex. One year later, Ohtani announced that it was time for him to surpass his former sensei, as well.

Benoit was a wonderful opponent for Ohtani, since Ohtani could play the impudent chickenshit and still draw sympathy from the fans who couldn't help but pity *anyone* who had to take Benoit's offense. Like Samurai before him, Ohtani would withstand all of Benoit's most brutal offensive moves, forcing Benoit to go to extreme lengths.

Climbing to the second rope, Benoit performed a jumping Dynamite-Kid-style tombstone piledriver that would decisively end Ohtani's hopes of a miraculous comeback. Ohtani's credibility in New Japan rose greatly just by compelling the legendary Wild Pegasus to deploy such firepower to defeat him.

Benoit's most meaningful tournament victory came in what has gone down in history as the most important night in the history of junior heavyweight wrestling. Despite the manifest popularity of junior heavyweight wrestling with New Japan's fans, Choshu and Inoki were reluctant to treat it as anywhere near the equal of the less flashy but more credible heavyweight division. At New Japan's large dome shows, it was common for even Liger and Benoit to be treated as undercard afterthoughts. To counter the conventional wisdom that the juniors were just a child-friendly sideshow, Yamada booked the 11,000-seat Ryoguku Kokugikan for the Super J-Cup, a one-night junior heavyweight tournament. If the juniors could sell out New Japan's home venue all by themselves, it would prove both the drawing power and mainstream viability of smaller wrestlers in Japan; if they failed, junior heavyweights would be relegated to their sideshow ghetto.

The Super J-Cup was the ultimate test of a wrestler's ability; the winner would have to win three matches against an all-star field of juniors from wrestling companies around Japan, all on the night of April 16, 1994. Even when the show sold out in one day, the pressure was still immense on each individual wrestler: anything less than a night of wall-to-wall spectacular performances would be seen as a disappointment for wrestlers known for their showmanship and athletic skill.

Before a crowd of 11,000, Chris Benoit advanced to the finals after victories over Eddy Guerrero and Gedo, a fat wrestler in a red belly shirt from the Wrestle And Romance promotion who resembled a piglet with a blond pompadour. The show had been incredibly entertaining, but the all-important finals between Wild Pegasus and indy wrestling sensation the Great Sasuke would determine if the show was a critical and symbolic success.

Before his third and final match of the night, the aforementioned most important match in junior heavyweight history, Chris Benoit was only passingly familiar with Masanori "Great Sasuke" Murakawa's work. Along with his reputation as the most spectacular acrobat and stunt artist in Japanese wrestling, Murakawa was also known as an incredibly reckless, stubborn, and egomaniacal bastard. Fixated on Antonio Inoki, Murakawa believed it was his destiny to best Inoki's achievements as a wrestler and a politician, a goal that seemed pretty farfetched for a masked indy junior whose costume resembled homemade satin ninja pajamas. Liger trusted Benoit to reel in this mercurial, spotty wrestler and ensure that the night ended with all-time classic.

The pressure on Benoit was evident when the announcer called his name before the match; as Benoit saluted the audience, his face succumbed to a swarm of nervous twitches. With a harrowed look in his eyes, Benoit gnaws on his bottom lip as the referee checks both wrestlers for foreign objects. Never has a wrestler looked more obviously petrified before a match.

The match was laid out as a tribute to the Tiger Mask versus Dynamite Kid feud that sparked the birth of modern junior heavyweight wrestling. This was an unreasonably tall order: Dynamite and Tiger Mask had perhaps the greatest chemistry of any two wrestlers in junior wrestling history, which they developed over dozens of matches together. Murakawa and Benoit had barely met, but somehow they managed to work together with uncanny timing and precision. Benoit played the straight man to Sasuke's balletic grace, seamless reversals, and daredevil dives, subtly controlling the flow of the match by cutting off Sasuke with short bursts of power moves. After a vigorous, crowd-pleasing battle highlighted by Sasuke's acrobatic stunts, Benoit cut off

Sasuke as he attempted to perform yet another elaborate top rope stunt and instead delivered an "avalanche" gutwrench suplex for the three-count. The match was fantastic.

The prolonged, explosive cheers that greeted Benoit's victory still stand as one of the most passionate crowd responses ever received by a foreigner in Japan. With this clutch performance, Benoit's career was made; he was immediately transformed from a pro wrestling star into a living legend in Japan, a wrestler who could rest on his laurels for years and years without ever having to worry about his job security. The victory reverberated in North America, as well, where the Super J-Cup became one of the two most bootlegged wrestling tapes of all time. For years, Chris Benoit's performances on April 16, 1994 would serve as the introduction for tens of thousands of American hardcore wrestling fans to Japanese wrestling. Benoit became more than a cult favorite—he became *the* cult favorite. From 1994 on, a common refrain on the Internet would be why WWE and WCW did not have the brains to hire and push Chris Benoit, *the best wrestler in the world*.

"It meant a lot to me...the best junior wrestler in the world," Benoit said of his J-Cup victory. "I never think of myself as being the best or the quickest. I don't look at it in that way, because to me wrestling is a form of art."

Benoit had to make sacrifices for his art. His discipline and self-denial became legendary. "Work so hard, train so hard, diet so hard, very strict person" was how Osamu Nishimura described Benoit at his New Japan height. Benoit will long be remembered for the time that he made a minor flub in an irrelevant match with Chris Jericho, "pulled his usual Houdini act," and fled to a secluded boiler room where, to Jericho's shock, he began to perform 500 hack squats as "punishment" for his mistake.

Benoit's "art" as the foreign ace of the New Japan junior division was entirely dependant on his enormous steroid habit. Booked in the role of the dominating powerhouse, Benoit had to look the part, and that required a regimen of steroid abuse that even dwarfed his consumption during the "Megadose" days in Stampede. "Benoit had to blow up [his physique] to be a wrestler," close friend Scott Norton told me. "Benoit knew he had to kill himself in the ring to get a chance, and he knew he had to take absolutely whatever it took to get a look that could get him a push. Failing was never an option with him."

Benoit's steroid abuse became so pronounced that it began to attract negative attention. Former *Pro Wrestling Torch* columnist John Williams wrote on the Internet about meeting a "juiced out of his mind" Benoit in Japan with *Wrestling Observer* editor Dave Meltzer. "It was the biggest Dave had ever seen him up to that point, and frankly Dave had been watching his career longer than just about anyone at that point...." said Williams. "'Alarmed' would be the way I would describe Dave's reaction to [Benoit's] size."

No longer a Young Boy, in industry terms, Benoit was an established veteran with greater prestige than any other foreigner in New Japan. As the informal dean of foreign juniors in New Japan, it was expected that he would keep the younger, more inexperienced members of the foreign crew disciplined and well behaved. This discipline typically took the form of corporal punishment.

Yamada, who at this time policed the junior heavyweight Young Lions, was known for getting carried away with his duties. "Liger kept them in line, I'll tell you that," a former New Japan heavyweight champion told me. "I've seen him just walk up and pop a couple young guys right in the face like it was nothing. He never hesitated to put his hands on a young guy and really hurt him. That's just how you do business." Benoit would supposedly take this policy of officially sanctioned corporal punishment as an excuse to indulge in sadism so twisted and cruel that it could compare with the worst behavior of Tom Billington.

John "Pee Wee" Moore was an aspiring referee that had secured a place at the dojo and on tour with NJPW. Since no one had taken the time to coach the very young and inexperienced Moore on the elaborate etiquette of the Japanese wrestling locker room, he repeatedly breached the code of conduct that New Japan expected of a young novice wrestler. According to the Nasty Boys tag team, a "kangaroo court" of veteran wrestlers convened and sentenced Moore to be "humbled" for the good of the business.

A posse of foreign veterans ambushed Moore. Holding him down, they shaved his head with a razor so rusty and dull that it left Moore's scalp skinned and bleeding. To treat the many burns, scrapes, and cuts across Moore's skull, the wrestlers applied generous dollops of stinging hot wasabi, which they slapped into the wounds. Lying prone, Moore wept and begged for mercy; the foreign crew responded by surrounding him in a circle and unzipping their pants. Told to do pushups, Moore rolled over and began to slowly count them off one by one. "Faster!" Moore went faster. "FASTER!" With wasabi-flavored blood burning his eyes, Moore tried to go even faster. He failed. He felt four or five streams of hot urine sprinkle onto his back and the top of his mangled head. Although two of the Nasty Boys spoke publicly about the incident in detail, another wrestler on the tour denied the story's authenticity, before slyly hinting, "I do remember that Pee Wee showed up one day with a shaved head, but *I* don't know how he got it."

According to a handful of sources, including to a Hall of Fame backstage personality close to the situation, one of the perpetrators of this travesty was The Silent Assassin, Chris Benoit. As always, Benoit had done the right thing as determined by the ridiculous code of honor taught to him by Billington, the Hart Family, and the despicable nutballs at the New Japan dojo. Business always came first for Chris Benoit, far ahead of his humanity.

Chris Benoit's idol, Tom "The Dynamite Kid" Billington, after a bloody brawl in Stampede Pro Wrestling.
(Photo Copyright by Bob Leonard)

A teenaged Chris Benoit during his first year of training with the Hart Family.
(Photo Copyright by Bob Leonard)

Benoit in 2002 with Bruce Hart (left) and Stu Hart (center), his trainers in the Hart Family Dungeon.
(Photo Copyright by Bob Leonard)

Benoit performing his signature flying headbutt in a Stampede Pro Wrestling ring. (Photo Copyright by Bob Leonard)

A chemically enhanced Benoit shortly after returning to Canada from his first stint in New Japan Pro Wrestling from 1986-1987. (Photo Copyright by Bob Leonard)

Antonio Inoki, Benoit's boss in New Japan Pro Wrestling.
(Photo Courtesy of David Layne)

Keiichi Yamada, Benoit's greatest in-ring rival, in his "Jushin Thunder Liger" costume. (Photo Courtesy of David Layne)

Kevin Sullivan, Benoit's archenemy and booker in WCW.
(Photo Courtesy of David Layne)

Benoit in the mid-90s in World
Championship Wrestling.
(Photo Courtesy of David Layne)

Nancy Sullivan Benoit as "Woman"
in WCW in the early 90s.
(Photo Courtesy of David Layne)

Paul "Triple H" Levesque,
Vince McMahon's son-in-law and
long-standing top star.
(Photo Courtesy of Adrian Guy Crook)

Eddy Guerrero, Chris Benoit's closest friend, shortly before his steroids-induced death in 2005. (Photo Courtesy of Colin Williamson)

Chris Benoit on February 2, 2006, four months after the death of Guerrero and well into his psychological melt-down. (Photo Courtesy of Danilo S. Nuestro)

Nancy and Chris Benoit at Owen Hart's funeral in May of 1999. (Photo Copyright by Bob Leonard)

Chapter VII
The Money Mark

"I heard [steroids] make you sterile.
Nothing's worth that. If you want to get
bigger, buy a Jane Fonda workout tape."

TED TURNER

Advising the WCW roster on how to handle the
professional pressure to use steroids.

THE BOTTOMLESS PIT

OF THE BILLIONS OF DOLLARS TED TURNER HAS
GIVEN TO CHARITY, NO CAUSE WAS MORE UNWORTHY THAN
WORLD CHAMPIONSHIP WRESTLING. The second largest
wrestling promotion in America was a misbegotten vanity
project that was not held to the standards of any other
division within the Turner Broadcasting empire, which
includes cable television giants CNN, TBS, and TNT.
Advised by management to discontinue the unprofitable
and disreputable wrestling division, Turner angrily
refused, announcing that as long as Ted stayed, so did
WCW. During Turner's years as an upstart television
tycoon, wrestling had been the cheap, time-filling staple
that drew reliably good ratings and kept his fledgling
"Superstation" afloat. Ted showed his gratitude by
indefinitely subsidizing the slumping U.S. wrestling
business with millions of dollars.

Newcomers to the CNN Center, the massive
Atlanta office complex that housed the headquarters of

TBS, Inc., were quickly let in on the dirty secret: WCW was above reproach, billionaire Ted's indulgent gift to himself. With his behavior, Tuner answered that timeless question: what do you give a man who has everything? Apparently, you give him an unforgivably bad wrestling promotion.

When Turner purchased Jim Crockett Promotions (JCP) in late 1988, JCP had established itself as the second most valuable wrestling brand in North America. At exorbitant cost, JCP had asserted itself as the flagship promotion and national television face of the age-old National Wrestling Alliance, the largely archaic network of old-school territorial wrestling promoters that included Stampede Wrestling. JCP was the home of old-school Southern wrasslin', a product that marketed itself more on the basis of classic, hard-hitting, serious athletic contests than WWE's mixture of celebrity crossovers, cartoonish superhero characters, kitschy comedy, and well-oiled bodybuilders.

To most American fans, JCP embodied the last holdout of the tough, redneck, 300-shows-a-year, blood-and-guts carny tradition of pro wrestling. In 1988, when Turner purchased JCP and transformed it into World Championship Wrestling (WCW), wrestling fans were of two minds: some felt it was the death and desecration of the last authentic wrestling promotion in the United States; others were ecstatic that Vince McMahon (known simply as "The Enemy" for his crimes against wrestling tradition) was finally going to face well-funded, professionally managed competition. When Turner's professed love for the old-school 1970's wrestling territories became publicized, even the skeptical fans were overjoyed that there was finally a national promoter who actually respected *wrestling*.

Unfortunately for wrestling fans, the media mogul had too many responsibilities to personally manage his beloved promotion. The Turner lieutenants who actually administered WCW did not hold wrestling in equal esteem.

In the past, wrestling on TBS was a junk-food ratings draw that filled up huge multi-hour blocks in the otherwise unprofitable weekend morning and afternoon hours. Though TBS now owned WCW and the commercial rights to all of its contracted talent, management still conceived of it as nothing more than a bargain-basement television production company—ignoring the tens of millions of dollars McMahon was making from licensing, merchandising, and touring. TBS management followed Turner's orders with nose-pinching contempt; they would purchase a pro wrestling company, but they weren't going to *run* a pro wrestling company.

Something as disreputable and sleazy as wrestling didn't fit within TBS' impressive, international corporate portfolio, and the experienced wrestling riffraff required to run such a racket were not presentable enough to be integrated into the elite Turner corporate hierarchy. Instead, real businessmen would run WCW.

"Turner basically bought this company because it was an investment in cheap programming, and they didn't give a shit or know anything about wrestling," says promoter Sheldon Goldberg. WCW's novice management certainly put it at a disadvantage in a competition with WWE, which was a multi-generation family business with roots dating back to prohibition. Future WCW star Scott Hall may have said it best when he compared WCW to watching wince-inducing amateur porn: "Turner, they put wrestling on their station, but Vince is a wrestling company that produces and programs wrestling shows. That's the distinction. It's not hard to tell the distinction when you watch the show. I mean, it's like watching good porn and bad porn."

"A normal white-collar businessman who attempts to manage a pro wrestling locker room is like a one-legged man navigating a minefield," one promoter explained to me. It should come as no surprise that a job in WCW almost immediately earned a reputation as the TBS equivalent of a diplomatic posting to Sub-Saharan Africa:

a one-way trip to an unmanageable backwater where promising careers went to die. According to WCW booker Dusty Rhodes, a top Turner lieutenant chose one president of WCW by simply walking up to a random guy he didn't know on the CNN Center's twelfth floor and asking him if he was interested in wrestling. That day, anonymous entertainment lawyer Kip Frye was introduced as President of WCW; he would quit in short order, realizing that his promotion was the worst thing that could have ever happened to his career.

The suits dumb enough to stay were men like Jim Herd, a former Pizza Hut executive who Dusty Rhodes called "the most untalented motherfucker in the history of the world." Imagine the learning curve the Pizza Hut executive faced when he was thrust into managing a national wrestling company without any prior wrestling experience. Like a Hollywood studio executive, wrestling promoter is an instinctual, creative right-brain management job. In addition to the usual administrative skills and dollars-and-cents business acumen, a good wrestling promoter needed creative flair, theatrical instincts, and an expert's ability to scout and judge talent. Unlike running a pizza delivery chain, WCW presented Herd with little quantifiable data or objective analysis to guide his decisions; he had to rely on instinct, of which he had none, and advice, of which he had too much.

Herd was mugged by some of the most persuasive bullshit artists in wrestling. How was clueless Herd supposed to know which liar to trust, let alone which liar was a more insightful judge of talent or more innovative pro wrestling booker? Completely unfamiliar with wrestling fans and their peculiar sense of what was ridiculous and what was not, how was Herd supposed to understand why the Undertaker's gimmick (a wrestling zombie in pancake makeup who derived power from a magical urn) was awesome and his idea for wrestling hunchbacks (their deformity prevented them from being pinned) was awful? When Herd suggested that Ric Flair start from scratch as a shaven-headed gladiator named Spartacus, booker committee member Kevin Sullivan responded, "After we change Flair's gimmick, why don't we go to Yankee Stadium and change Babe Ruth's uniform number?" Soon afterwards, Herd fired Flair for being stale and unmarketable; Flair was immediately hired by WWE and made their top star.

Corporate management for a wrestling company just did not work. Egotistical yuppie suits who looked down on wrestling were no match for the masterful charmers and manipulators in the locker room. The wrestling veterans that WCW management deputized as bookers to write the wrestling storylines and lay out each event took full advantage of their naïve mark bosses. Offered no possibility of corporate advancement by the condescending Turner bigwigs, the veterans treated the job of booker like outlaws suddenly made sheriff.

In addition to hiring friends and family, every WCW booker took special pleasure in humiliating his enemies with no regard for the health of the company. The behavior of Dusty Rhodes, who the Turner bigwigs gave multiple runs as booker, was characteristic of WCW office politics. Rhodes went down into history as making the worst first impression in booking history when he walked into the WCW locker room with a "shit-eating grin" on his face and announced: "Well boys, my name is 'the American Dream' Dusty Rhodes, and *I* the rake and *you* the leaves." He then immediately fired everyone in the room he didn't like.

Unsurprisingly, the WCW business model of clueless white-collar leadership assisted by corrupt, self-interested carny bookers failed. After losing nearly $25 million in four years, TBS finally decided that it might be a good idea to hire someone with a passing familiarity with the wrestling business to run things.

If anyone could be the savior of WCW, the educated wrestling fan believed it might be "Cowboy" Bill Watts. Watts, hired by Turner in May of 1992 to become the new boss of WCW, hadn't come to WCW to settle scores, play politics, or indifferently draw a paycheck. He was a man with work to do, someone who took his job seriously and damn well didn't need any on-the-job training. If anyone in wrestling besides Vince McMahon himself could reform the WCW it was Watts, a hardass ex-wrestler with a successful track record for writing fantastic television and running an unruly Southern wrestling promotion with an iron fist. Bill Watts would be Benoit's first American boss.

UNIVERSITY

CHRIS BENOIT MADE HIS AMERICAN TELEVISION DEBUT AMONGST FRIENDS. On June 16, 1992 in Charleston, South Carolina, Benoit teamed with his former "Mega-Doses" Stampede Wrestling partner Biff Wellington against his best friend from Stampede, Brian Pillman, and his greatest rival in wrestling, Jushin Liger. It aired across America in primetime as part of a "Clash of the Champions" TV special, seasonal free TV events that traditionally garnered WCW's largest ratings.

This international cruiserweight bout was booked as one of the first steps of Bill Watts' plan to restore WCW's legitimacy in the eyes of the fans. Watts invited established tag teams from around the world to compete in a tournament for the prestigious NWA tag titles. According to one confidential source, the Benoit/ Wellington team was booked in the tournament by Paul Heyman, the shifty character who played WCW's top heel manager, Paul E. Dangerously, and dispatched minor booking duties backstage. A long time fan of Benoit's work, Heyman allegedly sold the wrestler to Watts as a credible cruiserweight whose moves "looked punishing," who "bumped harder than anyone," and whose intensity was "animalistic." Benoit himself believed that he was booked in WCW for a reason that had nothing to do with Paul Heyman; he insisted that New Japan had arranged the booking so as to ensure their star Liger was handled in the most flattering light possible.

Despite facing opponents who had been his friends since he was a gawky teenager and could be counted on to make him look as good as possible, Benoit was still under immense pressure. The nationally televised "Clash of the Champions" match would be his introduction to mainstream American wrestling fans. Who knew when his next chance to make such an impression would come? The challenge was that Benoit had to make an impact without making himself the center of attention. The match wasn't about Benoit; he was brought in to sell the fans on the ability and credibility of Pillman and Liger. If Watts got the impression that Benoit was cutting a commercial for himself, then Benoit and Watts would never be in the same locker room again. The only way to promote himself was to enthusiastically showcase Liger and Pillman.

Entering the ring to the Canadian national anthem, Benoit was clearly the star of the team. Hyped by announcer Jim Ross as a "former IWGP Jr. Heavyweight champion" known for his "tremendous feud with Jushin Liger," Benoit was introduced to American audiences as an accomplished international competitor whose appearance on free television was a big deal.

Benoit let Liger and Pillman perform the flashy, crowd-pleasing moves; in fact, the most conspicuous move Benoit performed was a simple clothesline, which he delivered with such impact and ferociousness that it became one of the match's highlights. Instead of manhandling Liger and Pillman like he would in NJPW, Benoit garnered attention by taking the craziest, most self-destructive bumps possible off his opponents' moves— just like the Dynamite Kid. Though the fans were impressed with the intensity of Benoit's wrestling, his performance was geared to the locker room, where everyone knew how selfless Benoit was being with his body and his ego.

Though Pillman and Liger reciprocated as much as their role allowed, Benoit's performance was best spotlighted by the deflated performance of his tag partner, Wellington. The hyperventilating Wellington was so "dead on his feet" that he could not get himself up for a basic bodyslam or backdrop. Left with television time to fill and a finish to execute, Benoit stepped up, took far more than his share of the punishment, and singlehandedly saved the match. At the age of twenty-five, in his first match in the American big time, the no-name Benoit had established his reputation as a ring general and someone who could be trusted to do good business. With no charisma, no microphone skills, no star power, and no freakshow physical presence, Benoit had done what he needed to do to establish his value.

The political test was just as important as the in-ring match. Before the match, Benoit avoided the litany of mistakes made by young wrestlers in their big league debut: he introduced himself to everyone with a limp handshake, kept his mouth tightly shut in the locker room before the match, and after his triumphant in-ring turn, ignored his own great performance to instead, with the voice of a titmouse, thank everyone backstage for the opportunity to wrestle.

Benoit had handled himself flawlessly. In a promotion that was one month into a new regime that aimed to restore traditional backstage discipline, Benoit had played the humble, quiet, respectful young boy coming up in the business—even though he was already an established, highly paid star in two countries. Benoit knew what he was doing; his undeniable wrestling talent combined with an ego-free, no-questions-asked attitude made him an irresistible addition to a WCW roster that was looking to downsize the overpaid, troublemaking established roster in favor of cheap, hardworking, obedient talent. Bill Watts liked the young kid, and once he had more leeway to put new contracts on the books in the new year, he promised to give him an opportunity. Benoit started with WCW full-time on the first tour of 1993, understanding that he would be allowed to make the major tours for WCW's business partner New Japan. Benoit had begun his American career under the tutelage of Bill Watts, the booker with the best reputation in America.

Watts was a classic wrestling promoter, which unfortunately made him unfit for polite company. A stereotypical Good Ole Boy, Watts flaunted all of the positive and negative characteristics of the breed. He was a tough, hardworking Southern shitkicker with no time for bullshit, laziness, or excuses. Having worked in wrestling in all capacities for decades, Watts knew the business inside and out, knew every trick in the book and every worker's reputation; he knew how to book a card, write a TV show, book a tour, spot a lie, and knock some discipline into the boys.

However, Watts was as unprepared to work in a corporate environment as Jim Herd was to run a wrestling locker room. Watts was not exactly traditional management material for a name-brand corporation that took public relations, investor confidence, and political correctness seriously. In a boom period for sexual harassment lawsuits, Watts thought nothing of calling a female colleague a "cunt" or whipping his dick out in the parking lot to take a piss. The impression of Watts as an unreformed Southern cracker was reinforced by the cowboy's tendency to brag that he carried a pistol in his briefcase, smoked joints on the balcony of his high-rise Atlanta office, and occasionally took a piss from the top of the CNN Center atrium.

Most troubling of all for a company that owned a serious news channel and two major league sports teams, Watts was, if not a homophobe and a racist, ignorant enough not to know when he was performing a convincing impersonation of one. In an infamous interview with the *Pro Wrestling Torch* newsletter, Watts openly pondered, "Why should I have to hire a fucking fag if I don't like fags?" and remarked, "If I don't want to sell fried chicken to blacks, I shouldn't have to. It's my restaurant."

Even Watts' handpicked black champion, Ron Simmons, when asked if he could think of any defense of his boss' racism, could only offer that at least "he never wore the [Ku Klux Klan] hood right in front of us."

TBS Management overlooked Watts' character flaws thanks to an enormously successful territorial booking run during the 80s and the results of a $30,000 professional polling company survey of their own, which told them WCW's audience wanted a traditional, Southern, blood-and-guts, anti-WWE show—a Bill Watts show. Watts himself was thrilled to have the job; with Turner's media firepower, Watts believed they would be "able to snuff Vince out like a flea on an elephant's ass."

To a traditional kayfabe promoter like Watts, who thought wrestling should be portrayed as a legitimate sport, irreparable harm had been done to WCW's credibility by the corporate bosses' "throw shit at the wall and see what sticks" booking philosophy. Watts believed that WCW was so dysfunctional and unprofitable that it needed to be rebuilt from scratch to be viable. The first lesson for fans and boys alike would be to instill discipline, to teach them how to respect the promotion and take it seriously. This plan involved such hardships as fines for being late and breaking kayfabe outside of the locker room, severe budgetary cutbacks, and no more free backstage catering at WCW's unprofitable events.

Instead of uniting behind Watts to save their jobs and transform WCW into a legitimate competitor to Vince McMahon, the wrestlers responded to the new regime with the maturity of a toddler whose pacifier has been taken away for the first time. The Cowboy's professionalism provoked locker room discontent that manifested itself in melodramatic self-pity, scowls and pouts in the corners of the locker room, and long, drunken wrestling promos cut in bars and hotel rooms against "that fat bastard Watts." The WCW wrestlers could not believe they were being forced to treat their sport like a job. Fresh from New Japan, the most disciplined wrestling roster in the world, Chris Benoit's first tour-of-duty with WCW would be his education in how big time American wrestling worked—or in WCW's case, didn't work.

Benoit was obsessed with putting on a great show for the fans and contributing to the business, but he soon discovered that most of his colleagues were far more obsessed with the indignity of working under Watts. As far as Benoit could tell, however, Bill Watts was the easiest, most laidback boss he'd ever had.

Despite his reputation as a bully, Bill Watts was hardly intimidating compared to Riki Choshu or Dynamite Kid. For a graduate of the Hart Dungeon and the New Japan dojo, Watts' supposedly merciless discipline was in fact comparatively lenient. An unfailingly punctual and obedient employee, Chris Benoit was indifferent to how rules he never broke were enforced.

In the *Pro Wrestling Torch* newsletter, Benoit would describe his stay under Bill Watts as a great experience. "One of my big goals was to wrestle for one of the big promotions in the United States and get to know the style of the United States.... Ric Flair and Arn Anderson, they have wrestled in the States for so long, they are so good at what they do, I thought it would be a good opportunity to improve myself."

All that mattered to Benoit was that he was getting the opportunity to follow in the footsteps of his idols Dynamite Kid and Bret Hart, the contemporary who he most closely modeled himself after. Both Dynamite and Bret perfected their craft in Stampede, made a name for themselves as workers in Japan, and hit the "big time" in the United States, making six figures a year in the "major leagues." At that very moment in WWE, Bret Hart was holding the heavyweight title, showing that even a bland Canadian technical wrestler—albeit a larger one—had the potential to reach the peak of the pro wrestling industry. Although Benoit was making great money overseas, it had always been his intention to become a star in the American wrestling market, just like Dynamite. Just as important for a self-professed student of the game, Benoit desired the challenge of mastering yet another style of pro wrestling and, in his humble way, showing everyone in the world just that.

Benoit quickly learned that the American style was very different from the Stampede style, let alone the New Japan or lucha style. American wrestling fans in 1993, who had been conditioned by nearly a decade of WWE showmanship and colorful gimmicks, did not want to see some boring wrestler "work the arm" for fifteen minutes or lazily sit on the mat in restholds. They wanted action. Benoit would tell the *Torch* about learning this the hard way. "You are catering to a different crowd that is educated differently. Like in Japan a lot of times, if you take a Boston crab on someone, the people appreciate what you're doing. In the States if you do that at the wrong time, you're gonna get shouted at and screamed at. That's what I mean in terms of psychology, it's totally different." Benoit learned to rely more on his strikes, slams, and suplexes, instead of slowing developing storylines based around submission holds and weakening a specific body part of his opponent. Benoit learned to sacrifice his physical well-being in a hurry.

It was also Benoit's first experience on the road in America. After three years of touring in style with New Japan, it was a throwback to the Stampede days for him to be hitching a ride all night in the back of some filthy car to half-full arenas in glitzy metropolises like Thibodaux, Mount Joliet, and Hopkinsville. The rigors of the Stampede circuit were inverted in WCW. Instead of traveling in blistering arctic cold, the old WCW loop traveled through what, to a Canadian, must have seemed like hell in the swamp humidity of the American South and Southeast. In old cars with rickety or broken air conditioners, Benoit would sit for hours feeling the tickle of sweat dripping down every cranny of his body. Wrestlers who worked in the South started sweating before they got to the ring, before they got to the locker room, before they even got into the arena; they would step out of the car, walk into the steaming wet cricket-song air, and immediately begin to lose body fluid.

The road trips themselves were terrible in a different way than Stampede. The Stampede trips were spent stuffed into vans, sitting shoulder-to-shoulder and knee-to-knee. In WCW, however, the boys traveled in cars. The wealthier stars might have a luxury rental car waiting in every town that they'd share with their regular traveling partner; a group of three or four guys might pitch in to share a normal rental car; some of the cannier old hillbillies would travel in beat-up, jerry-rigged, fume-belching jalopies with busted-out windows and a half-million miles on the speedometer.

A young wrestler new to the territory like Benoit was usually expected to ride with some of the veterans, lest he get the reputation of thinking he was hotshit or better than the boys. It allowed the young wrestler to get schooled in the promotion, in the personalities of the boys, and in the peculiar little rules and faux pas that existed in each locker room. It was one of the many paying-the-dues-type aspects of the business that slowly transformed a green nobody into one of the boys.

The relatively straitlaced Benoit always preferred to be the driver if he had any suspicion about the reliability of anyone else in the car. Unfortunately, a new wrestler could not turn down an offer to ride with an established star if he wanted to last in the business. Some of these grizzled old coots didn't want a goddamn Canadian greenhorn behind the wheel, especially considering how well most of them thought they drove drunk. Packed in the backseat next to heavy suitcases the size of magician's trunks, an anxious Benoit would sit tense and knotted as the driver guzzled Wild Turkey, popped pills, pissed out the window, erupted into spasms of laughter that zigzagged the car across the road, and kept the vehicle flying as fast as the engine could withstand.

Harley Race, former NWA champion and then WCW manager, had an age-old driving policy: have a bottle of hard liquor in hand and keep the speedometer at a steady eighty-five miles per hour at all costs, no matter what part of town they were in. If a cop car swung behind Harley and flipped on the sirens, it took a very persuasive driving partner to convince Race to pull over instead of commencing a high-speed chase. Other wrestlers had a drunk driving policy: always keep a razor in the front seat so that, in case you're pulled over, you can blade your forehead and scream at the cops, "We're going to the hospital! Ahhh!"

Benoit was thankful, at the very least, that his friend Brian Pillman was an established WCW personality. Unfortunately, riding with mercurial, drug-addicted Pillman was an adventure just as nerve-racking as driving breakneck speeds with a soused Harley Race.

Though WCW, dating back to its territorial roots, primarily worked in the South, Benoit also got the opportunity to perform (in front of anemic crowds) in places like New York City, Chicago, and Detroit. Benoit's role was not particularly demanding for someone of his experience and talent. He worked in the undercards, putting on quick and intense matches that set the mood for Watts' hardhitting athletic shows. Usually he'd work against fellow New Japan dojo graduate and gifted wrestler 2 Cold Scorpio. For a complete nobody, Benoit acquitted himself well, earning the insider crowd's respect as a hard worker with the potential to be a star—if he learned how to talk.

And that was the question as far as the office was concerned: would Benoit ever be able to develop the speaking skills that every wrestler who wasn't a giant or a bodybuilding star needed if he wanted to get a high-profile job in America? Far more daunting than the task of adapting his wrestling skills to the American style, Benoit had to learn how to cut a big league pro wrestling interview. The prospect of being in one of these histrionic, over-the-top wrestling promos intimidated Benoit.

Overseas, business was done in the ring, but WCW was different; the ability to pick up a microphone and transfix an audience of millions was all-important. Despite its reputation for taking wrestling so much more seriously than WWE, like all American wrestling promotions, WCW made its stars based on their charisma and "mic skills." Ric Flair may have been a fabulous technical wrestler, but his superstardom was just as reliant on his cartoonish interviews as Hulk Hogan's. Yes, Flair could "wrestle a broomstick to a three-star match," but what made him a star were his raving, coked-up, wildly gesticulating, beet-faced interviews during which he boasted of his wealth, style, and unparalleled sexual skills.

The previously mentioned Dusty Rhodes was morbidly obese, boring in the ring, and ugly as an inbred pig farmer, but he was one hell of an interview; a lisping, jive-dropping, yarn-spinning bullshit artist who convinced the fans that he was the homely physical embodiment of the American Dream. Consequently, Dusty became a multiple time NWA heavyweight champion. Dusty's verbal charisma not only made him a multiple-time champion but also perennial backstage management.

If Chris Benoit wanted to succeed in WCW and American wrestling in general, he knew that he would have to somehow learn to give a good, engaging interview. This seemed like a frank impossibility—eight years into his career, he had still never been given the opportunity to practice, let alone perfect his skills. In his first run in WCW, he received few opportunities. Though Benoit was soft-spoken and intelligent in regular conversation, in front of a microphone he was a shaky, panicky wreck with jumbled syntax and terrified eyes. When Benoit did manage to speak in complete sentences, he came across as so phony and inorganic that fans began to joke that he might actually be a robot impersonating a human pro wrestler.

Understandably, a promotion built on a tradition of high caliber interviews was not likely to give a "deer in the headlights" talker a lot of television time to learn on the job. So Benoit just watched, sticking around at television tapings to watch the masters of the craft. In addition to watching established legends like Rhodes and the recently returned Ric Flair, Benoit also watched the guys who were *not* naturals and picked up on how they got by with as few words as possible. If he caught them in a friendly moment, Benoit bombarded them with questions: how to attack your opponent without lowering his value, how to take direction without sounding scripted, how to sculpt a promo that sounded organic while still being colorful and entertaining.

Like everywhere else Benoit had worked, everyone remembers a very focused, unobtrusive young man sitting in a corner or standing off to the side, "just watching everything like a hawk." Benoit was comfortable paying his dues in America, putting on good matches and patiently learning through experience on the undercard just like he had in New Japan. Watts was happy with this tough little bastard who worked until he was stiff, looked credible, and didn't give a damn what he was paid or where he was booked on the card as long as he got time in the ring. Since Watts gave him a chance to learn and perform, Benoit was "really happy" with Watts as a booker.

Unfortunately, no one else was. The backstage political scheming against Watts had been intense from the moment he was hired, but for nine months no one had succeeded in taking him down. While most wrestlers simply assumed that Watts had been vetted and his racist comments to the *Pro Wrestling Torch* forgiven, one conspirator bet that there was one particular TBS executive left out of the loop: black baseball legend Hank Aaron. When Major League Baseball's reigning home run king began to read the anonymous fax ("If I don't want to sell fried chicken to blacks...."), Bill Watts' WCW career was over. When he was told what had happened, the cowboy quit before he could be fired.

In the power struggle that ensued, the man who came out on top would be Ole Anderson, one of the many failed bookers that TBS chose to lead the WCW again and again. As overbearing and unlikable as Bill Watts was, Ole Anderson was the ogre that made Bill Watts look like Barack Obama. Another Southern wrestling legend, Ole was born one of the earth's most miserable and disgruntled creatures. He suffered from the "In my day...." bullshitter syndrome, lecturing young wrestlers about how wrestling used to be full of legitimate shoot grappling contests—even though Ole became a star in the 1960s, not the 1860s. Still, anyone more than a decade younger than Ole was a helpless baby who didn't know the first thing about working, the first thing about the road, and couldn't have lasted a full day in his generation.

As a boss, Ole was far more cruel and close-minded than Watts. With godlike confidence in his perfect judgment, Ole venomously ridiculed anyone who disagreed with him or wrestled in a manner that didn't fit within his narrow, outdated conception of pro wrasslin'. Outside of his longtime cronies and his family, few could spend time in Ole's presence without being told that they were useless, stupid, godforsaken pieces of shit that would be better off dead. If Ole had been born a king, everyone in his entire kingdom would have been beheaded within a week.

Ole hated all young wrestlers, but he especially hated *small* young wrestlers. And, by Ole's standards, Chris Benoit was very, very small. Ole had an infallible method to judge if a man was made out to be a pro wrestler: The old-timer would walk up to them and wrap his big meaty fingers around their wrist. If Ole's fingers could reach all the way around, then the wrestler was insufficiently built to be a credible wrestler. "Female bones," he'd snort before walking away and getting their release papers ready.

Chris Benoit was just an undersized Canadian who couldn't talk. As Anderson watched Benoit wrestle and familiarized himself with the young man's style, he became enraged; he felt Benoit's hard work in the ring was *disrespectful* to the company and *bad* for business. If Ole wanted Chris Benoit to hog the spotlight and show up the big name wrestlers, he would have put Chris Benoit in the main events. Undercard wrestlers were just supposed to know their role and fill time. Benoit was no longer paired with 2 Cold Scorpio and told to put on the best match every night; instead, he was jobbed out to a green Little Richard impersonator night after night in short, bland matches.

If Benoit hadn't already built up such a good reputation with the veterans, he would've been fired immediately. Instead, it took a little while. Though he was out of favor, Benoit was not too troubled by Ole's decision to pair him in a "jobber team" with Bobby Eaton, one of the most respected tag workers in history. Sporting a majestic blond mullet, "Beautiful Bobby" was an Alabama native known throughout the world as one of the most generous, kind, and beloved men to ever step into a locker room. Though their tag team primarily existed to fill TV time and put over other wrestlers, it was still a wonderful opportunity for Benoit to learn American in-ring psychology from one of the recognized masters. Despite great performances with Eaton, Benoit was fired in the summer of '93.

When asked in a *Torch* interview why Ole fired him, Benoit responded, "I have no idea. I just stopped getting booked, I stopped getting booking sheets in the mail, I stopped getting correspondence from them, and that was that." Despite this blatant disrespect, Benoit "harbors no ill-will toward Anderson," according to the article. "He subscribes to the 'one leader—one vision' theory of running a promotion and gives 100 percent backing to Anderson." That was what the old-timers called "doing good business"—kissing the boss' ass even as he kicked you out the door. "Doing good business" was what wrestlers did when they intended to return to a promotion in the future under better circumstances. Chris Benoit would be back. The insider fans, aghast that Anderson could not see Benoit's talent, voted him the *Most Underutilized Wrestler* in the 1993 year-end *Torch* awards.

Though many fans would never remember Benoit's first run in WCW, he did make an impression on one wrestling legend. Gordon Solie, the dean of wrestling announcers, remembered Benoit vividly for one peculiar behavioral tic. Years later, Solie would tell Howard Brody, then President of the NWA, "You know Howard, there are only two men I've ever seen who always make a point to come to a show early just to feel the ring. Those two are Chris Benoit and Brian Pillman." In each town along the circuit, a wrestling ring is rebuilt from scratch, and, in the process of being constructed, its character changes. "They would go into the ring to see how it felt, to see where the soft spots were, where the wood lay—when you put a ring together fresh, all of that stuff changes." To Solie's surprise, he would walk into an empty arena to set up his announcing table, and, oblivious to his presence, Benoit would be crawling across the mat, caressing the ring, seemingly listening for its secrets.

Chapter VIII
The Cult

"He's the David Koresh of wrestling; he is
the Jim Jones of the locker room; he is the
ultimate motivator. There wasn't just a
light at the end of the tunnel: there was a
fucking beacon, there was a rainbow, he
would be in the back standing on those
stairs telling you that we were going to
march to victory, everything was going to
be okay, the sun is going to shine, we were
all going to make a shitload of money, we
were going to have a ton of rats, everything
was going to be awesome. The ultimate
motivator, he made you want to go kill
yourself."

MARK "BUBBA RAY
DUDLEY" LoMONACO
On Paul Heyman

THE DOUBLE-CROSS

"LACK OF GLITZINESS HURTS HIM IN THE EYES OF
SOME U.S. PROMOTERS," read the *Pro Wrestling
Illustrated* 1994 scouting report on Benoit. Though
renowned in insider circles as one of the greatest workers
in North America, Benoit's short run in WCW had proven
that he was hardly an easy-to-market personality. For the
independent "money marks" who booked wrestling shows
in armories, YMCAs, and high school gyms across

America, Benoit was a wrestler who could be relied upon to put on a great match and have little effect on attendance.

Benoit's best prospects for work in America after his run with WCW was in the Northeast indy scene, which stretched from New England south to Philadelphia and was known for its high proportion of "smart marks" who read the insider newsletters, traded bootlegged international tapes, and participated in the nascent online wrestling scene. To the smart marks who had read about him in the *Wrestling Observer* and watched blurry fourth-generation VHS dubs of his matches with Jushin Thunder Liger, Chris Benoit was a trendy, flavor-of-the-month underground sensation. This counted for little: Benoit was lucky if he received $200 per booking.

Thanks to his New Japan obligations, Benoit's next match in America came more than six months after his departure from WCW. This did little to dampen the enthusiasm of the smart marks for what was billed as an "indy dream match," in which the two favorite stars of the newsletter fans would face off: Sabu vs. Chris Benoit. The nephew of legend The Sheik, Terry "Sabu" Brunk had become a big enough star on the indy scene to win the *Wrestling Observer* "Wrestler of the Year" Award for 1994—without ever appearing on national television. Billed as a native of Bombay or Saudi Arabia, Sabu wore baggy Aladdin pants and a long Arabian headdress that fluttered down to frame his deeply scarred torso, which (depending on the source) was either the result of super violent-weapons matches in Japan or Sabu's own attempt at improving his image through self-mutilation. Sabu wrestled an original "hardcore" style that revolved not around working holds and establishing a psychologically sound storyline, but a relentless barrage of high-flying stunts utilizing tables, chairs, and springy ring-ropes as props. On the 1994 independent scene, there was no hotter act than Sabu performing acrobatic dives onto opponents lying prone on thin wooden office tables. It was the wrestling equivalent of the comedian Gallagher building his entire act around the moment where he would smash watermelons with an oversized mallet. In Woodbury, New Jersey, Benoit would be appearing in the role of the watermelon.

Though both wrestlers utilized styles that were unique on the American scene, Benoit and Sabu adjusted to each other and managed to have an action-packed match that left the unsuspecting crowd "shocked at the intensity of the action." The infamously antisocial Sabu—who, like his uncle, would often attempt to convince even fellow wrestlers that he really was a crazed Middle Eastern immigrant who spoke no English—pulled Benoit aside and whispered his thanks for the match. Seeing an opportunity to network with the top independent worker in America, Benoit asked for referrals on promoters who would book him and let him build up his American reputation. Sabu nodded, mumbled "Paul E. Dangerously," and said he'd put in a word.

Benoit continued to work the New Jersey indy scene for local NWA promoter Dennis Coraluzzo, facing legends Jerry Lawler and Terry Funk in the two months after his debut indy match with Sabu. Coraluzzo was cooperating on a title tournament to crown a new NWA champion with Philadelphia indy promoter and former WCW manager Paul "Paul E. Dangerously" Heyman, whose Eastern Championship Wrestling ("ECW") was just another independent promotion with big hype and a couple hundred fans. Heyman and Coraluzzo were in cahoots on the NWA title tournament at the behest of old-school promoter Jim Crockett, who was planning to reenter the national wrestling market.

Impressed by Benoit's performances on his shows, Coraluzzo suggested to Crockett that Chris Benoit be chosen as the new NWA champion—there was no one else on the independent scene who could regularly put on the long, credible, and physically punishing matches traditionally expected of an NWA champion. Crockett, six years out of the loop since selling his promotion to Turner, had no idea who Chris Benoit was and vetoed the idea. Instead, in a decision that would change wrestling history, Crockett okayed Paul Heyman's candidate for the title: the blond, cherub-cheeked, blue-eyed babyface Shane Douglas, who had a longer if not particularly successful career in WCW, where he was best remembered for playing a "Dynamic Dude" who carried a skateboard to the ring.

With his name established on the Northeastern scene thanks to his appearances at Coraluzzo's shows, Benoit was nonetheless booked to participate in the NWA heavyweight title tournament to be held in the Philadelphia homebase of ECW. In a pleasant surprise, Benoit received a rabid reaction from the crowd—a tour group of hardcore Japanese wrestling fans had traveled to Philadelphia to support Benoit as a New Japan native. As they often did in Bill Watts' WCW, Benoit and fellow New Japan alumni 2 Cold Scorpio put on the best match of the night, with Benoit losing.

Despite that performance, Benoit's role in that infamous August 27, 1994 show would be so overshadowed that most fans familiar with the event do not even know he was there. After Shane Douglas won the tournament and the NWA title, the hoary-voiced wrestler from Pittsburgh cut a promo that would singlehandedly earn ECW's national profile. Lifting the belt that, until Vince McMahon's national expansion, had the been the most prestigious wrestling title in the world, Douglas invoked a long line of great NWA champions of the past and, throwing down the NWA belt like garbage, announced that "They can all kiss my ass!" This was not part of the script—the boys watched in shock.

"I am not the man to accept the torch to be handed down to me from an organization that died—R.I.P.—seven years ago!" screamed Douglas, referring to Turner's purchase of JCP, which gutted the NWA. "Tonight, before God and my father as witness, I declare myself, the franchise, as the new ECW heavyweight champion of the world! We have set out to change the face of professional wrestling, and tonight let the new era begin...the era of the ECW!"

In the past decade, wrestling had undergone many controversies, but none had the symbolic power of the NWA title—the sacred relic that embodied wrestling tradition—being tossed with contempt onto a dirty mat like a used condom. "When that NWA title hit the mat, I was like *holy shit*! I just saw something that wasn't supposed to happen," remembers the wrestler known as the Blue Meanie. Heyman had ignited a scandal that would dominate the wrestling newsletters for weeks, making his newly renamed Extreme Championship Wrestling the most controversial and talked-about promotion in America. Heyman had created a brand for himself and ECW: *Extreme*, the iconoclastic outlaw promotion that "broke all the rules and pushed the envelope," with Heyman as the revolutionary who carried himself like the Trotsky of the squared circle.

To do so, Heyman had backstabbed Crockett and Coraluzzo, two business partners who had trusted him with their investments. "As Paul explained it to me," remembers longtime Heyman business partner and announcer Joey Styles, "he was so proud. Said it was a classic wrestling double-cross. So you lied, and you screwed a whole organization."

Raised in a traditional NWA territory that treated the NWA title with sanctity as the most prestigious in the sport, Benoit took some offense to the double-cross. Nonetheless, Benoit kept his mouth shut; thanks to Sabu, this conspiratorial renegade was his new boss. Heyman offered Benoit $300 a show, which according one source, "blew him away." After six months on the indy scene, Benoit's estimate of his own market value was apparently very low; one year later, Benoit would one of the hottest free agents in America. Working for Paul Heyman had its perks.

THE PREACHER

Paul Heyman was a pro wrestling prodigy. Slathered in grease and pimples, rigged with heavy braces, the fifteen-year-old Jewish kid from Scarsdale, New York was the most loathed photographer on the WWE circuit in the early 80s. Brash and obnoxious, he thought nothing of barreling over sports photographers from Tokyo and Manhattan, elbowing them aside like "Dennis Rodman fighting for a rebound." Heyman's street fighter physicality alienated the ringside professionals to the point that they organized and petitioned for Heyman to be banned from WWE events. When Vince McMahon himself ran into the hated teenager and absentmindedly asked him where he worked, Heyman proudly declared, "High school." Taken by surprise, McMahon laughed his loud, blasting cinematic laugh. "That's a hell of a story, kid." With one deadpan line, Heyman made an unforgettable impression on McMahon and saved his coveted ringside spot. Even at fifteen, Heyman knew how to work the most seasoned carnies in the business.

The son of a wealthy attorney, Heyman developed the quick wit, verbal evasiveness, and parrying charm that come from being cross-examined by an attorney since birth. With his sly bright eyes and sinuous conversational fluency, Heyman had an electric intellectual presence—some coworkers said they would actually sweat just trying to keep up with Paul in conversation. Heyman had the resources and intelligence to be a conventional success in any profession he chose, but he was born for the pro wrestling business. With his average unathletic build, Heyman had no interest in fighting glory—only backstage glory. Paul Heyman wanted to be the new Vince McMahon.

At the time most wealthy kids attend college, Heyman broke into the wrestling business as a part of the Northeast independent scene. Veterans recognized that this was one kid with a god-given talent for bullshit—both for selling it and for believing his own brand. These were the prerequisite traits for being a great pro wrestling manager. By the time he was twenty-one, Heyman was a manager in one of the most successful territories in the country.

Despite his bourgeois background, Paul was quickly accepted as one of the boys. It's easy to imagine Heyman as the smartass kid in high school who ruthlessly brandishes his wit to attach himself to the popular jock crowd with the best girls, best parties, and best drugs. From there, it's an effortless transition to being a pro wrestling manager, where charismatic operators sans athletic ability can hitch a ride on the wildest, sleaziest traveling bacchanalia in the world.

Paul lived fast, told a great tall tale, and, if you believe AWA coworker Marty Jannetty, was one of the best pharmaceutical drug hookups on the circuit. Heyman has denied that, saying, "When I was in the AWA, I never did any drugs whatsoever. I was twenty-one. I didn't touch GHB until twenty-five. Smoked my first joint the week before my twenty-fifth b-day. And have *never* hooked anyone up. Feel free to put me in the room with that claimant. Why would they need me when Wahoo [beloved wrestling legend Wahoo McDaniel] was there, anyway?"

Lacking the Olympian genetics of most wrestlers, the road took an egregious toll on Paul's body. Initially named after a Michael Keaton film character, by twenty-seven, "Paul E. Dangerously" more closely resembled Jim Belushi's misbegotten lovechild with Gene Simmons from KISS. With his slicked-back receding frizzy black hair, vast ass-cheek forehead, round face, jowly chin, devious smile, and disheveled suits, Paul closely fit the stereotypical image of the untrustworthy used car salesman with a flask in his back pocket. He fit right in with the boys. "Paul didn't come from Hell's Kitchen," says Heyman's friend and former coworker, Dan Madigan. "But he's street smart, he's seasoned, he's this cinematic shyster character that's too charismatic to be real. Paul still has a street mentality. Paul's a hustler; he doesn't take shit, and, if he wasn't in wrestling, he'd be selling stolen cars or trafficking drugs. The boys can tell all of that, too; they know he's not some punk. He's a man; he can handle himself; and he got respect for it."

Hired in the late 80s by Jim Crockett Promotions, Heyman would survive JCP's transformation into WCW and quickly become one of the top announcers and managers in America's second national promotion—all by the age of twenty-five. Though focused on eventually becoming the boss of a major national promotion, Heyman's ambitions were stymied when his reputation was ruined by accusations that he leaked to newsletters and embezzled money from the company. Heyman sued WCW and told his friends that the charges—the first of many accusations of financial impropriety made against him during his career—were just a manifestation of Watts' anti-Semitism. "Hey, I own the banks and the media, too," Heyman said.

Heyman took his dream of becoming the next Vince McMahon to the smalltime, quickly backstabbing his best friend in the business, Eddie Gilbert, to engineer a coup for control of Eastern Championship Wrestling, a small Philadelphia-based independent. "It all came down to power," explained Terry Funk. "Paul wanted to be the boss. He wanted Gilbert's job. You know, Paul E. wanted to be in wrestling from the time he was a young boy, but his dream was not to be world champion—he wanted to rule the world, the way Vince McMahon had done in the 1980s."

Lacking the resources to sign outside wrestlers to exclusive contracts, Heyman realized that the only way he could transform ECW into a viable entity using uncontracted talent was by making the *brand* of ECW marketable. Since the talent would be transitory, the fans' loyalty would have to be directed to the company itself. Heyman's method of branding ECW was brilliant: with WWE and WCW marketing to a wholesome, child-friendly demographic, Extreme Championship Wrestling would stake out the territory as the Rated R wrestling promotion. ECW would be lewd, ultra-violent, sexually salacious, and countercultural, the wrestling embodiment of anti-authority, alternative 90's culture. The perfection of this rebellious brand came with the NWA double-cross, which put a gold belt that embodied everything ECW rejected into Shane Douglas' hands. When that belt ate canvas, Heyman created a visual that communicated ECW's essence with incredible force.

"We broke away from the NWA because the National Wrestling Alliance was old school when old school wasn't hip anymore," said Heyman in an interview. "We wanted to set our mark, we wanted to break away from the pack, we wanted to let the world know that we weren't just some independent promotion."

"If Vince is stadium rock, if Vince is Led Zeppelin, then Paul is punk," says Dan Madigan. Like punk rock fans, ECW fans were usually more committed to what they referred to as "the movement," the ECW philosophy and attitude, than they ever were to any single performer within the promotion. Their bestselling merchandise was a black T-shirt with the ECW logo and, when the fans at the ECW cheered a great performance, instead of the wrestlers' names they chanted the name of the promotion, "ECDub! ECDub!" Paul Heyman had made the fans more loyal to the promoter who booked the wrestlers than the wrestlers themselves, who became expendable.

Though Heyman concentrated on making sure ECW could survive the inevitable defection of its talent for the high-paying WCW and WWE, this strategy succeeded only because Heyman could create new stars to replace the old. Since ECW still couldn't afford to hire established stars, the potential new stars had to be constructed out of the rejects: the wrestlers considered too small, too crazy, too fat, too wild, too bland, or too green for WWE and WCW. Far from intimidated, Heyman flourished with the wrestlers that were unemployable in the big leagues; a confidential source close to ECW explained that Heyman relates "to broken people," and relished the challenge of getting "performances out of people [that] they didn't have in themselves." According to a WWE writer who worked with him, "Paul thinks of himself as St. Jude, the patron saint of lost causes."

ECW was the home of such pro wrestling superstars as The Sandman (a rheumy-eyed, potbellied, alcoholic ex-con in baggy pants and a T-shirt), Tommy Dreamer (a pasty Ben-Affleck-esque goofball with a Jersey guido pompadour, a pinchable baby-fat face, and slight double chin), and heavyweight champion Mikey Whipwreck (a nerdy, rail-thin, Ric Moranis lookalike so hopeless that his trainer refused to accept cash for training him).

"It's the old 'Anyone can fuck the good looking girls' theory. Hey, it isn't hard to get The Rock over. Hand him a mic, and sit back," explains a confidential source who is an ECW icon. Heyman, on the other hand, delighted in his ability to "take a lower midcarder like Shane Douglas and make him a Franchise. Take Tod Gordon's drunken buddy, who comes to the ring in a wet suit to 'Wipeout,' and make him the cigarette smoking, beer drinking, cane swinging Sandman. Take a masked high flyer ready to retire [Ted Petty] and his opponent on the indies [who ended up being Johnny Grunge] and make them The Public Enemy." Whenever Heyman conceived of a marketable and successful character for a wrestler that the majors had rejected as hopelessly unemployable, he would "Get so high!" exclaims this anonymous source.

To be fair, Heyman had an easier time getting new talent than most big league promoters. Overlooked by Heyman worshipers is that Heyman had a far deeper arsenal of "cheap heat" at his disposal, in addition to a far more homogenous audience. WWE and WCW floundered trying to make Shane Douglas a name largely because they couldn't give him a microphone and let him cut screaming, rebellious promos like, "Hulk Hogan, you can suck my dick!... You are a caricature from the 1980s; you sucked then, and you suck now!" It was much easier to make lumpen penguins like Ian and Axl Rotten popular when they were allowed to wrap their fists in double-sided tape, dust them in broken glass, and beat each other's viscera all over the mat.

Despite these advantages, it is hard to deny Heyman's brilliance in realizing that the faults of a wrestler in the 90's alternative culture were suddenly his most marketable traits. By accentuating the *negatives* of his performers, Heyman concocted characters that flouted convention and flaunted their faults at the exact cultural moment when such antisocial and unconventional behavior was most fashionable. When struggling wrestler J.T. Smith was berated by the fans for botching his moves, Heyman made him the wrestler who botched his moves on purpose—and got cheered for it. Heyman at his best could market any weakness until it was a strength and convince his fans that every flaw was really an inside joke between the promotion and the hardcore audience.

Frequently compared to a "mad scientist," "prophet," or "visionary," Heyman earned the reputation as the ultimate makeover artist in the wrestling business. Paul was the starmaker, and he saw more potential in Chris Benoit than anyone else in ECW. Benoit was going to be his promotional ace and heavyweight champion. And, unlike every other promoter in America, Heyman knew just what to do with Benoit's "dry image" and "lack of glitziness": exploit it, package it, and market it as grimy unrefined authenticity to fans sick of cartoonish WWE-style bullshit. After all, everyone knows that most dangerous people in everyday life are not charming, histrionic extroverts like Ric Flair or superhuman genetic specimens like Hulk Hogan. The axe-murderers, assassins, and mailmen who end up launching bloody rampages through the post office: they were always the quiet, awkward, insecure, white guys with a chip on their shoulders. They were just like Chris Benoit. Meet the Crippler.

THE CRIPPLER

BENOIT'S BIG CAREER BREAK OCCURRED IN SABU'S NECK. It was November 5, 1994, a couple months into Benoit's so-far-undistinguished run in ECW. Booked to face Sabu in a match-up that was by now familiar, Benoit was nervous: though their matches never lacked violence or intensity, they had problems with their communication and timing. Sabu was often an aimless, disorganized, uncommunicative worker, and it was easy to get lost working with him. In October, Sabu came into a match against Benoit with three broken ribs and, due to a miscommunication, cracked another across Benoit's knees. Sensitive to the trust placed in him by his opponents, Benoit entered his biggest match against Sabu determined to take care of his reckless, injured opponent to the best of his professional ability.

Viking Hall was home to Extreme Championship Wrestling and Philadelphia's meanest midnight bingo game. Lacking showers or air-conditioning, Viking Hall certainly wasn't equipped to be a sports venue. After writhing around on a dirty mat in the overcrowded, torridly hot arena, ECW wrestlers soaked with sweat slumped backstage already itching, knowing they had nowhere to rinse off and therefore little chance of stopping yet another outbreak of hives. Others simply collapsed on the way to dressing room from heatstroke and had to be carried to the back, where their cracking lips would be splashed with cold beer. It is no surprise that ECW Arena fans were always so eager to have the six-pack-toting Sandman douse them with Budweiser: it was sauna hot in the cramped arena, and most fans would rather smell like beer than the nostril-burning musk that filled the air as some of the most hygienically challenged wrestling fans in America began to sweat.

Even on a November night, the arena was "fucking steaming," and naive fans who dressed for colder weather were ribbed by the regular fans as their accumulated body heat raised the temperature. Benoit entered the ring with his body looking especially impressive: jacked-up and muscular yet still neatly cut and defined, a "best of both worlds" look that can be achieved only if steroid use is partnered with a Spartan diet and unrelenting workout routine. Benoit didn't pose or jaw at the fans or do much of anything to develop his character; his mind may have been occupied with thoughts of how he could possibly protect Sabu and still put on a match that would satisfy the ECW fans.

A half-speed, cautious match with the beat-up Sabu was not an option; it was never an option in the ECW Arena. "The fans of the Northeast were more bloodthirsty," explained ECW veteran Axl Rotten. "All they care about is action and violence.... The result was matches in the Northeast tended to be a lot cruder, because they'd hammer you if you tried to slow down even for a few seconds." The regulars at the ECW Arena considered themselves part of the show—just another element of the ECW brand. The hardcore Philadelphia fans commonly hung out with the boys every month at the cracked-out neighborhood Travelodge where Heyman left his wrestlers after shows. Passing around joints and talking about the business, these fans treated the wrestlers with the sadistic, ball-breaking familiarity of frat brothers. This crowd's chants were merciless: "You fucked up!" "End this match!" "You suck dick!" Legitimate tough guys who would never take shit on the street would ruin their bodies chasing the approval of the newsletter-reading, tape-trading nerd hecklers in the ECW arena: the self-professed hardest-to-impress wrestling fans in America.

Even if Benoit was comfortable disappointing the fans with a take-it-easy match, Sabu never considered it a possibility. His entire reputation was based on his determination to nearly kill himself every night—at any show, no matter how small.

Accompanied by Paul Heyman and a lumbering oaf billed as 911, Sabu sprinted out of the locker room without his usual theatrical entrance. Out for revenge, Sabu slid into the ring and made a mad dive at Benoit for a takedown. Benoit was prepared, cutting off Sabu and stomping him down on the mat. Without hesitating, Benoit pounced on Sabu's injured ribs, smashing him with a knee to the stomach and tossing him chest-first onto the top ring rope. Performing for the fans, Sabu writhed across the mat, howling in pain. Benoit had protected him so far, while still playing the methodical, ruthless injury-exploiting predator for the fans.

Lifting the still-selling Sabu to his feet, Benoit stooped down, bent Sabu's right knee, hooked it, and tossed him over his shoulder into the air. It was an awkward maneuver, some sort of sloppy kneelock-flapjack. Expecting Sabu to land on his stomach, Benoit threw his opponent, not straight up into the air so he could fall naturally on his stomach but up and *forward*. The storyline of the match dictated that Sabu should land on his front side to sell his injured ribs, so Sabu twisted to correct himself; there wasn't the time.

By attempting to land on his stomach, Sabu instead impaled himself headfirst into the mat like a javelin. This was *not* a good bump. Sabu rolled in a scurrying panic out of the ring to make sure Benoit didn't touch him before he could let him know he was hurt for real. Hunkered down on the ringside concrete, Heyman and 911 huddled over Sabu, shielding him from the fans. The first few rows could hear the foreign maniac who never spoke screaming, "I broke my neck! I broke my neck, goddamit!" The match was declared a no contest, and the injury was so obviously real that the callously cynical ECW Arena fans behaved themselves for once, wishing Sabu luck as he was carried to the back.

Somewhere in the melee, Benoit lived up to his "Houdini" reputation by disappearing in the midst of crowded arena and dressing room. No one could remember seeing him leave the ring or walk backstage, but Heyman was insistent that Benoit would want to accompany Sabu to the hospital. Heyman ran shouting through the small

ECW Arena, looking for where Benoit could possibly be hiding. Moments before deciding that Benoit must have simply ran out and hitched a cab ride out of town, Heyman opened up a closet door backstage and discovered Benoit crouched in the corner, his head buried in cleaning supplies. Benoit was rocking and weeping uncontrollably, mumbling that he had crippled Sabu in the ring. Heyman pulled Benoit up and sent him to the hospital with Sabu.

The hospital trip was beyond parody. There was reluctance at the hospital to admit this scarred-up Aladdin. First of all, there was no way to tell if he had health insurance since no one accompanying him knew his real name, and—broken neck or not—Sabu was reluctant to break kayfabe in front of a bunch of marks while still in his Arabian costume. He initially refused to even speak English, let alone give his real name. When sanity finally prevailed, X-rays of Sabu's neck revealed two cracked vertebrae—and a bullet in his face. Having already opened his mouth about his name, Sabu was adamantly keeping silent about the mystery bullet.

A few days later, Sabu was training at the gym with a neck brace; he spoke to Heyman and promised to appear at an ECW show in two weeks. With his top star still on the road, Heyman's creative fires had been sparked—he saw the gimmick that would transform Benoit into the most marketable character in ECW, his promotional ace. Heyman had been noticing some similarities between Stu Hart and his student.

Though Benoit would display exaggerated, mannerly respect to veterans he respected, Heyman had witnessed him being jarringly cruel to the young wrestlers hanging around ECW looking for a chance. Despite his reputation for shyness, Heyman watched Benoit at the bar after shows and noticed that the Canadian relished ribbing and mocking the inexperienced young wrestlers, especially the boys he saw as being less tough and less disciplined than himself. "Benoit had a dry, vicious sense of humor, usually at someone else's expense," a source from ECW remembers. Benoit had that "Stampede sense of humor" that was infamous throughout the business and used to describe any cruel, hazing prick that picked on those too weak and too inexperienced to defend themselves.

Heyman had made a habit of basing his storylines on reality—in the post-kayfabe era, it was much easier to get heat from insider fans if there was a superficial layer of truth to the storylines. In the 70s, Ray Stevens was a short in-ring technician who had made a name for himself by combining methodical, technical wrestling moves with wild, suicidal bumping skills. He had gone by the name The Crippler for his ability to pinpoint an opponent's weakness and incapacitate him. Combining characteristics of Stu Hart's reputation and Ray Stevens old character, Heyman envisioned an opportunity to create a 1990's version of The Crippler who could be exponentially more violent, over-the-top, and bloodthirsty in the "anything goes" ECW than Stu Hart or Ray Stevens had been in the 60s and 70s. Chris "The Crippler" Benoit was born: the cruel, mean-spirited, sadistic pupil of Stu Hart who loved to use his shooting expertise to "humble" and permanently injure his opponents. In Heyman's mind, The Crippler was just as close to reality as portraying the Sandman as a drunk.

Shortly after speaking with Sabu, while Heyman was still in a state of heightened creative frenzy, Benoit called ECW's booker to ask about Sabu's well-being. According to a confidential source, Heyman "knew Sabu was not suffering, or in great pain, or a victim of lasting damage" and hurriedly told Benoit, "Sabu will be fine, but this is a huge break for us," before launching into a wild, speculative revelry of all the angles they could run, all the feuds he'd book, and all the money they could make together. If his past behavior is any indication, Benoit had probably spent the last few days alternating between out-of-control weeping, vicious self-criticism, and brutal exercise regimes as punishment.

Heyman's four-word dismissal of what Benoit assumed was a career-ending injury had not satisfied Benoit's hunger for detailed information, but, no matter how many times he interrupted Heyman or attempted to steer him back to the subject of Sabu, Heyman could not be distracted from his new Crippler character. "It's going to be great; we'll have you suplex every opponent until he's paralyzed, and the ref has to end the match. As the emergency crew is dragging him to the back, you can run down and knock him and yank on his neck...It'll be *great!*"

Benoit would never forgive Heyman for what he saw as his unforgivable callousness and insensitivity. As far as he was concerned, Heyman was the ultimate unprincipled, unscrupulous, self-interested promoter looking to exploit the boys at any cost. Years later, when Heyman was Benoit's top proponent on the booking team, there were still indications that Benoit had not forgiven his former boss or gotten over his guttural distaste for his behavior. On the other hand, Benoit seemed to laugh off the issue on his WWE biographical DVD, and one former WWE writer, Dr. Ranjan Chhibber, is adamant that Benoit held Heyman in high esteem. When the news broke that Chhibber was leaving the WWE to protest the management's treatment of Heyman, Benoit pulled him aside and said, "You're doing the right thing for the right man."

For his part, Heyman could not understand Benoit's resentment. One person close to the situation explains, "[Benoit] was a vicious man in terms of 'paying dues' and would—like Stu Hart—enjoy stretching someone who wanted to break into the business, but he had all this compassion for someone like Sabu, for whom he had respect." It made little sense to Heyman how Benoit could be so merciless and unfeeling towards young wrestlers following their dreams, yet he would protect and coddle an awesomely reckless fool like Sabu just because he was a veteran in the business. Feeling sorry for Sabu for suffering yet another injury was like crying over a sideshow freak who accidentally gave himself a nosebleed while hammering a nail up his nostril.

Like all of Heyman's best gimmicks, the Crippler character directly addressed the parts of Benoit's persona that other promoters would have attempted to hide as liabilities. In any other promotion, a match where Benoit had botched a move so badly that it nearly paralyzed a popular wrestler would have never been mentioned again. In ECW, Heyman insisted that it be brought up repeatedly, along with endless slow-motion replays and even a "Pain Scan" segment, where Joey Styles used a TV sports analyst's pen to draw arrows on the screen indicating where and how the break occurred. Chris Benoit became the wrestler so dangerous to work with that he might one day kill someone in the ring. Joey Styles advised one Benoit opponent, "He better be leery of the Crippler—it can happen at any moment!" And Heyman made sure that, just like in the Sabu match, those moments came out of nowhere. Without any phony build-up or theatrical structure, sometimes Benoit just executed a suplex in the middle of a match, and his opponent stopped moving. It was over. Out came the stretcher.

Since Benoit still gave halting, robotic, colorless interviews, Heyman marketed the Crippler as a cold, dead-on-the-inside, unfeeling killer. "That man has ice water running through his veins!" screamed Joey Styles. When Benoit failed to convincingly sell that he was a malicious, evil killer, Heyman instructed Styles to accentuate that, as well. The Crippler became an unwilling victim of his own strength and predatory instinct. "Not that Benoit is trying to send people to the hospital, it just happens! He's just that lethal...! Not even Chris Benoit knows how dangerous he is," explained Styles.

To spice up Benoit's promos, Heyman exploited what he recognized as the sadistic parts of Benoit's personality that were cultivated throught his training under Stu Hart. Anyone who came up in the wrestling business during the 70s and 80s heard stories of Stu rubbing his hands together and licking his lips when a new football star or wannabe wrestler showed up at the Dungeon to be trained. In allusion to this, Heyman edited Benoit's promos over a superimposed image of his hands rubbing together in anticipation, just like Stu getting ready to stretch someone. The close-ups of these calloused, rough hands sold Benoit as a craftsman of violence. Heyman fed Benoit lines that accentuated the fundamental bitterness and insecurity of the Crippler; insecurity that Heyman felt guys like Stu and Benoit must suffer from since they were always needing to prove themselves as tough guys.

"Sabu, you're back in the ring; you're back here in the ECW," began Benoit's most famous ECW promo. "And people are starting to talk. I don't like what they're saying. They're saying that you're some type of tough guy. They're saying that the Crippler is unable to get the job done. Well, Sabu, the only reason you're back is because I want you back. Sabu, on any given night, I can take you out and end your career, permanently." It's not hard to recognize Stu Hart Jr. as the basis for the Crippler in this promo.

Whatever else can be said about Paul Heyman, it is undeniable that he crafted a character that made Chris Benoit a millionaire, a star, and a world heavyweight champion in the two biggest promotions in American history. The Crippler character worked; thanks to the promotional work of Paul Heyman and Joey Styles, by the time Benoit next appeared at the ECW Arena, he was met by fans chanting, "Break his neck! Break his neck!" For the rest of his life, Chris Benoit would be the Crippler.

PUTTING THE PRO IN PRO WRESTLING

"IF YOU *PASS* A DRUG TEST IN ECW, YOU'RE FIRED!" This was the motto of the ECW locker room. Walking backstage at the ECW Arena, Benoit encountered a casual and friendly, if rampantly hedonistic, scene. The Sandman, who by some accounts wrestled sober exactly twice out of his countless appearances in ECW, always brought along a large ice chest of beer that would be taken from and added to throughout the night. The boys gathered around the beer, drinking, ribbing each other, playing cards or shooting dice, laughing uproariously at the latest tall tale from the road. Known as the most relaxed and friendly locker room in wrestling, ECW had little backstage drama or politics. This was partially due to there being so little money involved, but it mostly came down the unique character of Heyman and his roster.

Since most everyone in the company found it hard to believe that *anyone* could intimidate, outwit, or out-carny Paul, there seemed to be no reason to scheme and even less reason to resent others' futile attempts. Just as importantly, ECW's roster was made up of wrestlers who, if they had been the sort of conniving and ambitious office politicians that normally get ahead in wrestling, wouldn't be in ECW to begin with. Most of the boys in ECW came into the company as working class nobodies with day jobs, and it was hard to develop superstar egos in what was still basically a penny-ante indy promotion that ran three or four times in a busy month. The boys knew that Heyman would do his best to get *everyone* over, make them recognizable to the audience, no matter how pathetic or unmarketable, so each wrestler would get his chance. Since Paul was alone among 1990's promoters who did not make stars on the basis of their physique, the ECW locker room was also free of the resentment and volatility caused by the steroid-abuse arms race between the boys.

Free from professional strife, the ECW locker room developed a fraternity atmosphere, or, considering the large number of naked women backstage, a frat party atmosphere. Since ECW had only one locker room and no showers, there was no space for the women to be separate from the men, so they simply changed in front of them. It was common for the ECW locker room to look like the backstage of a strip club, with gorgeous women in bras, panties, garter belts, and high heels having casual conversation with men in similar stages of undress. The

most outspoken and respected female member of the
locker room was Nancy Sullivan, Benoit's future wife; she
was notable for her utter casualness about her own body.

The ECW females were not the only half-naked
women in the locker room. Gangs of leather-clad
dominatrixes were occasionally invited backstage by ECW
moneyman Tod Gordon, who was active in the online
bondage scene. The vast contingent of ring rats who
serviced the ECW roster would also pass in and out
throughout the night, delivering drugs or beer or other
essentials. "Rats would come from far and near," says New
Jack in the ECW documentary *Forever Hardcore*. "Bra,
they'd be on ice boats coming over the border [from]
Alaska. They be comin' out of Africa with a bone in their
nose. Oh brah, *they come*. I'm talking 'bout midgets, blind
people—everybody. I loved the rats in Philly: I got credit
cards from these rats, I got my room paid for—even
though it was already paid—I got advances from these
rats which I've never paid back to this day, I've rented
cars for months! We used to toss [the rats] around like
beach balls." Most dangerous of all were the ECW crew's
steady girlfriends, who could be fiercely protective of their
men with all the rats and intoxicants around. Most of
them had risky behavior, to say the least: one infamous
girlfriend sported a serial number tattooed under her lip
by her boyfriend "owner" and went to federal prison on
serious cocaine trafficking charges. It was considered a
miracle she didn't drag half of the ECW roster with her.

Booze, marijuana, cocaine, and pills were used
openly before the matches with little worry. It was
common to see ECW wrestlers purge into a garbage can
before going through the curtain or, better yet, "take a
powder" in the middle of a match to slide out of the ring
and puke. ECW wrestlers subscribed to a *Drunken
Master*-style folk belief that guys like Sabu and multiple
DUI-wonder Sandman were less good, less relaxed, and
less reliable in the ring without their "gimmick." These
claims seem less credible when the numerous examples of
Sandman's drunken "reliability" are reviewed, such as the

night he staggered out to the ring without pants, forcing Tommy Dreamer to run up and cup Sandman's genitalia in his hands to prevent an obscenity charge that would have taken away ECW's promotional license.

The best Sandman story was perhaps the night when Heyman booked the too-bombed-to-wrestle Sandman to make the main event run-in as a compromise. With a head full of booze, Sandman charged out of the dressing room, slipped on the ringside concrete, and careened face-first into a steel ring post—knocking himself out cold. The intended target of his run-in used Sandman's limp, unconscious body as a puppet, engineering the world's least credible asskicking to uproarious laughter.

Drug use was more than tolerated; management supposedly endorsed it. According to a story told by Sandman, one night he showed up at a show bleary-eyed and high, and "Paul took one look at me and said, 'Go find New Jack and get some coke in you right now!'" Once again, Heyman denied this story. "I have never done coke in my life and have never encouraged it, either. Just a personal disgust I have for people on coke. That should put that claim to rest."

Benoit was never a wrestler who partook in drugs backstage before a match and, according to most sources, rarely afterwards. Especially as a young man, he took his body and physique too seriously to take recreational drugs; the only narcotics he would ingest were those he thought improved his body, if not his health. (Though Benoit would later claim that he never finished a full beer drinking with the boys, sources in ECW disagree.) Shockingly hard on himself for the minor mistakes he made in-ring that hurt no one, Benoit never wanted the responsibility for injuring another wrestler on his conscience. Being branded as the man who cripples other workers was extremely troubling.

But Paul Heyman had a way of dissipating the doubts of his employees. "You could want to shoot him in the head with a gun, and you'd come walking out [of a meeting] with his cock in your mouth," said Raven in one interview. In his memoir, Chris Jericho remembers that, "Paul waited for every single wrestler to come through the curtain so he could congratulate them personally for their contribution to the show. His encouragement meant more to his crew than money. I'm sure there were guys in the WWE who would've given a week's pay to get that kind of acknowledgment."

Heyman knew well how most promoters treated their wrestlers, and his promotion benefited incalculably from the loyalty of workers who treasured his appreciation and praise. He could convince even the most used-up jobber that, deep down, he loved them: "Vince is like 'You're mine until we get this angle over, until we get *Wrestlemania* over, and then you're shit,'" said Bam Bam Bigelow in an interview. "With Paul E., you're his family. Paul E.'s one of the boys."

This extravagant kindness extended to the newsletter writers who, in the days before the Internet, held so much influence in the industry. While Hulk Hogan burned copies of the *Wrestling Observer* live on pay-per-view, Heyman was wooing the newsletter writers with Clintonian charm. As a result, in addition to the couple hundred dollars Heyman could offer talent, he tempted them with priceless PR within the industry from dirt sheet writers who, in retrospect, were often preposterously biased. Many limited wrestlers got signed to six-figure contracts with WWE and WCW based solely on their ECW reputations and the hilariously inflated praise given to them by the hated newsletters that everyone in the industry unfailingly read. Even Stu Hart, the paragon of shooter grizzledness and old-timer kayfabe values, had his wife read him each issue of Dave Meltzer's *Wrestling Observer* newsletter the moment it arrived in the mail. And as far as Stu Hart or Vince McMahon knew, the newsletter writers that rated such ECW "classics" as The Gangstas vs. the Public Enemy a perfect five stars out of five were trustworthy.

"Paul had business skills. You can't look at what he did in ECW and not say he was a good businessman. He was brilliant in how he manipulated the Internet, the newsletter writers, and even other promoters," promoter Sheldon Goldberg has said. "The problem is his business changed, and he refused to change with it. He let his carny personality get in the way of the best interest of ECW at times."

Arriving at ECW shows, Heyman looked like he had just been plunged out of a toilet. Greasy faced, stubbly, red-eyed, permanently distracted and disheveled, Heyman bolted through the locker room ranting encouragement and hype with Waffle House napkins with booking notes scribbled over them falling out of his pocket. This whirling hobo shaman image inspired Terry Funk to describe Heyman as "an insane, crazy, Einstein type of moron." In one pocket was his best tool—a doctor's prescription pad that he used to write out bereavement notices that would garner his workers reduced airline fares and who knows what else. Wrestlers would be baffled when stewardesses bit their lips and made solemn pouting faces when they checked in at the airport, only to find out that their "brother" had died for the fifth time in six ECW shows. When they attempted to call Heyman and find out what the story was, the boys likely got Paul's "roommate" on the phone, whose voice sounded identical to Heyman's. The "roommate" promised Paul would call back; the Virgin Mary appeared in tortillas and pieces of toast more often than Heyman returned phone calls as promised. "Paul Heyman would rather climb a tree and tell lies rather than stand on the ground and tell the truth," said Dennis Coraluzzo.

In person, Heyman had a bottomless reservoir of words. In between his variably honest praise, Heyman specialized in unspooling elaborate fantasy vistas of immensely profitable success that lay in store for everyone who stayed loyal to ECW. These hallucinatory pep talks inspired such blind, stupid devotion that Heyman was commonly compared to suicide cult-leader Jim Jones, who persuaded his flock to drink cyanide-laced Kool Aid.

"He was the most charismatic guy," declared Raven. "He was like Jim Jones. I would've drank the Kool Aid. I would've drank the Kool Aid dripping out of his asshole." Workers became so convinced of Heyman's unique talent to make stars out of nobodies that they accepted it when Heyman told them that the only way to get accepted into ECW was for unsigned workers to travel from show to show *for free*, proving their devotion to the brand by spending thousands in travel costs. The dozens of foreign wrestlers in ECW worked on illegal tourist visas and, when Heyman failed to deliver their promised work visas, nonetheless continued to take the risk on themselves and cross the border illegally—except for Benoit.

Despite all the pep talks and sermons and promises that he would feud with fellow New Japan import Eddy Guerrero for the heavyweight title, Benoit could not forgive Heyman for repeatedly promising him a work visa that was always arriving at the next show and then the show after that and then the show after that. Benoit threatened to leave, but Heyman believed that Benoit was going to leave anyway, so why pay for his visa?

Benoit retaliated by committing a rare break of wrestling etiquette: he declined to personally inform the ECW office that he was accepting a tryout with WWE, set up by Bret Hart, who had been talking to McMahon about hiring Benoit and Steve Austin. Rumors abounded that WWE management was interested in tagging Benoit with Owen Hart or reforming the British Bulldogs with Benoit joining Davey Boy Smith as Dynamite Kid's replacement. On June 5, Benoit lost to Bob Holly in his first WWE match; on June 7, he had what was described as a far better match with his close friend from Stampede, Owen Hart. In Bret Hart's memoir, he describes watching Benoit beam with happiness as he listened to Owen talk about his wife's pregnancy while the two traveled together from Benoit's WWE tryout. "I realized then that these two were close," said Hart.

The June 10 issue of *Pro Wrestling Torch* reported, "Vince McMahon watched Benoit's dark match from ringside and appeared absolutely delighted with what he saw, smiling broadly throughout the match.... Benoit has a long way to go in improving his mic work...but if he signs with the [WWE], he brings a working ability perhaps never seen before in that federation." *Torch* editor Wade Keller reminded his readers that, with WWE's momentarily strict steroid policy, "Off steroids, [Benoit] still has a V-shaped build and a machine-like look, but he will be considerably smaller than many top WWE wrestlers."

Benoit's decision was made for him. Masa Saito informed Benoit that the New Japan office considered his negotiations with WWE to be a violation of their exclusive working agreement with WCW. Likewise, the monopolistic WWE outright rejected any talent-sharing agreement with New Japan or any other promotion. It would have been absurd for Benoit to abandon his extremely lucrative, prestigious, and secure position in New Japan for spot in a company known for doing very little with small wrestlers. On steroids for maybe a decade, the insecure Benoit probably did not want to risk his career on a company that would prohibit steroid use and reveal how small he naturally was, which would make it obvious for the rest of his career when he was using drugs.

Shortly afterwards, Benoit was stopped at the Canadian border by a sympathetic customs agent who advised him that officials were well aware of his visa violations and, if he did not immediately desist, he would be banned from entering the United States for five years. Benoit was left with no choice: he had to leave ECW, and there was only one promotion in America where he could work while maintaining his Japanese bookings. Though Benoit did not wish to return to WCW, which he had heard was more politically dysfunctional than ever,

Heyman's crackerjack business practices gave him no choice if he wanted to continue his American wrestling career. At the very least, Turner Broadcasting would obtain a basic work visa for its employee, and it was on that fundamental level that the decision to leave ECW was made.

"You can shuck and jive and maneuver yourself around certain things, but once you're playing with the big boys, there's a another level business that you have to deal with," explains Sheldon Goldberg. "And Paul wanted to play on the same level as the big boys, but he didn't want to change his style and organizational standpoint."

Benoit along with his friends Malenko and Eddy Guerrero bid farewell to the ECW Arena on August 28, 1995, as the fans uproariously chanted, "Benoit! Benoit!" Since Benoit was leaving for a good reason, they spared him the "You sold out!" heckles that normally accompanied exits from ECW. Heyman wished Benoit, Guerrero, and Malenko luck in WCW, hoping that the WCW would treat them so badly on their first day that they would immediately opt out of their contracts and return to Philadelphia at the end of the three-month non-compete clause. A sign in the crowd read, "91 Days & Counting!" Chris Benoit would never return to the building where the Crippler was born.

Chapter IX
Works & Workers

> "WCW was a great place for veteran stars
> to make easy money and be lazy doing it.
> However, it was an awful place for a young
> guy to try and make a name for himself."
> JIM "SINISTER MINISTER" MITCHELL

THE KEN DOLL & THE HULKSTER

"KID, YOU LOOK LIKE A MOVIE STAR!" cried WCW boss Jim Herd when he hired Eric Bischoff as an announcer. Despite being classified by Bill Watts as "a sorry, lousy booth announcer" and a "popcorn fart: all noise, some smell but little substance," within a few years the former meat salesman with the thick black soap star hair and high cheekbones had succeeded Herd and Watts as boss of WCW.

Sharp, stylish, and youthful, Bischoff sold himself as an up-and-coming producer with a corporate mindset that would easily gel with Turner management, the "person who could wipe the southern yolk off WCW and make it a national entertainment company." He would be the long-awaited savior who would finally achieve TBS' longstanding goal of bringing CNN-quality production values, professionalism, and mainstream credibility to the cultural backwater of Southern pro wrestling. Though few have debated that Bischoff made the right pitch, many have questioned just how TBS decided that Eric Bischoff—a third-string announcer whose only production experience came from putting together a never-aired wrestling game show—was qualified to run a multimillion-dollar company, let alone a company in such permanent disarray as WCW.

According to Executive Producer Bischoff, the first step to revitalizing the WCW brand was to hold television tapings at Disney World. Because the shows were held in front of Disney tourists indiscriminately herded into a television studio, most in the attendance knew so little about WCW that they had to look at the blinking "Applause" sign to know how to react. Holding matches at a well-lit soundstage filled to capacity with smiling, upbeat, upmarket Disney tourists certainly presented a more wholesome mainstream image than shows taped at the sparsely attended and darkly lit arenas across the South.

Bischoff found the rest of WCW's mainstream credibility in a balding bodybuilder with a rotisserie-orange tan. For a decade, Terry "Hulk Hogan" Bollea had been synonymous with wrestling as mainstream, child-friendly entertainment. He bodyslammed Andre the Giant in the most famous wrestling match in American history, fought crime with Mr. T and the rest of the *A-Team*, tossed Sylvester Stallone around like a Neanderthal-browed dwarf in *Rocky III*, and singlehandedly won the first Gulf War with a leg drop to the throat of the treasonous Sgt. Slaughter. Hogan was pro wrestling's only mainstream celebrity.

By the early 90s however, Hogan was seen as an outdated relic of the 80s, one of those childhood idols who become "God, we were lame" punchlines once the audience hits puberty. The commercial value of the Hulk Hogan brand was already in crisis when the steroid scandals of the early 90s exposed Bollea as a drug-using liar and a hypocrite who had misled an entire generation of children with his clean-living "Drink your milk, take your vitamins, and say your prayers" routine. Hulk Hogan was pronounced a dead brand, and a deflated, roid-free Terry Bollea was left standing next to Laurence "Mr. T." Tureaud and Robert "Vanilla Ice" Van Winkle in that open grave where celebrity decays into self-parody.

Hogan was drawing paychecks from such cinematic shit sandwiches as *Mr. Nanny* when he somehow conned MGM into producing *Thunder in Paradise*, a syndicated TV show where Hogan played an ex-Navy Seal crimefighter with a futuristic speedboat as his partner. Conveniently, *Thunder in Paradise* was filmed in close proximity to the WCW's Disney World studio. Bischoff pitched Bollea a mutually beneficial deal: in return for lending his star power and credibility to WCW, Bischoff would pay him tens of millions of Ted Turner's dollars and transform WCW into a star vehicle dedicated wholly to the glorification of Hulk Hogan. Hogan's ego had reached Antonio Inoki levels of megalomania during his run at the top, during which he had imbided so wholeheartedly of his own bullshit that he told McMahon he wanted to accept an offer to fight Mike Tyson in a fair, honest-to-god competitive fight. There was no way a fame junkie like Hogan could turn down Bischoff's offer to reclaim his superstardom, especially at the terms the inexperienced Bischoff was offering.

In addition to a contract that paid him, according to some estimates, over ten million dollars in yearly salary and perks in an industry without any million dollar contracts, Hogan retained full creative control over every aspect of his character including: absolute control over the storyline, length, and finish of every match; absolute control over every word spoken on WCW TV by Hulk Hogan or about Hulk Hogan; and absolute control of every television segment that could even be tangentially connected to Hulk Hogan.

The ramifications of this last clause in Hogan's contract were severe for WCW. It is impossible to improve on *Pro Wrestling Torch* columnist Chris Zavisa's elucidation of the creative control issue: "[Hogan] skillfully manipulated Bischoff to give him the one thing that no other wrestler had and that was control.... Eric Bischoff was so eager to be number one that he surrendered some of his very managerial power to Bollea to sign him on the dotted line. The result is that Terry Bollea is both labor and management and can run roughshod over every other wrestler in the promotion regardless of their athleticism, popularity, or ability to draw money." In delivering control of WCW programming to its top star, WCW became the vanity promotion of Hulk Hogan as opposed to the vanity promotion of Ted Turner.

At first, the Hogan investment seemed to pay off—pay-per-view (PPV) specials with Hogan enjoyed skyrocketing buyrates, television ratings spiked, and WCW received more mainstream publicity than was previously imagined possible. For the first time in its history, WCW was perceived as being on par with WWE despite a huge comparative deficit in revenue, due entirely to Hulk Hogan's spot on the roster. WWE was *the* name brand in wrestling, but WCW now had *the* name brand wrestler. The PPV events pitting Hogan versus Ric Flair in the ultimate American wrestling dream match were the most successful in WCW history. Bischoff was promoted to Vice-President and soon President.

This unprecedented burst of success and mainstream credibility reinforced the business lesson: when WCW is flagging, just spend money to purchase new, ready-made stars from WWE. With the Hogan deal blasting open the bank vault, Bischoff went in for another big-money signing: Macho Man Randy Savage, who was being utilized as an announcer with WWE. To keep Hogan happy, his entire circle of locker room buddies—all old, played out, and shitty in the ring—was imported into WCW and given guaranteed contracts with storyline pushes.

Hogan himself never received a uniformly enthusiastic response. This was largely due to Hogan's own self-parodying booking strategy. WCW's booking was still as bad as ever, only now the storylines were so fixated on Hulk Hogan that he could have filed stalking charges against WCW cameras. Hogan fought his own overexposure and reputation for hogging attention by insisting that WCW double-down and increase the coverage and praise of the Hogan character. This naturally only built more resentment for Hogan—leading to his desire for even more worshipful treatment. WCW's deification of the Hogan reached the point that he and his sworn buddy Savage would team against seven top heel wrestlers at once in a cage match—and win. Easily.

Insecure about his own waning popularity, Hogan mercilessly used his creative control clause and, just as importantly, his sway over Bischoff to systematically destroy any serious opponents in *his* company.

Hogan's first target was Ric Flair, whose longevity had proven his ability to withstand even the worst and most biased booking. Though Flair had personally pulled strings behind the scenes to bring Hogan into WCW and had volunteered himself as Hogan's first sacrificial villain, Hulk was merciless in extinguishing Flair's value as a wrestler. Within months of debuting in WCW, Hulk Hogan booked himself to beat Ric Flair repeatedly without ever giving a win back, en route to finishing Flair's career off in a retirement match. Hulk did allow the retirement to be lifted a half-year later only for Flair to return in drag and get beaten by Hogan again in a match he wasn't even booked to participate in!

The backstage abuse of Flair was just as cruel. When Hogan turned in the list of wrestlers he desired to be hired, he included only one WCW wrestler whose contract he thought should be terminated: Arn Anderson, Flair's best friend and longtime lieutenant. Though Bischoff had no intention of firing Arn, Hulk's suggestion was used as a way to intimidate Flair into going along with Hulk's plans. Once, when Flair began to speak up at a booking meeting, Bischoff would ominously remind Flair, "You could roll Arn Anderson in shit, and he

wouldn't draw flies." Chastened, Flair kept quiet, but
Bischoff still fired him from the booking committee. This
un-Flair treatment would eventually cause the wrestler
to suffer a psychological breakdown.

Amazingly, he may not have received the worst
treatment. Vader was a young monster heel with
incredible working talent, unbelievable acrobatic skill,
and a great look. Vader was the perfect long-term money-
drawing opponent for Hogan, as he was the one heel with
the credibility to convince the crowd that he could beat
Hogan with his devastating powerbomb finisher. Vader
was also a gifted worker who could cover for Hogan's
eggshell style and dwindling athletic skill with his stiff,
credible offense. Unfortunately, Hogan didn't like
wrestlers who used stiff, credible offense that hurt and
who were still young, athletic, and popular enough to
eclipse Hogan's star and steal his negotiating leverage. So,
after forcing Vader to sign a binding legal document
assuring Hogan that he wouldn't be rough with him in the
ring, Hulk wrestled Vader and, after taking his previously
fatal powerbomb finish—the move that had legitimately
broken a wrestler's back—bounced right back onto his feet
like nothing happened and started posing. In that
moment, Hogan made a mockery of Vader's character and
everyone who had lost to him. Vader's hard-won
credibility with the WCW fans was shot. After his one-
sided feud with Hogan, Vader would never main event in
WCW again.

At least Flair and Vader continued to draw
paychecks and get television time; after all, they had
name value and credibility that could be sacrificed to Hulk
Hogan. The young up-and-coming talents in WCW had
nothing to offer to Hogan as opponents outside of making
him look old and outdated in comparison. One of the most
charismatic and gifted promo artists in wrestling history,
Mick "Cactus Jack" Foley was a popular performer who
had reached the WCW main events well before the age of
thirty, but he didn't fit the giant freakshow mold that

Hogan thought was marketable in heels. Once Foley got the rap of lacking marketability, he was done.

Foley voluntarily left WCW, a small dignity never granted to Steve Austin. Sporting a mop of early 80's blond Hulk Hogan hair, Austin was recognized by insiders as "the next big thing" in wrestling. Instead, shortly after Hogan joined WCW, Bischoff decided that the man who within a couple years would become the biggest ratings and merchandise draw in wrestling history was also "unmarketable"—just like Foley. In less than thirty seconds, Hogan's buddy Hacksaw Jim Duggan squashed Austin and took his title. When Austin came down with a serious injury shortly afterwards, Bischoff fired him.

WCW was a company that ate its young and talented. This was the environment that Chris Benoit was entering—a place where the higher your upside, the more likely you were to be psychologically tortured, embarrassed in front of an international TV audience, and sabotaged by your own bosses. At least you made good money.

THE FAX AND THE FOURTH HORSEMAN

CHRIS BENOIT WAS ALLEGEDLY HIRED BY WCW AS A RESULT OF A RIB THAT REVOLUTIONIZED THE PRO WRESTLING INDUSTRY. A confidential source on the management side of the wrestling industry claims that he played a prank on Eric Bischoff that unintentionally transformed Bischoff into the top promoter in America. Knowing that Bischoff had unsuccessfully applied for a job with WWE before being hired by WCW, this disgruntled party obtained a document with Linda McMahon's signature, scanned it, and pasted it at the bottom of a form rejection letter on WWE letterhead. "Mr. Bischoff: Thank you for recent application for employment with the World Wrestling Entertainment...." Programming his fax machine to show a Stamford, Connecticut-area code, the prankster sent it to Bischoff's personal assistant.

Enraged, thinking that the McMahon family was intentionally mocking him and his attempts to reach parity with WWE, Bischoff ripped the fax from the machine and went to TBS kingpin Bill Shaw. "Look! They're mocking us.... They're pissing on our reputation. They're making Turner Broadcasting out to be fools. We need to fight back. Let me take them head-on!" Shaw nodded, and *WCW Monday Nitro* was born.

Of course, there are other versions of the story. According to Bischoff's close friends, Kevin Nash and Scott Hall, the truth is that, given WCW's continued failure to live up to expectations, the TBS heads decided the only way they could ever convince Ted Turner to get rid of the WCW tumor was for the promotion to fail so spectacularly and so expensively that even he would be forced to admit that WCW was a lost cause. The perfect pilot for this kamikaze mission was Hogan's towel boy, Eric Bischoff. When Bischoff pitched the idea of going directly head-to-head against Vince McMahon in a timeslot that WWE had successfully branded as their own for years, they saw the perfect opportunity. WCW's fickle, disaffected fans—the fans who were booing WCW top star Hogan at nearly every show—would never watch WCW if given another wrestling option on another channel at the same time. Going *mano a mano* with the most successful wrestling promoter in American history, the former lousy announcer and traveling meat vendor would fail horribly enough to convince Turner to finally dump the company that had lost TBS fifty million dollars and counting.

If true, this story would be a fitting commentary on the absolute incompetence of Turner Broadcasting. For five years, TBS hires what they see as qualified executives and approve what they see as competent creative programs; the result is always so awful that it seems TBS is intentionally trying to put WCW out of business. Fed up, Turner management hires a completely unqualified candidate to execute a preposterous plan that they feel sure will fail and kill off WCW once and for all—only to watch in disbelief as he transforms WCW into the hottest wrestling promotion in America.

Regardless of the reasoning, WCW gave Eric Bischoff a huge multimillion-dollar budget and a primetime Monday night TV slot on TNT to directly challenge Vince McMahon's WWE. The Monday Night Wars, the battle to see who put on the best show and grabbed the highest ratings every Monday night, became the focus of the entire wrestling business. The fake wrestling industry finally had an authentic, real feud for its fans to believe in.

Work ethic and locker room morale instantly improved. With TBS' heavy investment in beating WWE, many wrestlers also figured that TBS would have no choice but to introduce accountability and corporate oversight into a company they had previously treated with indifferent contempt. With this much money on the line, there would be too much corporate surveillance for office politics to continue to be as arbitrary and debilitating as before. Wrestlers outside of the Hogan clique would be given a chance, and, if they drew ratings, the desperate Bischoff would have no choice but to give them a chance to succeed. And if they didn't, WCW was hiring a bunch of hungry young wrestlers who were fighting to replace them.

The drive to sign Benoit came from Kevin Sullivan, who had assumed nominal control of the booking committee for Hogan and Bischoff shortly after the announcement of *Nitro*. Sullivan's vision for *Nitro* and the new WCW was, "Gimmicks on the top, workers on the bottom." The wrestler who played a Satanic cult leader in the 1980s believed that the top draws in wrestling are the "gimmicks": the colorful, over-the-top characters and freakshow physical specimens. Usually, these wrestlers— often stars made by the ultimate gimmick promotion WWE—were not particularly entertaining in the ring due to their cartoon likenesses, abnormal physiques, aged bodies, reliance on their microphone skills, or their prima donna aversion to working too hard. Sullivan therefore liked to balance the athletically lacking main events with fast-paced, thrilling, daredevil wrestling on the undercards so that the fans would get their wrestling fix and pop entertainment fix on the same show.

The wrestler Sullivan and fellow backstage power house, Paul Orndorff desired most for the more serious side of WCW primetime TV was ECW star Chris Benoit. "I saw him as a talent right off the bat," said Sullivan in an interview. "When he comes out *he looks real*." The glowing review given by Sullivan's close friend, Paul Heyman, made Benoit appear to be an ideal employee. With the approval of Bischoff, Sullivan contacted the three New Japan stars who were revolutionizing ECW with their state-of-the-art working ability and hard-hitting, authentic Japanese style: Chris Benoit, Eddy Guerrero, and Dean Malenko.

All three came under political pressure from New Japan—who was paying WCW $750,000 a year for the use of their talent—to sign with WCW, thereby strengthening the bond between the two companies and helping New Japan carry the load of their salaries. When all three ECW stars were promised that they could work their full New Japan schedule in addition to their WCW schedule, they reluctantly signed with WCW in the neighborhood of $75,000 a year, which was soon renegotiated for $135,000 a year.

Like the overwhelming majority of WCW contracts, Benoit was classified as an independent contractor to whom the company owed nothing. He received no benefits, no insurance, had to cover the cost of his gear, accommodations, and road travel, and if he missed time from injury, after a short while his pay could be cut in half. In addition, every ninety days WCW would have the opportunity to fire him without cause. This type of hilariously inequitable wrestling contract exists nowhere else in the world of entertainment or sports. A sports team could never void the terms of an athlete's guaranteed contract just because he gets hurt on the job. A Hollywood studio could never dock an incapacitated performer's salary at will while maintaining exclusive contractual rights over his career. Real actors and athletes have unions and lawyers; TV wrestling stars have garishly scarred foreheads from the countless times they've mutilated themselves with razor blades at their bosses' request.

Benoit's salary was structured to include moving costs to the vicinity of WCW's southern headquarters, so Benoit did not have to fly in from Canada for WCW's regular television tapings in Atlanta and Orlando. Living in Atlanta also meant that Benoit could use the plane tickets and chartered flights that WCW bought en masse to transport the WCW roster across America for *Nitro*. Whenever he was not on tour with New Japan, Benoit in theory was supposed to work a three-day week: Saturday to Monday *Nitro*, with occasional house shows on Tuesday. This schedule was made even lighter by the many workdays spent in comfort at the Atlanta or Disney TV tapings. With four consecutive days most weeks to recuperate and spend time with the family, WCW offered its employees a far lighter and less demanding schedule than WWE. This was not due to any humanity on the part of Eric Bischoff; WCW lost money on their tours. There were many weeks in 1995 and 1996 where Benoit drew his guaranteed $2,500-plus weekly salary while only working one or two short television matches.

September 4, 1995 was the day the entire industry was waiting for, the night when *WCW Monday Nitro* would be broadcast live from Minnesota at exorbitant costs in an attempt to run Vince McMahon out of business. On the biggest night in the American wrestling business, the night where the future of his new employer would be decided, Chris Benoit was in between shows on a minor New Japan tour, waiting for a house show in the hamlet of Gagamori. Meanwhile, in Minneapolis, WCW aired a show that was notable for both its extreme progress and its extreme backwardness. *Nitro* was held not in a linchpin WCW market where such a show could make money and build business, but in Bloomington, Minnesota. Why? For the exclusive reason that Hulk Hogan was opening a "Hulk Hogan's Pastamania!" chain restaurant in the Bloomington Mall of America, and Bischoff happily granted Hogan huge swathes of the most important show in WCW history to talk about his new mall business endeavor. In between infomercial segments for a food court restaurant with only one location on earth, Bischoff programmed main event level matches like Flair vs. Sting that had never been shown before on Monday night TV.

On the October 9 *Nitro*, WCW returned from a commercial break with a black limousine pulling up to the arena in daylight—despite *Nitro* airing after dinnertime, a typical WCW production gaffe. The live announcer delivered a voiceover to the segment: "A man who has made a name for himself all over the world—in Canada, in Germany, France, the Middle East, and certainly in Japan. A man who is coming to where the competition is. And he's here because he knows one thing like every athlete in our sport...."

A barrel-chested chauffeur opens the limousine door and out steps a plain, suit-wearing man whose most noticeable characteristic is the long, fluffy mullet that extends down between his shoulder blades. To no one in particular, Chris Benoit says, "WCW: where the big boys play!" in a seemingly bored voice before biting his lip, looking down, and walking out of camera range towards the arena. WCW's announcers, who every week earned their reputation as the worst in the business, crow, "Where the big boys play, indeed!" and "Well, at least he knows how to show up!" While Hulk Hogan was treated as if he was the balding walrus-mustached reincarnation of Christ on his debut WCW appearance, Chris Benoit was praised for at least managing to make it to the arena without hurting himself.

Two months after signing his six-figure contract, Chris Benoit made his WCW *Nitro* debut in Albany, New York. His opponent was Eddy Guerrero, sporting newly grown facial hair, who was picked specifically for his ability to keep up with Benoit in a showcase performance of Japanese-style wrestling. With neither given a storyline or character, the match was a simple wrestling exhibition, a venue for WCW fans to see a series of Japanese and Mexican style moves and bumps that they had never seen before. Hulk Hogan might kick, punch, perform a simple body slam, let his opponent run into his foot, and then leg drop him in an entire twenty-minute main event match. In just one eight-minute match on free TV, Benoit and Guerrero unleashed two huracarranas, a springboard huracarrana, a hammerlock Northern Lights suplex, a dive from the top to the floor, a backdrop suplex from the ring to the floor, a high-angle powerbomb, a dragon suplex and much more. After Benoit pinned Guerrero cleanly, announcer Bobby Heenan enthusiastically praised the newcomer as "A force to be reckoned with! He's no 290 pounder; he's not 6'8", but I guarantee he can beat anyone in WCW!"

On his first PPV with WCW, *Halloween Havoc*, which would boast a Monster Truck Match between Hogan and The Giant, Benoit was not given a spot on the card. The Giant was tossed off the roof of a five-story building at the end of the Monster Truck showdown, only to appear later that night unscathed, acting like Hogan's frail offense was killing him. Despite the incredible amount of television time and promotional firepower devoted to making Hogan the biggest star in America, Hogan's superman act was receiving an increasingly hostile reaction from the WCW audience. Crowds cheered heels for poking Hulk in the eyes or kicking him in the balls; free Hulkster merchandise tossed into the crowd to make the audience look pro-Hogan was tossed right back. It was an odd business decision to focus the entire promotion around resuscitating the popularity of an overexposed, leatherfaced wrestler who put on horrible matches.

Hogan eventually realized that even TBS' oblivious, negligent management would notice that their top-paid good guy was getting booed and heckled like a

war criminal. Hogan decided that his character needed a
break from television to freshen up his act and give the
spoiled fans time to cool down and overcome their
hysterical delusion that they were tired of "The Immortal"
Hulk Hogan.

In the meantime, a Hogan hiatus required that, for
the first time in well over a year, someone besides the
brain behind Pastamania! would have to hold the WCW
heavyweight title and anchor the television and PPV
events. Even Hogan had to admit that the only wrestler on
the WCW roster whose popularity had survived his
career-butchering rampage was the least likely survivor:
Ric Flair. The Nature Boy was the cockroach scurrying
over the ruins wrought by Hiroshima Hogan's ego; if
anything, the excessive attempts to kill Flair's popularity
had been so transparent and mean-spirited that they only
served to make him a sympathetic figure. Nonetheless,
Hogan believed Flair was still too old and too damaged to
threaten his preeminence, so he okayed a convoluted title
switch that would allow Hogan to drop out and go on
vacation without ever being pinned.

The WCW booking team unsurprisingly took the
easiest, laziest route possible to elevating Flair back to the
main events: they rehashed a storyline that worked in the
80s. Flair's legendary stable of wrestlers, the Four
Horseman, would be reformed to provide the reenergized
Nature Boy with a marketing hook and an on-camera
entourage to boost his credibility. Once it was decided that
the first two spots would be filled by Flair's longtime
henchman Arn Anderson and charismatic wild man Brian
Pillman, there was intense competition for the fourth and
final spot. In the pre-Hogan WCW, the Horsemen had a
stable reserved for the elite, for those wrestlers who could
uphold the best traditions of the NWA in the ring. Being a
Horseman meant credibility. Former world champion and
recent big-name free agent Lex Luger actively lobbied to
be drafted as Flair's third lackey, believing that the Flair's
upcoming title run guaranteed any one of the Horsemen

involvement in the main event storylines and thus high television visibility.

Booker Kevin Sullivan did not want to waste the final Horseman slot on a star who would overshadow Flair in his own group and didn't need the rub to begin with. Besides, Flair and Anderson were aging, and to prevent them from being worn down, they would be best paired with a young workhorse who could keep the matches moving and take the brunt of the beatings. With the approval of Flair and Anderson, Sullivan had decided on the perfect candidate, a wrestler who had paid his dues and would fit in seamlessly with the Horsemen's image as swank professionals with passion and respect for the art of wrestling.

The Fourth Horseman was introduced in a flat backstage segment that revealed the lack of sincere booking effort put into Flair's run on top. Anderson stood next to Pillman in a small, undecorated room. Without prompting, Pillman launched into a speech to an empty room: "Double A and myself scoured the global landscape, and we found ourselves a whiskey-drinkin', skirt-chasin', fist-fightin' son-of-a-gun that will knock your jock off!"

In a stilted druidic tone, Anderson intoned, "Enter the Fourth Horseman: the Crippler, Benoit!" As Benoit walked on camera rubbing his hands together and nodding his head, he had to believe that he had finally walked onto the big stage. Best of all, on his ride to the top, Benoit would be accompanied by one of his best friends. A decade after they broke into the business together during the downfall of Stampede Wrestling, Benoit and Brian Pillman were joining the most prestigious outfit in wrestling together. In a promotion notorious for its unwillingness to give promising young talent high-profile storylines, they were in line for one of the biggest and most innovative pushes of 1996—a push ordained from the top by Eric Bischoff and Kevin Sullivan.

The two young Horsemen had staked one of the plum spots for new talent: feuding with the booker, in this case Kevin Sullivan. Between his membership in the

Horsemen and the Sullivan storyline, it seemed Chris Benoit would have every chance to make himself a star. For the first time in his career, he was playing for the highest stakes in wrestling: a high-profile storyline, regular national TV time, and monthly PPV spots in a major American promotion.

Benoit was playing under far more pressure than ever before, which meant he was matching wits with a far more dangerous breed of gambler than ever before. His experiences in Stampede (where he presented a threat to no one), New Japan (where he was a favorite of management), and ECW (where little politics existed) had not prepared Benoit for the backstage political game, let alone at the Jedi level practiced by WCW's apex predators. He would not prove up to the challenge; Benoit would be busted. While he floundered, Benoit would watch one of his best friends outwit, outbluff, and outplay everyone in the American wrestling industry—from Sullivan to Bischoff to Heyman to McMahon. Benoit could never hope to be one-quarter the player that Brian Pillman was.

And look what happened to Brian.

THE UNCANNY GENIUS FOR FAILURE

BRIAN PILLMAN FOUGHT, FUCKED, AND PARTIED HARDER THAN ANYONE ELSE IN PRO WRESTLING. Naturally thin and less than six feet tall, Pillman possessed a physical charisma—a hot-blooded feral presence—that cast one of the biggest shadows in locker rooms full of giants. Never a huge star to fans, Pillman was a backstage legend; in a subculture that fed on gossip and tall tales to pass time on the road, Pillman's reputation among the boys was towering, mythological. The most salacious rumor about Pillman was simply that the stories about him were actually *true*. They didn't call him "Flyin' Brian" just because he performed a few top-rope moves. In retrospect, his surname seems like a malicious cosmic joke.

Brian Pillman was always a legend. In high school, he was the rebel jock with the rabid libido and fearless reputation as a street fighter and drag racer. In college, the 5'10", 200-pound Brian Pillman was an NCAA All-American defensive tackle in a position where his closest rival was the 6'2", 335-pound William "The Refrigerator" Perry. His reputation as the campus seduction artist with intense, mesmerizing Rasputin eyes was unparalleled; he became a folk hero for "having sex with a woman who was hanging upside down from a chin-up bar while wearing gravity boots." When NFL scouts said a defensive tackle that weighed 200 pounds never stood a chance of even being drafted, Pillman flooded his body with steroids until he was swollen to the bursting point with muscles. With his impressive new body, Pillman signed with his hometown Cincinnati Bengals as a "street" free agent, a "camp body" brought in just to make the numbers even for practice drills, and shockingly made the team. Pillman fulfilled his dream.

His dream lasted six entire games before he was cut; steroids made the small guy bigger, but steroids also made the big guys enormous. There was no room for a player Pillman's size in the NFL, roids or not. After two more years of vain struggle, Pillman quit football and broke into pro wrestling, which of course was just as size-prejudiced as the NFL. Fresh from a stint with the Calgary Stampeders Canadian Football League team, Pillman entreated the Hart family to train him as a wrestler without knowing of the Hart family's predilection for making an example of professional football players.

Little did they realize that attempting to bully Brian Pillman would only steel his determination to defy them. Pillman's imperviousness to pain stupefied the Hart family's attempts to make him scream and beg, and, no matter the abuse they lavished on him, Pillman always arrived the next day with chipper nonchalance. Pillman flouted his fearlessness in the face of the Hart family, which always provoked maximum retaliation. They set

Pillman up to be "humbled" by getting ambushed by a far larger, jacked-up tough guy in an empty locker room. As the entire roster waited outside to see Pillman dragged out bloodied and broken, the football vet suddenly swaggered out with a smile. The little guy who spent his football career steamrolling huge offensive lineman demolished the Harts' tough guy, leaving him blood-soaked with an eyeball dangling from the socket.

Pillman further proved his manliness by bedding the entire female populace of Western Canada. Pillman's close friend Kim Wood told author Scott E. Williams, "You know those *Penthouse* letters that run every month, how they all seem like they're all fiction and all written by the same person? Well, we realized we were half-correct— they *were* all written by the same person. That person was Brian Pillman, and all those stories were true." Other Stampede vets might boast sleeping with a pretty ring rat in one or two godforsaken redneck towns, but Pillman had gorgeous rats on his roster in every town on the circuit, and their quality was of a jawdropping world-class level thought impossible to procure in places like Milk River and Medicine Hat. The most famous of Pillman's catches was nineteen-year-old Trisa Hayes, a faultless goddess who would go on to ECW fame as Beulah McGillicutty, one of the sexiest women in wrestling history.

Unfortunately for Pillman, he was facing a gang of bullies, and no one in either Bruce or Dynamite's clique could risk looking weak to his comrades by backing off. No matter his toughness or popularity with the ladies, Pillman was never given a reprieve from the veterans' ribbing, hazing, and ridicule. Stuck permanently at the bottom of the totem pole, Chris Benoit was one of the few to truly accept him as a friend and equal. Perhaps awed by Pillman's daring personality and physical toughness, Benoit became Brian Pillman's closest compatriot in Stampede and his self-appointed babysitter, a role that Benoit would later play with his next best friend, Eddy Guererro. They made a symbiotic odd couple: Pillman the uncontrollable wild man and Benoit the shy, disciplined dreamer. They were united by grave insecurity over their size and an implacable determination to nonetheless succeed in pro wrestling.

Thanks to his NFL background and slightly larger build, Pillman would get his first break in America long before Benoit. Since WCW management had a special preference for football players, Pillman was quickly scooped up and given television time as "Flyin' Brian," a linchpin of the WCW first cruiserweight division. His work in the ring was pretty good by global standards, but a groundbreaking series with Jushin Liger on American TV inflated his reputation to world-class levels. His popularity with the boys and the smart marks skyrocketed when he beat the shit out of the loathed giant Sid "Sid Vicious" Eudy in a bar brawl, which sent Eudy into a humiliated rage. Desperate to avenge his defeat to a much smaller man, Eudy instead unconsciously nominated himself for Biggest Dumbass in Wrestling History when he retreated from the bar to obtain a weapon and returned menacingly brandishing a squeegee.

Pillman's combination of in-ring and backstage exploits earned him a spot tagging with Stunning Steve Austin as The Hollywood Blonds, a combo that was instantly heralded as the next big thing in pro wrestling. However, WCW politics continually postponed the long-promised main event push for Austin and Pillman, who naturally threatened WCW's established older stars. When Hogan was signed, the uncomfortably talented Austin was driven from the company, leaving his smaller, less charismatic, and less talented tag partner with little hope for long-term survival.

Pillman needed his regular paycheck provided by his WCW contract; he actually needed more. Pillman's private life was a lecherous, irresponsible mess. For years, he was wrestling's premier "MILF hunter," the man who deputized an army of stagehands to babysit the kids of the mothers he seduced at the arena and escorted to sleazy pay-by-the-fuck hourly motels. Already a father at least once, Pillman impregnated and married a crackhead prone to disappearing for days on binges in the ghettoes of Cincinnati. After the inevitable divorce, Pillman promptly seduced, impregnated, and married a *Penthouse* Pet, who got into an argument with his first wife that lead to her retaliatory suicide. Including his *Penthouse* kids from previous relationships, Pillman was responsible for five young children. There was no way to support five children on an indy wrestler's salary.

As Pillman's contract wound down in 1995, he began to panic. His body was already breaking down from two decades of football, wrestling, and steroids, to the point that his voracious painkiller addiction required him to cycle through forty local pharmacists to procure a supply large enough to dull his pain. Coming off a flat exit with WCW, he would never have a chance at making real money in WWE, which at the time was testing for the steroids that made him look credible as a wrestler. Realizing that his body would fail him within a couple years at the most, Pillman had no choice but to quickly stockpile enough money to support his wife and kids after his imminent retirement from pro wrestling. Somehow, Brian Pillman had to transform himself from a worthless, soon-to-be-fired flameout into the hottest free agent in wrestling—and do so, while nearly crippled, in WCW, the promotion with notoriously little upward mobility.

Focusing on the man who controlled his destiny, Pillman had a revelation. "Bischoff was always trying to convince people he was a tough guy," Kim Wood told Scott Williams. "He was into martial arts and all that shit. The guy was a complete mark for himself, which told Pillman he could definitely be worked." Bischoff's constant boasting of his martial arts skills exposed his fatal flaw: an insecurity that the boys thought he was a weakling. Compared to the third-generation promoter and aspiring Orwellian dictator Vince McMahon, Eric Bischoff would always be a half-ass punk announcer, an outsider mark to be bilked and worked. If Pillman wanted to win over Bischoff, the easiest way would be to conceive of a plan where Bischoff's need to prove himself to the boys would manifest itself in pushing Brian Pillman.

The pitch was a brilliantly pinpointed blow to Bischoff's weakness: Pillman would give his boss the opportunity to prove his carny credentials by fooling the entire wrestling world. The mechanics of the scheme would have Pillman work a contentious, violent feud with his bosses Bischoff and Sullivan on national TV...without telling the boys it was fake. Bischoff's ego would be tickled first by the opportunity to look tough by firing his disobedient employee, and then later Bischoff could prove he was smarter than all the dirtsheet writers and wrestlers by revealing that the entire scandal was as fake as any other wrestling angle and that he had fooled them. As an incidental side effect of Bischoff's ego trip, Brian Pillman would become the hottest story in wrestling, the batshit crazy freak who told off and physically assaulted his bosses on live TV.

The storyline fittingly started offstage, at a company meeting where Pillman interrupted Bischoff to complain about Sullivan's behavior backstage, leading to a tense scene. The plan was an initial success—they could tell the boys had been fooled because the backstage politicians came up to Sullivan to talk shit about Pillman and then went to Pillman to talk shit about Sullivan. The plan went national live on PPV when Pillman seemed to lose his mind during a match with Sullivan and began to punch and eye-gouge Sullivan "for real," only to inexplicably run out of the arena after committing wrestling blasphemy by calling Sullivan "booker man" over the microphone. The crowd was baffled, the announcers seemed legitimately confused, and there was an uncomfortable period of dead air while Arn Anderson conferred with a shell-shocked, panting Sullivan in the ring. The stunt was an instant sensation among the insider fans; no matter how many times *Wrestling*

Observer editor Dave Meltzer told his readers that the feud was a work, many were reluctant to believe him.

Fired in the storyline, Pillman began to show up at WCW and, thanks to an under-the-table deal, ECW shows and cause disturbances that would lead him to be ejected and arrested. Playing a strung-out, drug-mad, broken-down wrestler who had been manipulated and exploited by his bosses one too many times, Pillman went postal. Capitalizing on the scandal, Pillman set up his own 1-900 hotline, making $10,000 a week from fans calling in to hear the latest rantings and ravings of pro wrestling's authentic madman. The "Loose Cannon" role was hardly much of a stretch for a manic-depressive drug addict, who was unable to support his children and on the verge of being fired.

Suddenly the most talked-about wrestler in America, Pillman pulled the oldest, dirtiest trick out of the carny playbook—screwing your own partner after a big score. With an offhand comment, Pillman convinced Bischoff that the only way the storyline would have full believability was if he granted the Loose Cannon a legitimate release from his contract. Bischoff immediately called up his assistant to prepare his release, fully planning to sign Pillman to a new contract in a couple weeks, so starting Pillman and Benoit's revolutionary "anti-Horseman" stable.

Pillman knew he was a player in WCW when, in March, he was told that the ultimate heat-seeking parasite, Hulk Hogan, had requested to face him at the next PPV. McMahon even bought into the controversy and offered Pillman the first guaranteed, big-money contract in WWE history. Figuring that McMahon's sensationalist, scandal-mongering business philosophy would be more suited to promoting the Loose Cannon character than Turner's more uptight corporate culture, Pillman decided to sign with WWE for his last, nest-egg-building run in the business. If Pillman had accepted Bischoff's offer, Benoit would have immediately found himself working a two-man angle against the biggest star in wrestling history, Hulk Hogan; instead, his friend and prospective meal ticket was leaving him by the wayside in WCW. Benoit understood that it was just business; he was more concerned that Pillman might not even survive to sign on the dotted line.

Benoit could see that his friend's "act" was at least half-reality; the drug abuse was real, and his real-world mental disease and the suicide of his ex-wife informed the psychotic breakdowns he performed for TV. Worryingly, the success of his elaborate, farfetched con game was inflating Pillman's sense of infallibility; he was an adrenaline junkie cackling as he careened out of control. On his manic upswings, Pillman was the most ecstatic, outright giddy person Benoit had ever met; he was triumphant, vindicated. When Pillman's mood dropped, however, fueled by downers, pain pills and whatever else was available, all of his success seemed like a trap, a tightrope act that he couldn't possibly follow through to its fruition. His body was falling apart; so was his mind, it appeared.

For days, Pillman could not sleep. Like a blocked writer, he wore himself out with anxiety trying to formulate the perfect ending. He had increased his salary 300 percent and went from being a jobber to a main event star in a matter of weeks, all without wrestling a single match. This was already the most incredible swindle in memory, but Pillman had too addictive a personality to stand pat and cash in his winnings. He had become addicted to the con; he was like every drug dealer who made his millions yet couldn't drag himself away from the high-octane rush of the game. Pillman just had to study Bischoff and McMahon, discover their weaknesses like he had before, and find the angle that would blow their checkbooks wide open. Sleep-deprived, high, and terrified for his future, Pillman got into his car for a mind-clearing drive that he hoped would reveal the winning move; instead, Pillman hallucinated that his dead wife was staring at him in the rearview mirror, crashed into a tree, and soared through the windshield.

The car wreck shattered in Pillman's face like a piece of china and crushed his right ankle down to powder; his head swelled to the size of a pumpkin. Pillman became a locker room laughingstock, the self-destructive fool who won the lottery and wasted the winnings buying more lottery tickets. Pillman had that uncanny junkie genius for failure, that allergy to success.

His doctors had never seen blood work results like Brian Pillman's; how does a man stand up, let alone wrestle, with ten times the maximum dosage of the strongest painkillers on the market in his bloodstream? With a reconstructed ankle made of steel and fused with "eggshell" fragile bone, Pillman was told he'd be lucky to walk again and that the pain of wrestling would be too much for any human to bear. Not surprisingly, the man who had overcome absurd odds to become a NFL defensive tackle and a sudden main event star in pro wrestling did not accept their diagnosis. Pillman felt he had no choice but to fight to provide for his wife and five children, and he began working out with psychopathic, sleepless fervor; he took mammoth dosages of painkillers that could have killed a basketball team. To maintain his pro wrestler's body, he shot himself up with double-barrel loads of steroids that would have intimidated the Dynamite Kid.

Relying on his body's superior athletic physiology, Pillman wrestled for WWE, but his face aged decades. There were times when he would look into the camera, and wrestling fans would see a strained, contorted, awful face—the face of a man desperately clinging to consciousness as he suffered unimaginable physical pain. Fueled by self-loathing, he became abysmally depressed, lethargic, and even suicidal. His wife began divorce proceedings and locked him in the basement the few days he was at home.

Compensating for his pain, Pillman's drug abuse reached the miraculous level of becoming scandalous even for 1990's pro wrestling. One wrestler told writers Shaun

Assael and Mike Mooneyham, "As long as nobody pushed the envelope, Vince [McMahon] was willing to let dope smoking or casual coke use ride. But Brian threatened that whole status. Two of the boys took him out back and roughed him up, you know, saying stuff like, 'Listen asshole, don't you fuck it up for the rest of us. We know how to handle it. Don't screw us just because you don't.' Everyone knew what was going on with Brian. They were just afraid to do something about it."

Chris Benoit heard updates from his friends in WWE, the Harts, about Pillman's rapidly disintegrating state. Owen Hart had been Chris and Brian's contemporary on the Stampede roster and a blood brother to both. Owen, like most of the Hart family, tried to convince Brian to clean up, but he was past the point of positive thinking. In his "Rehab is for Losers" T-shirt, Brian admitted he had a problem and admitted that he'd always have one. He was an old-fashioned, unapologetic addict. Owen and Benoit had watched Pillman live at supersonic speed for a decade, and now they watched their friend die in achingly slow motion. There was no mystery, no denial on any side; undrafted in the NFL, Brian Pillman became a top draft pick in the WCW roster's annual dead pool. Hours before his death was announced, Pillman was discovered curled up in the fetal position on the locker room floor, unconscious. Like so many undersized wrestlers who abuse steroids, Pillman died young of a heart attack. The autopsy found a stressed, unhealthy heart inflamed by steroid use to an abnormally huge size.

When news of Pillman's death spread backstage at WWE's October 6, 1997 *Badd Blood* PPV, Leon "Vader" White angrily dismissed the reports and said, "We can worry about that after the match. I've got to come up with a fucking finish!" The WCW reception was even less inspiring; wrestlers resentfully cursed Pillman for fucking up and tempting Turner to enforce a drug policy that would ruin their fun.

The next night on *Raw*, WWE hyped a no-holds-barred, uncensored interview with Brian Pillman's widow for the duration of the show. More creepy and vulgar than ever, Vince McMahon himself conducted the interview, leering at the crying, wincing *Penthouse* Pet who sat vulnerable and barefoot on her couch. The mother of five fatherless children, she had just found out that she was pregnant with a sixth. "I just want everyone to know it's a wake-up call," Melanie Pillman offered in her first main event TV appearance. "For some of you it could be your husband. Or it could be you. And you don't want to leave behind a bunch of orphans like my husband did."

Chris Benoit had lost one of his closest friends. Brian Pillman was a small, hardworking overachiever who withstood crippling punishment and a poisonous flow of steroids just to make it in pro wrestling. In return, he died a pathetic, mentally disturbed junkie at the age of thirty-five. Benoit watched as his friend's death was crassly exploited in the most disturbingly blatant fashion imaginable; he saw his friend's colleagues shrug off his death as an occupational hazard. If Chris Benoit learned any lessons from the death of Brian Pillman, it was not evident in his behavior.

Chapter X
The Devil

"What amazed me about Kevin Sullivan
was that he really was that heel he played
in Florida all day. He was for real. He really
wanted people to think he was the Devil,
and his friends would walk up to him and
be like, 'Hey, what up Devil?'"

CHAD DAMIANI
WCW Announcer

TURD POLISH

THE OLD FLORIDA TERRITORY HAD NEVER SEEN
ANYTHING LIKE KEVIN SULLIVAN BEFORE. "I was
intelligent enough to pull it off," Sullivan bragged in an
interview. "There were rednecks wrestlers spitting
[tobacco] into their cups saying, 'I think he really a devil.
He's gon' putta spell on us.' If you can fool the boys you can
certainly fool the people." Short, balding, stumpy-legged,
and weasel-faced, Sullivan looked more like Dr.
Frankenstein's hunchbacked manservant Igor than a
wrestling main eventer in the era of Hulk Hogan. By any
objective analysis, Sullivan with his comical blue-collar
Boston accent and mediocre wrestling skills, did not have
the look, charisma, or athletic talent needed to be a
wrestling superstar. All he had was his guile, and that
turned out to be enough. Sullivan fooled everyone into
taking him seriously against the top stars in the business.

It simply took convincing everyone—the boys and fans alike—that he was Satan himself.

It also took a five-ring circus worth of tricks, stunts, hype, and cheap heat; it took a whole lot of turd polish to make Kevin Sullivan look like a star. In his mid-80's heyday in the Florida territory, Sullivan deputized an entire carnival troupe to make him look like something special. As Michael Jackson's "Thriller" played over the arena sound system, Sullivan would be preceded by two face-painted zombies in Druidic robes with giant boa constrictors around their necks, a manager in a tropically-colored jumpsuit sporting a Mount Rushmore-sized version of Kenny Rogers' hairdo, and an S&M sex slave outfitted in a black leather studded bikini with garters, stockings, and black high heels. Around her neck was a dog collar with a steel chain leash that led back to the least interesting member of this hellish Renaissance fair parade: Kevin "The Prince of Darkness" Sullivan himself in his plain black tights. Though Sullivan also wore face paint and a giant snake as a necklace, his personal presence was hardly imposing; the Fallen Angel at his side had the star power.

The Fallen Angel commanded the attention of redneck Southern audiences like only a dog-collared Satanic sex slave can. Stepping up to the ring ahead of Sullivan, she would seductively lower her bikinied ass to the middle rope, symbolically spreading the ring ropes for her man. After Sullivan splayed his near-naked body across the mat, the Fallen Angel would step between his legs and place all three writhing snakes on strategic spots across his body.

With her bed-tousled hair, sandblasted makeup, and swimsuit model body filling out her tight dominatrix gear, the Fallen Angel was the darkest and dirtiest sex symbol pro wrestling had ever seen. In the era of child-friendly Hulkamania and lumpy female wrestlers whose matches looked like a catfight on the *Golden Girls* set, the Fallen Angel was an insatiable sex demon who wanted her man to dominate and beat her. Before she left the ring to let her man get on with his anticlimactic match, Sullivan would yank hard on her dog leash and maybe give her a slap or two to the face as she moaned and pouted in ecstasy. In a business as shameless as pro wrestling, there was no one who sold sex and depravity as shamelessly as Kevin Sullivan. Sullivan was more than a decade ahead of Vince McMahon's soft porn marketing of his bombshell "divas," and his Fallen Angel character was the wrestling business' first high-profile queen of smut. The Fallen Angel was a sex-crazed vixen straight out of the era's hard rock music videos, and only Kevin Sullivan was smart enough to bring that authentic heavy metal menace to the hopelessly conservative and behind-the-times wrestling territories of the day.

The Fallen Angel was Nancy Toffoloni, a nineteen-year-old receptionist plucked from the front row by a wrestling photographer and duped into joining the business. Enticed by offers of "becoming a model," the lithe, deeply tanned, black-haired Toffolini posed for nude cheesecake photos and wrestled other bikini-clad girls in the photographers' apartments. As soon as the boys became aware of Toffoloni, a locker room-wide ring rat hunt commenced; who would bag the teenage knockout who resembled a sultrier Valerie Bertinelli? The winner was Sullivan, the gray eminence of corrupting influences, who dumped his wife, lured Nancy into becoming his valet, and broke up her marriage to her high school sweetheart within months, maybe weeks. Soon Nancy Toffoloni became Nancy Sullivan, and Kevin was selling softcore photos of her through the wrestling magazines.

The Sullivans were a fascinating couple to visit. In private conversation with friends, Sullivan had a hilarious caustic sense of humor that was delivered in a staccato Boston Irish patois. The tiniest mention of someone he disliked would ignite an epic verbal onslaught; a fast, fluent, and profane George Carlin-style tirade that dismembered his target one fault at a time. Nancy was his pet "stoner hyena," according to one friend and former boss, splayed in scanty clothes over a couch, cackling at Sullivan's jokes and nursing a joint as he hosted company. In the midst of his brutal rants, Sullivan would pause and bark "Nancy! Roll me one the size of my finger!" in his grizzled voice. Within moments, Nancy would deliver a giant, expertly wrapped joint to her husband before plopping back down.

Although it was a rare occassion when someone got a word in with Kevin Sullivan around, when Nancy did engage workers in conversation they were amazed at how canny, smart-to-the-business, and incisive Sullivan's eye-candy was. Sullivan was quick to quiet Nancy; he felt it was in the couple's political interest to stay in character and play the roles of authoritarian husband and obedient sex-kitten wife even in front of friends. Many of his friends have said that Sullivan only "lived his gimmick 24/7" because his depraved, bullying wrestling character was more or less identical to his actual personality. Nonetheless, while silently listening, Nancy learned an incredible amount from Sullivan, who was undeniably one of the sharpest manipulators in the business.

When the Florida territory was absorbed in Jim Crockett Promotions in 1987, the twenty-three-year-old Nancy quietly deployed her own talents for deception. In Sullivan's words, Jim Crockett was "a churchgoing Baptist" who feared that promoting the Prince of Darkness and the Fallen Angel would send his family's "souls to damnation and Hell." Nancy was told immediately that she would never appear on television and that not only Sullivan's gimmick but his job were in peril. Seeing that Crockett himself was hopeless, Nancy took it upon herself to charm Crockett's second-in-charge, Jim Barnett. "She was a power broker behind the scenes," one close friend of the Sullivans divulged. "She was a key to Kevin's relationship with Jim Barnett because she was one of the few people with whom Barnett was open about his homosexuality, and Nancy having 'girl talk' with

Barnett kept Kevin as a favorite of his. She was very savvy, and an astute politician behind the scenes." Kevin not only kept his job but was promoted to assistant booker at Barnett's insistence.

After her scandalous reputation had faded, Nancy returned to TV in 1989 as a modest good girl in glasses who went from ardent fan to manager of the gullible simpleton Rick Steiner. Eventually, the too-sweet-to-be-real fan-slash-manager betrayed Steiner and revealed herself as Woman, the evil, sultry harlot behind the masked African-American tag team Doom. Sashaying to the ring to the accompaniment of Bob Seger's "Her Strut," Nancy proved herself to be a success without her husband. Nancy was the center of attention with Doom, the "heat magnet" manager who pissed off the fans and provided charisma and personality for the faceless tag team. Unlike most great wrestling managers like Paul Heyman or Jim Cornette, Nancy succeeded through her physical presence instead of her verbal acuity.

"She was, to be frank, a below-average interview," one of the great wrestling mangers of this era has said. "And was not good at physicality [bumping]. But she was a most unique performer whose presence was so captivating that no one in the crowd seemed to notice or care about her shortcomings—her understanding of how an angle should play out. Nancy had a booker's mentality but was always very careful not to let too many people know it."

In 1990, one of WCW's many backstage coups drove the politically conniving Sullivans out of the company. On the indy scene over the next few years, Nancy made a movie star impression. Indy booker Don Laible, who called Nancy "by far...the sexiest lady that ever stepped into a ring," was stunned by her style, class, and flawless grooming. "Wearing a black, skin-tight dress, black hose, and matching pumps, she not only looked fabulous, Nancy smelled out of this world. For some reason I began to sweat at an alarming rate. After a few minutes, Nancy looked up at me and asked, 'Donny, why do you always sweat so much around me?'" Nancy would show up at the airport for a 6 a.m. flight dressed "as if she was ready for a photo shoot."

In 1993, the Sullivans joined the ECW roster due to a request by their close friend from WCW, Paul Heyman. Though Kevin would shortly return to WCW, he could not convince management to hire Nancy. By this point deeply enamored with the business, Nancy chose to stay in ECW on her own, where she managed 2 Cold Scorpio and the Sandman, opening Sandman's beers and lighting his cigarettes on the way to the ring. In the comparatively green locker room, the thirty-year-old Nancy became a mentor and elder statesman.

"Nancy was a positive influence on the rest of the locker room and a pleasure to have around," one ECW insider told me. "She was such a strong personality that most of the guys, who see nothing but tits and ass, would sooner or later get past that and end up in philosophical discussions with her about the business. That's how clever she was. After a while, the boys got past drooling over the tits and ass aspect, and would say 'Nancy said the most interesting [thing] today about this finish I was putting together.'"

In her absence, Sullivan had maneuvered his way into booking power in WCW by shamelessly flattering the pretensions of two new powerbrokers, Bischoff and Hogan. One legendary booker has said that Sullivan, as the Devil, was "Shrewd beyond description. Kevin always understood the changing of the guard, and was always on the lookout for the next wave. He never had aspirations of *creating* the next wave. He was always looking to spot it before anyone else."

When it became clear that Hogan wanted to replicate his WWE-style superhero battles against cartoonish heels, Sullivan concocted a stable of B-movie monsters called the Dungeon of Doom, hell-bent on "destroying Hulkamania." This corny squad of punching bags for Hogan would be led, of course, by the Prince of

Darkness himself; what good-versus-evil story could be more basic and obvious than Hulk Hogan versus the Devil? Though the Dungeon of Doom was so cheesy and ridiculous that WCW talent hosted backstage roasts of Sullivan's promos complete with drinking games and comedic overdubbings, Hogan loved the idea. Not only did Sullivan become the top heel on WCW TV, he also became a backstage toady whom Hogan felt he could trust with his interests.

When *Nitro* was launched in 1995, Kevin Sullivan was the only man trusted by both Hogan and Bischoff to run the *new* WCW—at their bidding. One of his first acts in power was to get Nancy a tryout to be the *Nitro* color announcer. When that failed, he got her hired as a manager for the Four Horseman, who he was planning to feud himself en route to building up Pillman's stable of loose cannons.

To the surprise of no one, Sullivan quickly earned the reputation of being a particularly crude, dishonest, and conniving boss. He spoke to lower card talent like an abusive husband, hiring Hugh Morrus by calling him up and asking "You still fat?" and introducing himself to new manager Jim Mitchell by looking at his gimmick and screaming, "No! Don't do that shit! It looks fucking stupid!" New talent with political power or star potential he treated with ingratiating flattery and chumminess, only to "buttfuck them with extreme prejudice" at the first opportunity. "Sullivan seemed to take pleasure in backstabbing people, as if it added to his character's (his *fictional character's)* credibility," says Chad Damiani.

"I think professional wrestling was Kevin's life, and somehow life became wrestling to him," continues Damiani. "Wrestling is all about lying to the public and getting over on the marks. I think that's how he looked at the locker room, and I know that's how he looked at the bank [anyone from Turner, or from the office that wasn't a talent]."

Fancying himself a successor to 24/7 workers like the Sheik, carnies who were never out of character and never showed their true feelings, Sullivan loved nothing better than to "work the boys," sometimes just for the sake of the con. Since the death of kayfabe and the rise of newsletters and the Internet, Sullivan was convinced that the fans cared less about wrestling, and that the only way to recapture the mystique would to be convince them, somehow, that the angle they were watching on a openly fictional TV show was real. With the boys ratting out storylines to the newsletters, the only way to keep the veneer of authenticity was to dupe the boys in addition to the fans. Instead of concentrating on writing the best TV he could, WCW's booker was obsessed with somehow subverting the essence of fictional, scripted entertainment.

After his pet "worked shoot" angle with Brian Pillman became the most talked about scandal of early 1996, Sullivan was convinced that faking authenticity was the wave of the future in pro wrestling. With Pillman gone, Sullivan moved on and started feuding with his partner, Benoit. Since Benoit's interviews barely convinced audiences that he was a carbon-based life form, Sullivan did not expect him to dupe millions of people with the visceral authenticity of his acting skills. Sullivan would orchestrate the work from behind the scenes, letting the boys and newsletters publicize the storyline for them.

Beginning in earnest in April of 1996, the Sullivan/Benoit feud would peak two months later at the *Great American Bash '96* PPV with the best match on one of the best all-around shows in WCW history. Kevin "The Taskmaster" Sullivan (hailing from "the Iron Gates of Fate," whatever that means) faced Chris Benoit in a "falls count anywhere" match. Benoit and Sullivan engaged in a wild, stiff brawl that carried itself into the crowd, up the steps, and into the men's restroom, where Benoit showed his devotion to authenticity by writhing shirtless across the floor of a crowded Baltimore public restroom. As Benoit and Sullivan slammed each other's heads into stall doors and attempted to dunk each other into the urinals, their antics even a drew a female fan into the men's room, which sent announcer Dusty Rhodes into a melodramatic meltdown as if he were covering the Hindenburg crash. *"There's a lady! There's a lady in the men's bathroom!"* On the way back to the ring, Benoit was tossed down the aisle, rolling down the concrete arena steps to the floor. Finally, after a battle that Rhodes would describe as one of "the most unbelievably fought, vicious contests seen in WCW," Benoit suplexed Sullivan from a table on the top rope for the victory.

Benoit and Sullivan laid on the punches in the *Great American Bash* match, attempting to make the fight look, if not real, then fueled by real hostility. This was the essence of Sullivan's worked shoot: to convince the fans that the clearly fake proceedings were infused by authentic hatred. Stiff punches would hardly do the job by themselves; Sullivan needed to give the fans a reason to believe in their real-life feud. Sullivan's idea was simple: while booking Benoit to steal his wife on TV, they must also convince the boys that Benoit was fucking his wife behind the scenes and wait for the story to leak to the newsletters and Internet, creating a buzz about their matches together.

Sullivan's entire wrestling career hinged on the success of this asinine angle. In a promotion informally owned by Hogan, Bischoff had arbitrarily decided that bookers shouldn't also be wrestlers since it leads to a bias in their favor. Sullivan learned, without warning, that his angle with Benoit would be his last as an active wrestler. Since only an angle as controversial and hot as Pillman's could convince Bischoff that he was too valuable a talent to relegate to backstage duties, Sullivan insisted that Nancy and Benoit go past the limits of reason in convincing the boys that they were really cheating on their spouses together in the hopes that it would ignite a scandal.

According to friends of Nancy, she resented Sullivan's insistence that she spend time with Benoit,

whom she knew without any particular affection from
ECW. Though they shared a love for the business, Nancy
was an upbeat and laidback pothead, and Benoit was an
uptight, shy workaholic with a cruel streak and vicious
sense of humor. Being forced to spend hours and hours on
the road with a dreary, introverted bore in a futile attempt
to fool the boys, who were usually too drunk or high to give
a shit about Kevin Sullivan's marital life anyway, seemed
like a ludicrous waste of time. What type of husband
encourages his wife to pretend to cheat on him in public,
to lie even, especially to their friends? The road was
crappy enough without having to act at all times.

Kevin and Nancy's relationship had been volatile
for years, ever since Nancy had grown out of being Kevin's
unthinkingly obedient sex kitten. Her personal success in
the business had emboldened her, and joints were no
longer enough to cool her fiery temper.

"Nancy held her own; she could be a bitch with
Kevin. But, unlike Kevin, she wasn't vindictive," says
former friend Howard Brody. Violent, "falls count
anywhere" fights became a frequent event at the Sullivan
household; their neighbors had the police on speed dial.
Kevin and Nancy regularly struck each other, allegedly
both in anger and in play, though only Sullivan himself
knows how much of the widespread rumors about their
S&M proclivities was work and how much was sincere. A
major source of discord was the thirty-two-year-old
Nancy's desire for children, an idea that gave the Devil the
dry heaves.

By the mid-90s, it was an open secret that Kevin
and Nancy were cheating on each other, which is one
reason why Sullivan's worked shoot angle seemed so
misguided. I have yet to speak with anyone connected to
the Mexican wrestling industry who has not heard the
Nancy and Heavy Metal "biting" story. "Nancy was a good
friend of mine and wanted to go to Mexico," explained
ECW/WCW luchador Konnan. "So I brought her in as
Psicosis' valet [on a tour of lucha promotion AAA]. I told

Kevin I would take care of her and everything. At the time, I was booking and helping to produce [AAA] TV. We finished a show in Tijuana. The next day we were going to have a show in a place called Aguas Caliente. I went there to set up TV and got a call from Kevin. He asked where his wife was, because she had not called him. I had a wrestler who was supposed to pick her up and bring her to the next town, but she never made it there and she didn't know how to get home, so he got mad. There is more to it, but I'm not going to get into it...."

The rest of the story allegedly is that late on the night of the Tijuana show, Konnan heard screaming and panicked knocking on his hotel room door. When Konnan or one of his roommates opened the door, they saw a half-naked, heavily bruised, weeping Nancy Sullivan. She explained to Konnan and his roommates that she had gotten high with lucha heartthrob and notorious bad boy Heavy Metal as a prelude to sex. However, Heavy Metal was so incapacitated that he failed to perform and compensated for his limp dick by taking a huge, bloody bite out of Nancy's ass. A scuffle ensued in which both took some solid blows and, though Konnan sympathized with Nancy's swollen face and bleeding asscheek, he could not confront her assailant because the gay boss of AAA had a passionate (and some sources say "satisfied") crush on Heavy Metal. Instead, he sent her home early to avoid further incident. Years later, when one lucha insider joked with Konnan that Kevin Sullivan would have castrated Metal if he had heard about the story, Konnan supposedly responded, "Not really, he probably beats her up even worse."

Sullivan seemingly had little reason to fear that his wayward wife would be seduced by Benoit, who was known as a conspicuously well-behaved family man in a company of voracious whoremongers. To outsiders, Benoit seemed happily married to his wife Martina, who was pregnant with their second child, Megan, at the time. [Author's Note: I have intentionally avoided discussing the details of Martina and Benoit's marriage because there is nothing to be gained by violating the privacy of Martina and her two fatherless children. All that needs to be said about them is that Benoit, by all accounts, was very much loved by Martina and the two children, regardless of whether that love meant enough to convince him to curb his maniacal touring schedule or stay faithful. In the aftermath of the murders, Martina would be quoted as saying, "Chris was the most loving person anyone could imagine."]

The feud dragged on and on and on. Benoit's steady career ascent had been stopped dead; he seemed to be stuck in wrestling's version of *Groundhog Day* all by himself with Kevin and Nancy Sullivan. It galled Benoit as a performer to be "married" to Kevin, a limited-to-shitty brawler, in all of his matches. As bored as Sullivan may have been with Benoit, he could not let the feud end, because his career was preordained to end with it. The con would go on for as long as it took for someone to give a damn.

Increasingly desperate, Sullivan faked a fight with Benoit at a hotel bar and put more and more pressure on his wife and his "hostage" to make their dalliances more believable, more passionate. Neither one known for their acting skills, Chris and Nancy's blatantly phony, intelligence-insulting affair actually engendered a backlash from their coworkers. "The locker room resentment against Kevin Sullivan, Nancy Sullivan, and Chris Benoit grows as they continue to stick to their, by all educated assumptions, worked feud to try to fool the wrestlers for unfathomable reasons," read the February 15, 1997 *Pro Wrestling Torch*.

Friends of the Sullivans claim, while booking Nancy to fictionally cheat on him, Kevin was actually cheating on her with *his* fictional mistress, Jacqueline Moore. Though Benoit and Nancy had grown fonder of each other after having worked together for so long, by most accounts their relationship was strictly platonic. No one took Sullivan's stupid work seriously...besides Kevin Sullivan. Racked by his guilty conscience, Sullivan ironically was conned by his own con. In his funhouse world of trick, gimmicks, and straight-up bullshit, even Kevin Sullivan got confused about which reflection was real. Watching Nancy and Chris together, he slowly became convinced that these two crappy actors were for real.

Unfortunately for Sullivan, his elaborate scheming had tied him in a knot: he could not separate his cheating wife and her supposed seducer without summarily ending the angle that was prolonging his career. So, instead, Sullivan went mad with jealousy. How dare his employee abuse the opportunity given to him by Kevin Sullivan to *pretend* to fuck his wife by *actually* fucking his wife! A nasty bastard under the best of circumstances, Sullivan turned venomously against Nancy, subjecting her to constant accusations, taunts, insults, and passive-aggressive behavior. Faithful—at least when it came to Benoit—Nancy naturally took offense at her husband's behavior, leading to what one close friend described as a "a mutually-violent incident in Tokyo [which was] the final straw."

Another friend of the Sullivans agreed that the April 1997 incident in Tokyo, held during a New Japan tour in which Sullivan and Benoit would take their feud global, was the turning point from work to shoot. "Sullivan was tearing into Nancy relentlessly for cheating she wasn't doing. Finally, he just lost it, couldn't control himself anymore, and he beat the *shit* out of her in a Tokyo hotel room. At that point, Nancy decided to get even; if she was going to get her ass kicked for fucking Chris Benoit, she figured she might as well fuck Chris Benoit. Either way she'd get punished for it, so why not do it?" Living without female companionship in lonely hotel rooms for half the year, Chris Benoit—with his grossly heightened testosterone levels—had little hope of resisting the focused seductive talents of the Fallen Angel. Chris and Nancy became a real couple; though management feigned outrage, most in the wrestling industry were immune to being scandalized. "I wasn't surprised," one wrestling legend told me. "WCW was like Fleetwood Mac: everyone was fucking everyone and their wives, and the wives were even fucking each other."

Sullivan was in an absurd "carny who cried work" conundrum; after pretending to be hurt and outraged by his wife pretending to cheat on him for a year, now Sullivan was actually hurt and outraged and no one believed him. Though, characteristically, he would later try to fool interviewers and claim that he was not bothered by Nancy's infidelity, in reality Sullivan entered an emotional, psychological, physical, and professional nosedive. Within a month of the Japanese incident and the earnest beginning of the affair, Sullivan had fallen into such obvious drug-addled disarray that Eric Bischoff, one of the most permissive and indifferent bosses in history when it came to chemical abuse, insisted that Sullivan take time off before he overdosed.

Two months later, Sullivan returned for his long-awaited retirement match against Benoit in Florida. The wrestler who Mick Foley dubbed "the least sympathetic character in the business" was booked to turn babyface in front of his theoretical longtime fans, but, despite his plucky perseverance and courage, Sullivan could not get the crowd on his side. After a thirteen-minute match in which Sullivan disrespectfully sold Benoit's offense like an impervious "tree trunk," Sullivan was pinned by a flying headbutt, began to weep, and walked backstage an involuntarily retired wrestler. Shortly afterwards, he would be an involuntarily divorced, publicly cuckolded, retired wrestler.

Despite his time off, Sullivan did not regain his psychological stability or sobriety. "Sullivan can't string a coherent sentence together with anything resembling proper syntax. He has passed out twice on the job under suspicious circumstances in recent months. He slurs his words when he is on TV. His conduct is completely unbecoming that of a top executive in any world other than WCW," wrote Wade Keller. In his memoir, Bret Hart describes having to step over Sullivan, his boss, as he convulsed from a GHB-induced seizure on the floor of the locker room. In 1999, when fellow bombshell Missy Hyatt told Nancy that she planned to dance on Sullivan's grave when he died, Mrs. Benoit responded, "Well, that's going to be a long conga line."

The announcement of Chris and Nancy's divorces and subsequent engagement did little to harm their reputation with their coworkers. Their careers, however, suffered heavily: Nancy was taken off television permanently, and Benoit was condemned to years in the mid-card doldrums. Within weeks of Nancy and Chris' affair, the much-hyped "Apocalypse" angle that was going to make him the leader of his own stable of wrestlers was unceremoniously scrapped. After a sixteen-month marathon feud with Kevin Sullivan, Benoit transitioned into two years of meaningless time-killing storylines. Management punished him for his indiscretions (and his shortness and lack of interview skills) by giving him as little to do as possible while not overtly burying him enough to guarantee that he'd leave when his contract was up. Some of these filler feuds and storylines would get over through Benoit's hard work; a meaningless best-of-seven series for the otherwise irrelevant TV title with tag wrestler Booker T was elevated from obvious time-killer material into a notable feud, due solely to its spot on free television. These rare successes would earn Benoit either a few weeks off or a feud with the worst wrestler available; it wasn't in management plans for Benoit to succeed. Like so many WCW wrestlers in the late 90s, Benoit's job was simply to draw a paycheck without threatening any backstage power brokers' spots.

As frustrating as this career purgatory was to Benoit, he carried the burden gracefully. Like his teachers taught him, Benoit worked hard, did not ask questions or complain, and never missed a show unless he was completely incapacitated. Regardless of WCW's lack of good faith, Benoit had a code to uphold.

CASTE

"*NITRO* USED TO BLOW. *NITRO* USED TO SUCK. And
they couldn't even put their highest paid guy on TV
because the fans were booing. ...I mean, to have 20
thousand people chanting, 'Hogan sucks! Hogan sucks!
Hogan sucks!'" Smart about the business if nothing else,
Scott Hall accurately diagnosed the all-consuming
dysfunction of WCW in 1995 and early 1996.

WCW was not a wrestling promotion; it was an
anti-promotion. What it most wanted to promote (Hogan,
Sullivan's Dungeon of Doom) floundered, and what it
wanted to bury (Flair) became more popular. Unable to
make his own stars, Eric Bischoff spent millions
purchasing established WWE stars at exorbitant costs,
sustaining business on their leftover drawing power.

As Benoit began his marathon feud with Kevin
Sullivan, it was the turn of WWE stars Kevin Nash and
Scott Hall to cash in. Both were former hostages of
WCW's incompetence who had obtained their releases
with the set purpose of joining WWE to become stars in a
real promotion. Despite little wrestling talent, Kevin
Nash became WWE champion because he was naturally
huge in an era when a federal indictment prevented
McMahon from pushing steroid abusers. Scott Hall had
the "rocket strapped to his back," because Vince had
never seen the movie *Scarface* and thought Hall's Pacino-
as-Tony-Montana impression was a wholly original
charismatic creation.

In addition to being WWE stars, Nash and Hall,
along with their buddy Shawn Michaels, had been genius
backstage politicians. Pooling their professional leverage
and considerable charisma, they concentrated like no one
since Hogan on obtaining maximum power, maximum
pay, and maximum privileges from McMahon—for which
they should be commended. Their calculated mind games
against their colleagues were less worthy of plaudits: they
would shit in the food and bags of the women who rejected
their advances, berate workers who did not use speed and

pain pills, and use their near hypnotic pull on McMahon (who was commonly rumored within the industry to have a psychosexual fixation on Michaels) to get away with power trips that shattered the confidence and morale of their competition. To Nash and Hall, the wrestling business was a cutthroat team sport in which ruthless self-gratification was the only goal, and they played this sport with skill and killer instinct. They were good enough to play Vince "Emperor of Carnies" McMahon like a hapless mark, and in 1996 they were again facing authentic hapless marks in WCW.

"I never met James Dean and Frank Sinatra, but from every indication, they and Elvis (Presley) were about as cool as you could be in their day," WCW star Konnan has said. "Scott and Kevin were *that* cool." Chad Damiani, a young announcer in WCW, similarly described the duo, saying, "In their heyday, [Hall and Nash] wanted to be (and were) the coolest kids in school. Everything was a joke, and they were in on it. Nash especially. Nash was near seven foot tall, good looking and had real charisma backstage. The younger guys idolized him, and the older guys—although weary—wanted to be associated with the coolest guy in the company."

"We knew we had the cool factor; we were hip, and [Hogan] just wasn't hip," said Kevin Nash in an interview. "We could smarten him up to pop culture, and he could smarten us up on how to get more money." With Sullivan acting as the devil on the Hulkster's shoulder, they convinced Hogan to dump his good guy act and embrace their wiseass, cooler-than-thou, degenerate rock star attitude. They were New World Order ("nWo"), an irreverent army of stripclub sleazeballs sent to destroy WCW ostensibly by Vince McMahon. With their new act, Nash, Hall, and "Hollywood" Hogan did the impossible: they set the WCW business on fire and made WWE look passé. After years of losses, the nWo-driven WCW made a fifty-five-million-dollar profit in 1997.

"Everyone was in such great spirits," recalls Damiani. "The shows were like electric. The nWo was so popular that the rest of the show could be shit and, as long as the nWo ran in at the end, everyone would go apeshit and [leave] satisfied. It was like a traveling rock 'n' roll show." Even though he was too mired from his Mexican standoff with Kevin Sullivan to play a major role in the nWo feud, Benoit witnessed the rapid transformation of WCW from the most spectacular failure in wrestling history to the greatest success. Suddenly, the Boy Scout from Edmonton was surrounded by a drug-fueled orgy of jaw-dropping decadence that would result in a heavy body count.

"The thing that always kills me is people say wrestlers party like rock stars," says Nash. "I'm thinking, I've partied with rock stars. Rock stars don't party anywhere near what wrestlers do. The quote should be that rock stars party like wrestlers.... We partied hard, man. We partied harder than everybody ever. I've been an athlete, I've been around the rock business a little bit, as far as doing security and stuff like that; nobody partied like we did. We partied like wrestlers and that was pretty much the pinnacle."

"It was like a traveling glam band, like Def Leppard in the early 80s," says Nash clique member Damiani. "Only wilder. They attracted really sleazy, excellent girls. Strip club girls were their demographic. You felt like a king. Since Bischoff was the roster's partying buddy, everything was strictly expense account. Money was out of control: I went out with the group and had a $2,500 night out when I was still just a freelancer, but they comped all my food and drinks. I was just a freelancer! It's like taking your plumber out for a complimentary night on the town.

"It became a VIP scene; it no longer was just the hotel bar. We'd go to places like Vegas, and it was just *madness*. Just imagine a herd of 250-pound guys, the worst dressed guys on the planet, Melrose shoppers walking around with these garish fanny packs where they kept their pharmacy. Guys like Konnan would pull out their bags, and it'd be like narcotics trail mix, all these multicolor pills, powder, and bundles."

"Was there anybody at that time on our roster that wasn't getting whacked every night?" Kevin Nash once asked himself. "Not that we were hanging out with! *Every single night....* It's amazing: a lot of guys died—it's amazing it wasn't ten times [more]."

"I've been places with my cock you wouldn't go with a pistol," says infamous WCW partier and sexual predator Jim Mitchell. Mitchell's favorite pastime while on the road with WCW was to film comedic home porn with ring rats and hold viewing parties for the boys at the hotels. When one of Mitchell's traveling partners fucked a rat whose virginity Mitchell had intended to take on video in an elaborate pseudo-Satanic ritual, he retaliated by convincing the wrestler that the girl had a terrible venereal disease that required him to inject Monistat 7 vaginal cream up his asshole for seven days lest his dick turn into a "a stalk of cauliflower." For the rest of week, the wrestler would come to the shows "looking like he had been raped" while all the wrestlers that Mitchell had clued in snickered around him.

Unlike in WWE, where extracurricular depravity never intruded on the strict professionalism of McMahon's events, in WCW the party never stopped, even for the TV and PPV events on which millions of dollars hinged. At first, all of the partiers would bring their own coolers and six-packs of beer so that, by the time the show began, everyone would be too shitfaced to wrestle safely or give coherent interviews. The drunken wrestling especially galled Benoit, who loathed the idea of entrusting his safety to wrestlers like Nash who were careless and indifferent when *sober*, let alone when they were too drunk to stand without leaning on the ropes.

Since Hogan had creative control, it was not uncommon for him to waltz into the arena ten minutes before showtime, veto everything in the script offhand ("That doesn't work for me, brother!"), and force Bischoff to *improvise* the show live on air. If the WCW announcers seemed clueless, it was because they were: they'd be on TV without a script, an outline, or sometimes any idea at all what matches would take place. It didn't matter; business was so hot that WCW drew great TV ratings even when a fluke satellite feed malfunction turned one show into a scrambled, incomprehensible mess. WCW's fans just sat in front of the static-swamped TV screen, waiting patiently for the problems to get cleared up.

Though Bischoff was hailed as the genius who beat McMahon and was rewarded with huge raises, he was essentially just along for the ride. "I flew with Eric all the time in private jets," one former world champion told me. "He'd show me the script for that week's *Nitro* and say, 'Not one thing on this is going to happen. You know why.' And that night, he was right; not a match on that paper happened. Bischoff wasn't much of a boss: he jumped in the backseat and tried to drive."

After working so closely with a formidable leader like McMahon, Hall and Nash had no respect for a company as naïve and helpless as WCW. "I'll never forget the first couple of times me and Kev went to the ring and did interviews," Scott Hall once said. "We'd come back, and they'd go, 'Great great, excellent excellent!' I looked at Kev and went, 'What the fuck? That was fuckin' brutal. If we did that for Vince, we'd get fuckin' yelled at.' But [at Turner] you hear, 'That was great. Really good job. Thanks.'

"I said, 'Fuck, they don't even know,'" Hall continued. "WCW was so used to being a failure that they didn't have a clue, so basically we just raped 'em." Hall and Nash's contempt for the company was hardly hidden; they announced it regularly. Hall even made a point to do so in Bischoff's face. "One time I remember walking into a production meeting when Bischoff was sitting there. I walked in and said, 'Hey, Bischoff. You know what, I ain't no lawyer, but I have read my contract, and there is no

Asshole Clause. There is no alcohol policy. In fact, all I have to do is show up on time and pass your piss test and I get my money.'"

Since Bischoff had granted the top talent guaranteed, no-cut contracts, his leverage was nonexistent. All he could do was hold meetings where he could "stick it to Hall and Nash" by announcing, "There are only three wrestlers in this company who've ever put asses in the seats. Those three are Hulk Hogan, Randy Savage, and Roddy Piper." In addition to outraging roster members like Ric Flair and Dusty Rhodes who had sold out hundreds of buildings as world champions, this comment had the added effect of telling popular mid-card wrestlers like Benoit and Eddy Guerrero that their own boss didn't realize that they were helping draw the cards and entertain the fans.

If the president of WCW was this powerless in the face of the main event stars, then imagine the plight of the average wrestler. When Hall and Nash slammed the trunk of their car and picked up their bags to walk into the arena, they became different people. TV was just a lark; backstage was the real competition, where they got "their game face on." Working, portraying different characters, provided them with the most sadistic entertainment. In their own words, their first thought upon entering the locker room was simply: "It's time to stir some shit!"

Nash would corner some nervous rookie or foreigner, look down at his ring gear, wince, and say "You're not wearing *that*, are you? Is this dumb shit your gimmick?" Even gentle-hearted Eddy Guerrero, the devout Christian who would perform acrobatic turns of phrase to avoid saying a bad word about even the biggest asshole, could not restrain himself when it came to Kevin Nash's behavior. "Considering how little talent he had in the ring, Nash is one of the most arrogant people I've ever had the displeasure to know," Eddy wrote in his memoir. "He'd walk right past you and not acknowledge your presence unless he thought there was something he could get out of you. I don't say this lightly, but I genuinely feel Nash is evil."

One motivation behind Eddy's criticism may have been Hall and Nash's treatment of his best friend. Benoit was a favorite target since he took wrestling so seriously. He was just a "$400,000-a-year champion," their term for wrestlers like Benoit and Bret Hart. While Nash and Hall were getting paid millions for doing nothing, Hart was happy in WWE working his ass off for $400,000 as long as Vince gave him a championship belt and treated his fictional character well. Hart had become a famous punchline in the locker room for the match where he broke his sternum, shattered his ribs, began to suffocate, and nonetheless refused to let his opponent pin his imaginary wrestling character, despite his needing immediate medical attention.

Deranged marks like Hart and Benoit were the easiest targets imaginable. Hall would walk up to Benoit backstage "real friendly like" and say, "I love your finish! What is it, the diving headbutt? I can't wait to kick out of it!" On another occasion, Hall began talking to Benoit in a casual, chummy manner, relaxing him, making him feel special like a nerd in high school who is finally getting treated like a human being by the jock bully. Midway through the conversation, Benoit realized that Hall had covertly taken out his dick and was pissing on Benoit's cowboy boots. Since Hall and Nash were politically untouchable, Benoit simply walked away, humiliated in front of his colleagues and his girlfriend. Benoit was the ideal doormat wrestler that trainers try to create with every new student.

Benoit proved Hall and Nash right: he was a hopeless mark. Benoit could forgive urinating on him in public, but it was another thing altogether to disrespect the business! Benoit and Guerrero, two men with unhealthy Hart-esque mindsets who enabled each other, were driven mad by the WCW caste system, in which the talented young wrestlers getting paid around $250,000 put on great matches in the undercard while the old, incapacitated, and lazy wrestlers getting paid one million dollars or more would wrestle each other in the main event. In WCW, your worth to the company and the opportunities you received were not decided by how talented or popular you were but simply by how much they had been dumb enough to agree to pay you. For wrestlers like Benoit and Guerrero who lived to perform in the ring and burnish their legacy, working in a company where they were predestined to be nobodies was hell.

When Benoit was given a rare main event cameo in the headlining tag match of the *Uncensored '97* PPV shortly before his affair with Nancy became serious, Bischoff told him that he would be booked to win the match for his team. At the last moment, as Benoit stood behind the curtain ready to enter the ring for the biggest victory of his career, Hogan "called an audible" and said that people wanted someone they bought tickets for to win, not a nobody like Benoit. Hulk Hogan won the match instead.

The mid-card wrestlers were not even given a good faith opportunity to become popular in the mid-card. When Benoit and Guerrero lobbied for Malenko to be allowed to book an annual showcase tournament for the smaller wrestlers like there was in New Japan, the tactful Bischoff told Malenko that it would be pointless since the fans didn't give a damn about smaller wrestlers. When Benoit and Guerrero got over on their own accord, it only served to *lessen* their chances for advancement; you could get punished for being unexpectedly popular in WCW. As soon as Arn Anderson became involved in a successful storyline, he started worrying about getting fired. Perennial whipping dog Ric Flair shocked management by drawing one of the best PPV numbers of 1998 and was immediately taken off TV for making the company so much money that it lowered Hogan and Nash's negotiating power.

Unlike WWE, where an unexpected breakout star like Steven Austin received management's full support, the only wrestlers allowed to get over in the mid-90s WCW were the wrestlers Hogan, Nash, and Bischoff had deemed worthy. When Benoit and Guerrero's names were included in online polls asking what the best match on PPV was, a vote for them would be tallied as five for Nash or Hogan's preferred match; sometimes their vote total would actually *decrease* for every vote they received. Even a mid-card tag wrestler like Booker T would get offended when he was told that he was working with a smaller wrestler like Benoit, grimacing "as if he would get leprosy from touching us," according to Chris Jericho.

For a while, Benoit thought that his two mentors on the road, fellow Horseman Ric Flair and Arn Anderson, would intercede on the behalf of himself and other young wrestlers. After all, they were traditional, old school workers who claimed to appreciate guys that "did business the right way" and promised to be on his side when he needed them. Benoit was sorely disappointed: Arn and Ric kept their mouths shut no matter how badly he was treated. Prone to idealizing his elders as he was taught, Benoit felt deeply betrayed by two men whom he had admired and felt stood for what was right in the business.

The Horsemen further alienated Benoit with their own incredibly unprofessional backstage behavior. The nearly fifty-years-old Flair was legendary for marathon thirty-hour boozing sprees, exposing his genitals in public, and the unremitting barrage of sexual harassment he aimed at waitresses and stewardesses. While Benoit blushed at his side, Flair might peek under a waitress' skirt before explaining himself by saying, "Just checkin', honey, you know what they say: *no hair, no Flair!* Whooo!" One behind-the-scenes WCW talent remembers watching a nattily dressed Flair load up a plate of food in catering, zero in on a young female stranger, and nonchalantly declare, "I wanna be with you!" Confused, she stared awkwardly at this old man "with a mouth full of broccoli" who thought the sincere declaration that he wanted to fuck would be enough to persuade her to hike up her skirt and bend over a cafeteria table.

Arn Anderson had a well-known reputation for allegedly tricking naive young female talent like model Tylene Buck into sleeping with him by pretending that he was the booker in control of their career. Chad Damiani remembers speaking with a female office employee when Arn casually intruded on their conversation to ask her, "Would you like a cat bath?" Apparently a "cat bath" was Arn Anderson's pet term for his oral sex services.

Without any friends in management or the upper card, Benoit kept close to the others in his mid-card caste. For the first few years, in addition to Guerrero, he traveled and shared rooms with laidback cutups Chris Jericho and Dean Malenko, two guys who, while accomplished wrestlers, did not take wrestling over-seriously. They helped to keep Benoit and Guerrero lighthearted and distracted from their resentment over their stalled wrestling careers. Eventually, Benoit and Guerrero's strict dietary discipline and mandatory 7:00 a.m. daily workout drove the foursome apart. The wisecracking, comparatively lazy duo of Jericho and Malenko traveled together, and the grimly determined wrestling nuts Benoit and Guerrero formed a feedback loop of obsession, frustration, and resentment. Today, one pair is financially secure and in good health; the other pair suffered from enormous amounts of drugs and periods of suicidal depression, eventually finding the hell out of Jesus and dying by the age of forty.

Working for WCW was humiliating and demeaning on a daily basis for Benoit and Guerrero. Guerrero had been the headliner during one of the greatest boom periods in Mexican history, and now he worked for Eric Bischoff, who told him things like, "You are lucky that you aren't working back on a ranch for one hundred dollars," ignoring Guerrero's reminders that he was a natural born middle-class American whose first language was English. Benoit had been paid a lavish salary and treated as a superstar by New Japan, and now his career was the personal plaything of Kevin Sullivan, a miserable face-painted prick who had beaten his new wife in their previous relationship. Benoit and Guerrero worked with broken bodies on the tiniest shows in Moose Taint, North Dakota without being noticed by management, while Kevin Nash missed the biggest show of the year with indigestion and was made world champion.

Going to work was enough to knot their muscles, lock their jaws, and curl their toes; the sight of Bischoff or Nash or Hall or Sullivan filled their roid-riddled minds with a near irresistible fantasy of punching these guys straight in the fucking face. Wrestling was everything to Benoit and Guerrero, and these know-nothing pricks had ruined wrestling for them. Together, Benoit and Guerrero stewed, and then they exercised to exhaustion to expend all of their pent-up rage and frustration. Over the years, Eddy managed to get Benoit to fully open up and express himself with a level of candor and vulnerability that he never displayed with anyone else. Eddy and Chris were family, and it may be that it was Guerrero's friendship that prevented a Chris Benoit tragedy in WCW.

Even with Guerrero's companionship and empathy on the road, Benoit underwent a noticeably serious psychological change in the aftermath of the Sullivan scandal. Once one of Benoit's closest friends while riding high in Japan, Scott Norton had his touring schedule with New Japan written into his WCW contract. Since he was huge and Bischoff looked at him as "one of his boys," Norton was given a contract for roughly $800,000 a year while working little for WCW and notching up world title reigns in New Japan. As the years passed in WCW, Norton found his good friend Benoit acting cold, paranoid, and disturbed.

"When he started making some dough in WCW, he wouldn't even acknowledge me," Norton has expained. "This guy was like a brother to me, and overnight he'd just look right past me, snub me, give me these cold looks. This business is a bitch, and some guys handle it differently. It completely changed Chris, clear as day. Something went wrong with him.

"I confronted him about it, and he'd just say, 'The business is tearing me up. I'm so wound up I can't think straight. I get so paranoid. The politics are driving me crazy. I think everyone's out to get me.' I understood where he was coming from—Sullivan and the nWo and all that bullshit—but why take it out on me? He'd make plans with me to catch up, and he'd pull the Houdini shit and leave me stranded. He could never remember an appointment, and it used to drive me crazy.

"I think the business wore Chris out. There's no doubt about it. That's an understatement—in WCW he started to get really depressed, quiet, and out of it. He looked like he could barely get up the energy to move. Then they'd ring the bell, the match would start, and he'd be shot out of a cannon. You hear that a lot, that someone lives for their time in the ring, well, I think Chris got to the point when that was *all* he was living for. He was a good friend, someone I thought I could count on, and he just let me down so many times. It got to the point that the guys on the New Japan bus would ask how he was doing, and I'd just say, 'Don't know, he's being a dick!' and that was it. I was done with him. This was a decade before the whole thing [the murders] went down; whatever was up with him wasn't fresh."

There are many feasible explanations for this dark personality shift: the stress of a divorce, Catholic guilt over how he had won Nancy, an abusive workplace, incredible professional frustration, the painful degeneration of his joints and spine, nonstop steroid abuse for over a decade, the death of his close friend Brian Pillman, or the festering hatred of Hall, Nash, and Sullivan that he could never act on. By themselves, any of these stimuli could induce severe depression.

There is one more ominous explanation: concussions. Along with the Crippler Crossface submission hold that Dean Malenko had taught him as a gift, Benoit had made Dynamite Kid's flying headbutt his trademark move. There was rarely a match, win or lose, where Benoit did not fall from a great height directly onto his forehead. In addition to causing such massive spinal degeneration that the move's inventor, Harley Race, went out of his way to warn both Dynamite and Benoit not to use it, the diving headbutt frequently led to concussions.

One WCW opponent of his, Chris Kanyon, remembers Benoit suffering two concussions from performing the move in matches he had with Benoit. "Both times they resulted in bloody noses from the move and when we got to the back to congratulate each other for the match, he told me that the headbutt had caused the bloody nose as well as a concussion," wrote Kanyon on his website. "I am [only] one opponent. Chris probably did that move well over 1,000 times in his career. He has also done it off the top of a steel cage a few times. He has taken tons of chair shots. Believe me, he has had a bunch of concussions." Benoit's close friend Bret Hart also vouches that Benoit suffered many concussions in WCW and a countless number over his long career.

According to a peer-reviewed posthumous scientific study of his brain, this great multitude of unhealed, untreated concussions led to extensive damage to all four lobes of Benoit's brain and brain stem. The widespread degeneration and death of Benoit's brain tissue through repeated concussions has been tied by doctors to extreme shifts in personality, morbid depression, paranoia, and an increase in homicidal and suicidal impulses. In light of the catastrophic brain damage Benoit gradually accumulated over his career, Scott Norton's complaints about his increasing depression and forgetfulness—which Benoit would complain about himself in the coming years—were given validity.

For a brief moment, it had seemed like the mid-carders in Benoit's clique might get the hope they'd been desperate for: in August of 1998, Kevin Sullivan, with his "Gimmicks on the top, workers on the bottom" philosophy, was finally toppled. He had been done in by his own drug abuse and psychological instability; Benoit and the feud had indirectly brought him down. This brief flash of hope was answered with the worst-case scenario in typical WCW fashion: Kevin Nash, Head Booker. Nash had spent two years proving that his only concern was raping and pillaging WCW down to the last penny, and now he was boss. The only person with the power to oppose Nash, Hulk Hogan, was going on vacation to run for president on the platform that ex-wrestler Jesse "The Body" Ventura had become Governor of Minnesota and therefore Hulk Hogan, a much more popular wrestler, deserved to become President of the United States.

While Jay Leno was quizzing Hogan about his proposals for the nation (answer: "Flat tax, brother!"), Nash completely subjected the interests of WCW to the financial interests of Kevin Nash. At the time, the entire company was making a profit despite unimaginably bad booking solely due to the popularity of one wrestler: the undefeated juggernaut Bill Goldberg. With the entire company hinging on Goldberg continuing his record-breaking streak, Nash did the obvious: he personally beat Goldberg in as ridiculous a fashion as possible as quickly as possible, For good measure, he booked his non-wrestler boss Eric Bischoff to pin Ric Flair.

Kevin Sullivan knew that WCW was doomed the night that Bischoff let Jay Leno wrestle a competitive match with Hulk Hogan ("It's all over now! Jay Leno has Hulk Hogan in an arm bar!") on *The Tonight Show*. It was management's purely ego-driven decision to put themselves over Goldberg and Flair, the two most popular stars on the roster, when the company flew clear off the edge of the cliff.

For Eddy Guerrero, it was the end.

"Nash didn't give a damn about how much money Goldberg was drawing for WCW—all he was concerned with was being the Number One guy in the company," wrote Guerrero in his memoir. "When he screwed Goldberg for the title, it hurt the business for everybody. No one has the right do that. No one has the right to affect how the rest of us feed our families, just because their ego tells them that they need to be the big man."

Less than a week later, on the last day of 1998, Eddy decided that he was "tired of life and wanted to die." His inability to get a push in World Championship Wrestling was enough for this father and husband to decide to abandon his family. "I had given up believing. I had tried to fill the empty place in my heart with wrestling." With his heart in despair over the wrestling business, Eddy consumed five caps of GHB while driving, sped up to 130 miles-per-hour, and crashed into a ditch. Catapulted through his windshield, Guerrero landed 100 feet away with a broken right hip socket and a left calf shredded to bloody, glass-dusted ribbons. By the time he made it to the hospital, the doctors saw no point in lying to his family: he would probably die in around forty-eight hours. If he did live, he would never walk again.

Guerrero would prove the doctors wrong, of course, returning to the ring through the voracious use of painkillers, steroids, and other drugs. "It didn't make a dent on me at all," Guerrero said of Brian Pillman's death only one year earlier from drug abuse following his own life-threatening car wreck.

New Year's 1999 began with Chris Benoit's best friend fighting for his life. Things would only get worse.

DANCE MACABRE

GUERRERO DID NOT SEE THE POINT IN LIVING WITHOUT WRESTLING. Always an alcoholic and congenital addict, Guerrero had been scared away from downers when his pillhead tag partner Art Barr died in his sleep while cuddling his small son. Now that both of his legs were in excruciating pain at all times, Guerrero had no choice but to consume whatever he could get his hands on if he wanted to push his body beyond its natural capacity and return to work. Like the Dynamite Kid and Brian Pillman before him, Guerrero lived on a round-the-clock diet of booze, steroids, and pain pills. Guerrero was terrified that he would not be able to resume his wrestling career, and Benoit was terrified that he'd lose another friend to a madcap rush back into wrestling. Benoit waited for "the call."

He received the call, but it wasn't Eddy's turn yet. On May 23, 1999, WWE held a PPV show unfortunately titled *Over the Edge* in the Kemper Arena in Kansas City. The Hart-family baby, Owen, was scheduled to wrestle as the Blue Blazer, an annoyingly self-righteous masked superhero whose gimmick was that he would make an incredible entrance by descending from the ceiling of the arena like Superman only to botch the landing and fall flat on his face. During a previous performance of this silly stunt, Owen had taken too long to unstrap his ponderous harness after landing, causing a brief few seconds pause in WWE action. To forestall such a waste of airtime on a PPV event already purchased by its audience, WWE asked its regular stunt rigger to outfit Owen with a quick release snap shackle that could drop Owen to the ring instantaneously, without the lag of having to undo his harness. When the stunt rigger absolutely refused to use snap shackles because they were highly unreliable and dangerous, WWE dumped him and hired a cheaper, less principled rigger who outfitted Owen with a harness designed for use on sailboats. Raised in the Hart wrestling dynasty, Owen thought it was ridiculous to ask an accomplished wrestler to perform treacherous and risky stunts despite having no stuntman training. Dangling from the ceiling of an arena on the end of a fishing line, waiting for his cue with an eight-story drop under his feet, Owen was terrified. Though he complained to friends, Owen kept his feelings away from WWE management; he didn't want to get a reputation as being a "pussy."

Benoit's relationship with Bret and Owen Hart, the two most talented and successful Hart brothers, was the closest of any of his remaining Calgary friendships. Besides Dynamite, Bret Hart was Chris Benoit's favorite wrestler and greatest inspiration; Benoit recalled standing behind Bret in line for concessions at a Stampede show as a child and shaking with nerves. Bret was one of the Stampede babyfaces who had treated the teenage Benoit as one of the boys, and, though he was already in WWE by the time Benoit broke into Stampede, he frequently visited the boys back at home and had done his best to tutor Benoit.

Much more so than quick flameout Dynamite, Bret was a comparatively healthier role model for Benoit's American career. Despite having little charisma, mediocre size, and a safe technical wrestling style, Bret became the most popular WWE star during the steroid-embargo years because of his authentic, unembellished underdog character and his masterfully executed wrestling. Bret proved that Benoit, if he kept his integrity and worked hard, could eventually become a star without having to perform Dynamite Kid-style bumps, and Bret constantly reminded him that the point of wrestling was *not* to get hurt or hurt his opponent. Hart not only hated Benoit's crazy bumps and flying headbutt but even told him that his chops to the chest were a bullshit move because slapping someone so hard on their pectorals that their blood vessels burst wasn't a *work*. It actually hurt. Benoit "had forgotten who the marks are and who the workers are."

Of course, Bret Hart today is more famous than anyone else for forgetting that the business itself is a work. On his way to WCW, WWE world champion Hart refused to lose the title to his rival Shawn Michaels in Canada, but McMahon, showing the difference between his business practices and Bischoff's, took creative control and screwed Hart out of the title live on television. "Bret Hart, smarten up!" colleague Wayne Farris said in disbelief. "You didn't beat anyone for those belts! A fucking promoter gave it to you, you fucking cunt!" Arriving in WCW as the hottest, most controversial star in wrestling, WWE's "$400,000 a year champion" was paid $3 million dollars per year to have his career sabotaged by Hogan and Nash.

Owen Hart was Benoit's contemporary and close friend in Stampede. One Canadian wrestling personality described their relationship as "Jan Brady and Marcia Brady; Benoit was very good because he worked so hard, but Owen was a natural. He was uncanny." A wrestler out of economic necessity only, Owen was so gentle, fun-loving, and funny that Benoit could not envy him. According to Bret, Benoit forged a bond with Owen during the interminable cross-country rides in the Stampede's babyface van that was stronger than Owen's bond with some of his own brothers. Unlike Chris and Bret, Owen was satisfied making a fool out of himself as long as he got paid; Owen saved every penny so he could retire long before he was forty.

Clad in his superhero's cape and a mask, the thirty-four-year-old Owen Hart swung back and forth from the rafters like a hypnotist's pocket watch, waiting for his lower-card comedy match with a wrestler portraying a shuck-and-jive caricature of a black pimp. While Owen waited, the hairtrigger snap harness that WWE's stunt rigger had refused to work with malfunctioned and dumped him nearly eight stories down to WWE's hard ring. Some audience members in the Kemper Arena believed Owen Hart's death plunge had been the work of a stunt dummy. Some shouted "Bullshit! Bullshit!"

While announcer Jim Ross was attempting to convince WWE's incredulous at-home audience that Owen Hart was dead, Vince McMahon was busy making one of the most fateful decisions in wrestling history. Surrounded backstage by weeping and shell-shocked employees, Vince chose to finish the show as planned without telling the audience in the Kemper Arena that Owen Hart had died before their eyes.

Jericho heard what happened and immediately called his mentor, Benoit, who did not pick up the phone. Panicked, Jericho left a message that helplessly asked, "What are we going to do?" Benoit didn't know. As Bret Hart has said, "I don't think anybody took Owen's death harder than Chris."

It is hard to imagine any other type of fictional theater in which the gruesome onstage death of a performer would not result in the cancellation or at least postponement of the rest of the performance. Not even the most serious stage rendition of *Hamlet* would continue to its conclusion if Hamlet himself was accidentally impaled on a prop sword. A porn director would be apt to postpone a shoot if there was a sudden fatality during a gangbang. But Vince McMahon decided that the most appropriate course of action would be to hide Owen's death from the fans in attendance at the Kemper Arena and complete the show as planned. McMahon did not even see fit to the cancel the storyline where a wrestler was thrown into a coffin that was then bludgeoned with a sledgehammer.

McMahon's justification that "Owen would have wanted the show to go on" was widely ridiculed by the wrestling community and contested by Owen's widow and family, all of whom asserted that Owen—if he even considered the possibility that he would *die* in the ring—would probably have preferred to avoid the grotesque spectacle of his traumatized colleagues lifelessly tossing themselves around the bloodstained mat where he had died. The next night, on WWE's flagship television program *Raw is War*, McMahon planned a show-long tribute to Owen that the widow and most of the Hart family—who believed that Owen died thanks to WWE's criminal negligence—vigorously opposed. Against the wishes of the Hart family, the tribute show went on as scheduled.

Two hours of memorials to Owen Hart were sandwiched between frivolous wrestling skits and matches. Two of Owen's closest friends, Jeff Jarrett and Mick Foley, gave particularly moving, heart-wrenching speeches. Compared to Jarrett and Foley's honesty, the tributes delivered by wrestlers who chose to stay in their silly wrestling characters seemed foolish and inappropriate. "Mr. Ass" Billy Gunn's concise eulogy of "If you're not down with Owen Hart, I've got two words for you: *suck it!*" drew some uncomfortable winces and laughter, and wrestling "porn star" Val Venis' dedication to Owen Hart would have been more meaningful if it didn't begin with the long, growling come-on of "Hello-o, ladies!" Even the Rock could not help himself from adding that the immortal soul of Owen Hart would want him to kick his opponent's "rooty-poo, candy ass!" Near the show's close, there would another ugly moment: as announcer Jerry "The King" Lawler told a tearful story about holding Owen's corpse in the ring, the smiling fans in the front row behind the announcers' desk wildly gestured for the camera's attention and ecstatically waved a novelty-sized foam middle finger.

At WCW *Nitro* that night, there was no ostentatious memorial show out of respect to the wishes of the Hart family. Benoit wore a black armband bearing Owen's initials: O.H.

One week later, Benoit attended Owen's funeral in Calgary, along with an all-star cast of mourners that included Hogan and McMahon. The eighty-four-year-old Stu stumbled about, consoling himself by locking random attendees in shoot holds. Chris Jericho chatted amiably with Hogan after years of snubs in the WCW locker room, telling him that he was finally escaping to WWE. With a deadpan look, Hogan asked, "Can you take me with you?" The proceedings were tense thanks to Martha Hart, Owen's widow, who insisted that McMahon attend to see what his callous disregard for his employee's safety had done to her family. "There will be a day of reckoning! This is my final promise to Owen," Martha howled from the pulpit during her eulogy for Owen as the entire church shifted their gaze to the unbowed McMahon. McMahon retaliated by secretly taping and airing footage of the funeral on the next *Raw*, despite Martha specifically stipulating that the funeral be a strictly private affair.

A few weeks later, Eddy Guerrero returned to television to the torpid indifference of the announcers. Barely able to stand without heavy pharmaceutical assistance, Guerrero's courageously stupid return was barely noticed by Bischoff: he was too busy paying one million dollars for rapper Master P to show up at five shows and yell "Hootie hoo!" and $400,000 a year for one of his bodyguards (who couldn't wrestle) to stand next to him. With Eddy doped up to the brink of death just to work for WCW, Kevin Sullivan was tempting fate backstage by allegedly referring to the "heavily armed" rappers as "monkeys," which made some uncomfortable since Master P had promised Bischoff that he would "cap [his] ass" if anything went wrong. Busy with the chaotic bullshit happening backstage, no one noticed the pale, enervated, incoherent Eddy Guerrero tottering around and doing his best Brian Pillman impression.

Benoit became Eddy Guerrero's chauffeur, handler, babysitter, and nurse. No longer did Benoit and Eddy share the driving duties; Benoit could not ever trust that his friend could safely take the wheel. After Eddy drank and pilled himself into an incoherent stupor, Benoit carried him through hotel rooms and locker rooms and meetings, doing his best to keep an eye on Eddy and protect his job so he could support his family. In Eddy's own words, Benoit specialized in rescuing Guerrero from the consequences of his addiction, buying Eddy time to clean up. His selfless, patient support of his best friend through repeated bouts of addiction was admirable.

Benoit's treatment of another close dying friend, referee Brian "Mark Curtis" Hildebrand, was also uncommonly compassionate and generous. Hildebrand was a gentle, sweet-natured goofball who was consumed by a pure, childish love for pro wrestling. Resembling the world's tiniest Jeff Foxworthy, Hildebrand's minuscule size prevented him from getting jobs as a wrestler but that didn't stop him from getting as close to it as possible. Addicted to the business, Hildebrand took a day job at a shoe store so he that he'd have enough money to support his expensive international wrestling tape habit and work for nothing at small indy shows as manager "Hymie P. Schwartz" or as a referee. While working on the indy scene in whatever capacity he could, the sunny and earnest Hildebrand became friends with his heroes Chris Benoit and Eddy Guerrero, two of the best small workers in the world.

In 1995, Hildebrand joined them at WCW as referee, and finally Eddy and Chris had a friend and traveling partner who held the wrestling business in the same sacred esteem as they did. According to Dave Meltzer, Hildebrand was part of Benoit's "support system" and one of his two or three closest confidantes; the normally reclusive Benoit even went on vacation with Hildebrand and his wife, who was a close friend of Nancy's, where they all apparently enjoyed a KC and the Sunshine Band concert.

In October 1997, Hildebrand was diagnosed with stomach cancer. For the next two years, the unflappably optimistic Hildebrand fought valiantly while retired colleagues and wrestlers did everything they could to help one of the most genuinely beloved characters in the business. Benoit was an especially attentive friend, working benefit shows, calling regularly, and offering any help that he could financially or professionally give. By the summer of 1999, it became clear to everyone besides Hildebrand that he had lost his battle. When he saw Hildebrand on one public occasion, Benoit was so overcome by the sight of his gaunt, obviously dying friend that he began to weep uncontrollably, emitting loud gasping sobs, all while the oblivious Hildebrand asked him what was wrong. Brian Hildebrand died on September 8, 1999. Shortly afterwards, Chris announced to his closest friends that Nancy was pregnant.

In the light of Hildebrand's incredible bravery and toughness, Eddy Guerrero decided that it was time to "be a man" and quit drugs cold turkey. If Hildebrand could stay optimistic while being eaten alive by cancer, then surely the son of the legendary tough man Gory Guerrero could at least *try* to get over an addiction to pharmaceutical pills. Unfortunately for Eddy, he didn't realize that going cold turkey with a drug habit as massive as his was risky. Five straight days of wired, buzzing withdrawal followed, so Eddy decided to take a "small" dosage of three GHB pills to help him sleep. Eddy's body immediately went into shock, and his lungs collapsed. He spent the weekend on a hospital respirator, but he characteristically ignored doctor's orders for prolonged rest and arrived at *Nitro* on Monday.

It had taken six months after his younger brother's tragic death for the inconsolably devastated Bret Hart to return to wrestling and deliver his official tribute. When Bret decided to return to the wrestling ring in October of 1999, he courageously chose to do so in the Kemper Arena in Kansas City: the site of Owen's death. This match would be Bret Hart's tribute to Owen and the official Hart family rebuke to what they saw as WWE's face-saving, disingenuous tribute show.

For his opponent in this most meaningful of matches, Owen's superstar older brother chose an adopted member of the Hart wrestling family, Chris Benoit. "I actually had to talk WCW into letting me work with Chris Benoit in honour of Owen," Bret wrote in his memoir. "Like anything else that made sense, it took them a while to even get behind it, and it was Chris who got them to do it. Chris had never forgotten that Stu, and Bruce, had got him into the business. Wrestling, old style, was all about trust and respect, the business of very tough men who could set aside those prized reputations when they needed to do so in order to make each other and the business. Benoit, despite being a young man, was old school. I wanted the Benoit match to honour my dad, the workers of his generation, the boys in the dressing room, those old-time fans—and, most of all, Owen."

To be chosen for such a heavy responsibility by a wrestling legend and universally admired performer like Bret Hart was a far more prestigious honor than any title or tournament Chris Benoit had ever won. On that night, there's no doubt that Benoit, with his obsessive in-ring perfectionism and already strung-out mental state, was beside himself with the pressure of living up to Bret Hart's expectations and honoring his blood brother Owen Hart's memory.

Benoit entered the arena for the highest-profile match of his career to the accompaniment of the thunderous, driving drums of his theme song, looking grim with wet, slicked-back brown hair, a homemade white Owen T-shirt, the glittering, gold WCW TV title on his shoulder, and a blank, unmoving expression on his face, his eyes empty and heavily lidded. Walking down the aisle to the ring, Benoit beat the left side of his chest with a closed fist, a gesture that he would make iconic in yet another memorial match to a fallen friend six years later. Interspersed with Benoit's entrance are camera shots of the Kansas City crowd holding up white cardboard signs with tributes like "Long Live Owen" and "We Miss You, Owen" in glitter or thick black Sharpie marker. Many of these diehard wrestling fans had witnessed Owen's death firsthand six months earlier in that very arena.

Bret and Benoit's tribute match began with a gentlemanly handshake and proceeded along the archetypical "good guy versus good guy" format of the Hart family's Calgary wrestling territory, in which two honorable fan favorites engage in a vigorous and violent yet cleanly fought athletic contest. Unlike most modern wrestling matches, where clearly choreographed wrestling moves are performed one after the other with little visible strain or resistance from either wrestler, Benoit and Hart made a point to bitterly struggle against every wrestling move and hold. It was a long, rambling, old-fashioned match that the announcers sold as an epic, grueling sportive contest.

Unfortunately, WCW announcer Bobby "The Brain" Heenan undercut the solemnity of the tribute. Once one of the great comedic minds in wrestling, Heenan by his own admission had "lost all desire to work, didn't care anymore or anything" in 1994. For the next seven years, Heenan made it manifestly clear that he held WCW programming in utter contempt, slurring blindly through hour-after-hour of TV tapings in a zombified drunk haze, compulsively repeating the same stale vaudeville jokes and "insights" with a senile obliviousness to WCW storylines or what was going on around him. While the rest of the equally unprofessional WCW staff attempted to rise to the occasion for Bret Hart, Bobby Heenan cracked jokes at grieving father Stu Hart during the memorial match to his dead son and suggested that Benoit "reach into his tights and pull out something that weighs about 45 pounds and tape it to his fist, and hit [Bret] right between the running lights and knock him out cold." Rest in peace, Amen.

After Hart's clean submission victory in the twenty-eighth minute of the match, Bret Hart cast his eyes to the ceiling of the Kemper Arena and saluted. After this gesture to Owen, Hart lifted up the stooped-over Benoit, who was still selling the damage done to his back during the match, and raised his hand in victory. Bret hugged Benoit to his chest and, as Benoit cried uncontrollably, told him, "Chris, he's up there right now watching us." They walked backstage linked arm-in-arm.

The Harts would receive eighteen million dollars in a "wrongful death to negligence" civil suit settlement with Vince McMahon. One year later, in the very same Kemper Arena, in front of many of the same fans, WCW had one of their wrestlers fake a fall similar to Owen

Hart's and be carried on out on a stretcher while the announcers worried about his life.

WELCOME TO ALTANTA

THE OFFICIAL WCW BUSINESS CARDS AND STATIONERY PRINTED FOR 1999 STATED THAT THE COMPANY WAS BASED IN ALTANTA, GEORGIA. It would be a fitting start to the year when the most inefficient, incompetent, wasteful, indulgent, and slapdash wrestling company in history self-destructed in the most hilarious fashion imaginable.

Kevin Nash proved the most catastrophic booking failure to that point in wrestling history. A show at the TWA Dome in St. Louis at the beginning of his booking regime had sold 30,000 tickets; a major PPV show held at the same venue six months later sold less than 7,000—a seventy-seven percent collapse in business during an industry-wide boom. To fail this badly with bottomless resources is not normal incompetence; this is revolutionary incompetence. Kevin Nash was the Henry Ford of alienating fans, developing new streamlined methods to repel wrestling fans with unprecedented speed and efficiency.

Nash transformed WCW into a vanity vehicle for his comedic sketch writing talents. Nash was convinced that wrestling itself was passé with the fans, so he booked shows that had hour-long stretches with nothing but interviews, sketches, and silly angles. Having a group of wrestlers write multiple multi-hour variety shows every week resulted in *Nitro* reviews like this one from the February 20, 1999 *Pro Wrestling Torch:* "Three hours of wrestling hell. The worst show in the history of *Nitro.*... A total embarrassment." The *Wrestling Observer*'s post-show poll of one Nash PPV actually achieved a perfect negative score, receiving *zero* thumbs up; the show was so bad that even smartass teenage wrestling fans were too traumatized to cast an ironic thumbs-up vote. Ratings collapsed.

Nash let it be known at a booking committee meeting that this monstrous across-the-board failure was due largely to how "those vanilla midgets, Benoit and Malenko" were driving wrestling fans away with their boring wrestling. When this comment reached the dressing room, Benoit had to be physically restrained from becoming an infamous murderer eight years early. After his matches, Benoit went backstage to discover that commercial breaks had been suspiciously inserted over his performances.

The only men who could stop Nash—Eric Bischoff and Hulk Hogan—treated WCW like a drunken college one-night stand they wanted to forget. Bischoff rarely showed up for TV or read the scripts; he was too busy jetsetting with his *Wonder Years* pal Jason Hervey, chasing his dream to be a Hollywood producer on Turner's expense account. Bischoff was so indifferent to WCW that he let the company pay millions of dollars every year in "Mailbox Money" to wrestlers that he never used but hadn't fired. Not only did Bischoff keep upwards of 150 wrestlers under contract when only forty at most could be effectively used, he even signed off on the purchase of plane tickets to *Nitro* every week for the 100 wrestlers who were never used. WCW was purchasing *thousands* of unused plane tickets every year without anyone suggesting that it might be financially irresponsible.

"[Bischoff] was absolutely out of his fucking mind," said Kevin Sullivan in an interview. Sullivan and his booking ally, Terry Taylor, compared themselves to *Titanic* crew members bailing water out of the sinking ship as Bischoff told them, "This is the most expensive, beautiful, unsinkable ship of all time! Shut up and keep putting more coal into the furnace."

Hulk Hogan realized that, with WCW in the midst of a garish full-company meltdown, it was in his best interest to keep Nash around as a heat magnet and fall guy whom he could conveniently blame for his own creative failures. When Hogan nonetheless received criticism for his stale act and the deflated ratings it drew, he too blamed "Malenko and the rest of the midgets."

Since Benoit and Malenko had been mid-card fixtures during the nWo boom period, it was apparently Nash and Hogan's belief that sometime in late 1998 the Vanilla Midgets had developed an entirely novel way of sucking that made viewers change the channel, not during their own segments, but during Hogan or Nash segments in which they did not appear.

"It is impossible to really communicate just how badly the wheels had gone off WCW by mid-1999," one insider told me. "In late 1997, this company was beating WWE so badly that they could not afford to pay their world champion, Bret Hart. Less than two years later, WWE was doubling our ratings, drawing four or five times the attendance at live events, and had completely blown us out of the water when it came to hipness and street cred. Though the WWE boom had a lot to do with its own success—I mean, they had guys like Steve Austin and the Rock, who were just light years ahead of our crew when it came to charisma—the damage done to WCW was almost all self-inflicted through laziness, stupidity, and, with guys like Hogan and Nash, this knowing self-aggrandizement. Those guys knew burying Bret Hart and Ric Flair and Chris Benoit and Chris Jericho was bad for WCW's business, but they knew it would raise their own value come contract negotiations. And the hilarious thing about WCW's downfall is guys like Hogan and Nash really, truly did not give a shit *at all*. They seemed to think it was funny."

While running WCW, booker Nash appeared on TV pilled-up and shitfaced more often than Eddy Guerrero. His best friend and creative partner, Scott Hall, went off on a marathon drunken streak in which he crashed at least six cars, missed countless shows, publicly groped a fifty-six-year-old woman, was arrested for attacking a limo outside a strip club, slipped and nearly cracked his skull during an enraged attempt to rip the windshield wiper off an announcer's rental car, and was run over by a WCW employee's car while drunkenly passed out in the parking lot of a bar. Hall earned his nickname as "the Keith Richards of wrestling" by surviving intact and continuing to draw his hefty salary.

"There would be times where Hall literally couldn't put sentences together," Hall's buddy Chad Damiani verified. "His skin would be bloated. You'd see him in the lobby of a hotel, trying to talk to a fan, and he couldn't seem to tell their faces were registering with horror.

"Hall used to have this trick when he was really high on pills," Damiani continued. "He didn't want to have to leave the bar to take his pills, so he'd palm drugs in his hand and cough, dropping the pill in his mouth as he covered his cough. It worked like a charm when he was sober. But as he got high, he'd just get *slower*; eventually, Hall would cough and clear-as-day lift the drugs right in his mouth like he was eating a pretzel. In his head, I'm sure he thought he was still doing his trick, but in reality everyone was staring at this dumbshit getting high in public like it was nothing. It was mind-boggling that they put him on TV."

The history of WCW during the late 90s reads like the cliché rise-and-fall-of-a-rock-band story arc. After years of futile stabs at making it big, WCW suddenly hit upon the right formula with the nWo and rocketed to unprecedented wealth and popularity. Isolated from moderate influences by a year-round touring schedule, the entire roster embarked on a two-year hedonistic rampage, indulging in booze, drugs, strippers, and Hollywood ego trips. Having lost their hunger, WCW lazily repeated the same formula until it was passé and the audience moved to the next hot thing. By the time the company's popularity had entered its nosedive, the primary creative forces behind its original success were too burnt out, complacent, jaded, and distracted by their new toys and friends to muster the energy save the company from its descent. By the fall of 1999, WCW's version of a *VH1's Behind the Music* special had come to the point where all the stars begin to OD or run off to ashrams in India—or the point where wrestler Raven bet on himself in WCW's annual dead pool and then "set the record" by staying continuously high on ecstasy for fourteen straight days, doubling his dosage each day to maintain his high.

After Jericho's escape to WWE in the summer of 1999, Benoit's clique of disgruntled mid-carders primarily consisted of Guerrero, Malenko, Perry Saturn, and former ECW stablemate Shane Douglas. Guerrero had repeatedly asked Bischoff for his release, at one point provoking a fit of rage in which Eric "accidentally" slapped his coffee into Guerrero's lap and squared off like he wanted to fight.

Usually deferential in the extreme with his superiors, Bischoff and Nash infuriated Benoit to the point that he no longer acted like himself. On WCW's own radio show, Benoit promised the fans that he intended to get the hell out of the company as soon as he was contractually able, an admission that drove Bischoff to pull the plug on the program. When Benoit was asked during a promotional appearance in the Canadian media if he thought there was a conspiracy within WCW to destroy itself, he smiled and responded, "It appears that way."

Benoit took the unprecedented measure of publicly flirting with Paul Heyman and asking for him to engineer his transfer to ECW. Heyman was eager to reclaim the man who he thought would be the ideal ECW world champion and supposedly convinced Acclaim, who produced ECW's video games, to put up the money to pay Benoit's salary. After leaking the story to the newsletters, however, Heyman backed out, claiming that there was a hang-up with "merchandising" that made the deal no longer feasible.

On August 23, 1999, Eric Bischoff held a backstage meeting in which he offered anyone in WCW their unconditional release if they wanted it. With recent raises to $450,000 a year, Benoit and Guerrero were not among the few wrestlers who took up Bischoff on his offer, which he immediately withdrew anyway. The Bischoff/Nash regime, despite having to book a month's worth of primetime television shows ostensibly building to the next

PPV, actually forgot to put together a card for the PPV until the day of the show. Previously purchased advertisements for the show read, "We're the advertising agency and they won't even tell us who's going to be there! For God's sake don't miss it!" The mystery PPV, in which fans were treated to the surprise of Eddy wrestling the Insane Clown Posse and Benoit losing to the awful Sid Vicious, drew the lowest buyrate in WCW history and received a perfect 100 percent thumbs-down vote on the *Wrestling Observer* post-show poll.

Four days later, Eric Bischoff was finally removed from WCW and paid his full salary to sit at home. Realizing that his time in power was short, Nash had executed a brilliant gambit shortly beforehand: he booked himself to lose a retirement match. With a contract that made it impossible to fire him, Nash had booked himself an indefinite paid vacation until it was in his best interest to return.

To replace Eric Bischoff, Turner made the questionable choice of promoting Bill Busch, who had previously been the financial wizard who assisted "ATM Eric" Bischoff with contract negotiations and budgetary matters. "Busch was this helpless, clueless, spineless, needle-dicked little Gilligan-lookin' fucker," according to one WCW employee. "I mean, I guess he was a nice guy, but it was clear from moment one that he was going to be eaten alive."

On October 3, 1999, Busch hired Nash's replacement: WWE head writer Vince Russo. This hiring decision produced a noticeable spike in roster morale: WCW had actually chosen a booker without a track record of failure, a personal stake in WCW office politics, a wrestling career to promote, or a long record of putting his own interests above the company's. Russo was the hip young wunderkind supposedly responsible for the greatest boom in wrestling history.

Russo was a hairy, bug-eyed, egomaniacal Italian New Yorker who followed Quentin Tarantino's trailblazing path by teaching himself how to write from watching sleazy B-movies in the video rental store where he was employed. Brought to the WWE writing team in a time of incredible desperation, Russo appealed directly to McMahon's basest attention-grabbing carny instincts. Russo's pitch was simple: dump tradition, dump serious wrestling, dump family-friendly TV, dump long wrestling matches, and embrace a completely shameless pornographer's aesthetic. Vince's only concern should be seizing the public's attention by any means necessary, and the most reliable strategy to was to sell a fast-moving MTV blend of sex, scandal, blasphemy, obscenity, misogyny, and violence.

Soon, Vince Russo was writing *Raw* with his partner Ed Ferrara, using four-hour blocks of the white-trash geekshow *Jerry Springer* for inspiration. Meanwhile, WWE was drawing the highest cable ratings in wrestling history. Paced to appeal to those with the tiniest of attention spans, WWE became Caveman TV, a relentlessly loud barrage of stunts, giant tits, catchphrases, shock tactics, and *Rocky Horror Picture Show*-style sexual deviance with a wink. Outside of PPVs, where wrestling mastermind Pat Patterson ensured the fans were entertained, the wrestling itself became almost irrelevant, as it would be hard to promote "serious wrestling" with characters portraying pimps, porn stars, cross-dressers, vomit freaks, and genital piercing fetishists.

Luckily for Russo and Ferrara, no one at the time realized that their publicity stunts and sleazy freakshow acts were only succeeding because of their environment. When plugged into the WWE machine with its incredibly charismatic performers, superb production values, and strict quality control, Russo's ridiculous ideas served only to catch the attention of curious channel browsers who were converted into repeat viewers by the charisma of Steve Austin, the Rock, Mick Foley, or Vince McMahon himself. Russo was the carnival barker who brought the fans into the tent, but he was not a ringmaster who could keep them there.

At the time, Russo's arrival elated Benoit, Guerrero, and the rest of their crew. Within days of Russo's arrival in Atlanta, rumors were already spreading that at his first agent meeting Russo had announced that Piper and Savage "were done" and that he was placing Hogan and Flair on an indefinite suspension from television. Russo would lead a youth movement that would reenergize WCW programming and rebrand the company known for pushing old, out-of-touch, lazy stars. Word quickly passed through the locker room that Russo's favorite among the existing WCW roster was Chris Benoit, the young star who had gotten over without management's help due to his work ethic, wrestling skill, and credibility in the ring.

Russo's first *Nitro* elicited hosannas and hallelujahs, all because Russo displayed the tiniest speck of professionalism. After four years of Bischoff, Sullivan, Hogan, and Nash as the primary creative forces in WCW, the revelation that Russo actually *wrote detailed scripts* and *prepared production notes* and *listened to suggestions* made him seem like Orson Welles to WCW employees. When Russo handed the crew his production notes, everyone had the same response: *What are production notes?* Like WCW's hapless announcers, the cameramen and producers had been ad-libbing their duties live on air due to a creative team that was too lazy to give them instruction. Eager to erase their incompetent reputation, the WCW office staff greedily leafed through Russo's detailed notes for the show and slowly felt the blood drain from their faces. They were working for a maniac.

Russo's booking plan seemed to be that, since WCW was already an unsalvageable brand, the only way to attract viewers was to make it such a spectacular travesty that they tuned in out of incredulous disbelief. For example, Russo's idea for the $850,000-a-year ex-WWE star Dusty Rhodes was a character with an ambiguous taste for child molestation. Russo filmed expensive mini-films of a costumed Rhodes apparently

stalking children and instructed the production crew to
conceive of an elaborate, expensive entrance as if Rhodes
were the Louis XIV of child rapists. Preparing his actor for
the angle, Russo, the sleepless, stubbly, bug-eyed golem,
rambled in what was described as "a coked-up fury" to
Rhodes about how he should stop on his way to the ring,
find a small child in the first few rows, and "quietly
whisper with him as if they were sharing a secret."
Turner unsurprisingly vetoed the entire storyline.

If the child molesting wrestler failed to make
television, Russo ensured that every other half-baked idea
he had was televised. Russo's scripts read like unedited
dictation of a raving schizophrenic. "In Russo's world,
there are no rules, there are no consistencies, and there is
no internal logic," wrote a columnist in the *Pro Wrestling
Torch*. "He thinks to eliminate internal logic is to be brash,
irreverent, and cutting edge." *Nitro* became an
incomprehensible angel-dust blitzkrieg of constantly
interrupted two-minute wrestling matches, split-second
backstage interviews, and juvenile sex jokes. The surreal
vignettes in which wrestlers openly discussed the scripts
for that night's matches were so irreconcilable to WCW's
storylines, characters, and narrative conventions that
they seemed to have been an intentionally awful parody of
pro wrestling.

Only two wrestlers seemed to actually benefit from
a coherent, sustained push: Chris Benoit and Bret Hart,
two longtime victims of WCW booking. Treated as a star
for the first time in his WCW career, Benoit was given
legit victories over Scott Hall and Ric Flair and was
booked to reach the finals of the WCW heavyweight title
tournament against Hart in the main event of the
Mayhem PPV. Before a partisan Canadian crowd in
Toronto, Hart and Benoit were allowed to wrestle a clean,
simple, and unimpeded wrestling match that gave Hart
his first WCW world championship and Benoit his first
American PPV singles main event. The storyline was
perfect: the Canadian national hero, after two years of

tragedy and abuse, finally redeems himself in his homeland in a moment that he shares with his greatest pupil and ally.

Of course, the brief "good booking" interlude was merely a ruse to set up Hart's own irrational heel-turn a month later—because who doesn't want to boo Owen's still publicly grieving brother? At the December 19, 1999 *Starrcade* PPV, Hart suffered a severe concussion from a kick to the head in the main event, dangerously inflaming his brain.

Hart continued to wrestle, suffering small concussions every time he took a bump and his swollen brain collided against his skull. Two nights later, Hart confided in Benoit about his condition and asked him to wrestle a very safe, protected match with him on that night's TV taping; as world champion, Hart could not take time off to heal. Russo booked Goldberg to chase Hart from the arena after his match and slam his fist through Russo's limousine in frustration after Hart escapes. Thanks to a prop malfunction, Goldberg sliced a foot-long gash down his forearm and lost thirty-one and a half liters of blood; WCW's biggest star would miss the next six months of TV. As the heavily concussed Hart drove away at top speed, his limo skidded over a patch of ice and nearly collided with a WCW production truck. Six months after his brother had died in a pointless stunt he wasn't trained for, Hart was furious that he had been asked to play stunt driver on an icy road with a concussion.

Displaying his inability to learn from the near-death of his two top stars from non-wrestling stunts, on the next show the apparently insane Russo asked the woozy, incoherent Hart to *drive a monster truck over a car containing another wrestler*. As Russo was explaining to the concussed wrestler with no special driving training how he could drive the truck just right so as to avoid killing his coworker, Hart momentarily regained enough coherence to ridicule Russo and walk away. A week later, a doctor would tell Hart that his career was over thanks to brain damage from repeated concussions. For putting the business first, Hart would be rewarded by a series of debilitating strokes in the coming years.

In what was beginning to seem like a premeditated murder spree, Russo next booked his last two remaining main event stars, Benoit and Jarrett, in a cage match with the ancient Jimmy "Superfly" Snuka on free television. With no buildup, Russo asked both Snuka and Benoit to dive off the top of the tall cage onto Jarrett below, which predictably resulted in a concussion that sidelined Jarrett as well. Shortly afterwards, when Russo suggested that WCW place the heavyweight title on potbellied UFC washout Tank Abbott, he was finally demoted from head writer. He would be re-promoted within months.

As with the previous WCW booking changes, Bill Busch managed to elevate the one possible booker less popular than the one he was replacing: Kevin Sullivan. Chairing the WCW booking committee with Kevin Nash as his assistant booker, Sullivan immediately proposed that Nash should win the WCW title after Number One contender Scott Hall forfeited his title shot, deciding to drink at a bar instead.

The mood of the undercard wrestlers became morbid when they heard that their two foremost oppressors had returned to power. During the four years that Sullivan and Nash had booked WCW, no young, foreign, or junior heavyweight wrestler had been given a chance to become a major star within the company. "The thing is, all these guys were pissed off because I segregated them—well they're supposed to be," Sullivan said in an interview. "Good workers should be with good workers, and the gimmicks should be with the gimmicks." Since Sullivan's hatred of Benoit for stealing his wife and sending his life into a tailspin had never subsided, most of the undercard wrestlers expected the proudly vindictive Devil to retaliate mercilessly against both Benoit and his friends in the undercard that had supported him through the Nancy controversy.

Chris was disturbed by the promotion of his wife's abusive ex to become his boss. He called his old mentor Bad News Allen and asked him out to lunch. Since Bad News was a former employee of Vince McMahon, Benoit sought his counsel on whether it would be advisable to try to leave WCW and join WWE. "You know, if there's anything I can do for you, 'cause you're like my son, man—I'd do it," Allen said before advising Benoit that McMahon was not to be trusted.

On Saturday, January 15, 2000, Benoit and thirteen other mid-card wrestlers met together to discuss how to react to Sullivan's elevation. Since Bill Busch had promised to grant a release to any wrestler who requested one, all fourteen wrestlers made a pact to ask for their release as a group.

The next night in Cincinnati at the PPV, seven of the original fourteen kept their promise and asked Busch for their release: Chris Benoit, Eddy Guerrero, Dean Malenko, Perry Saturn, Konnan, Billy Kidman, and Shane Douglas. According to Konnan, "Saturn just told Bill Busch, 'You told us we could have our releases if we don't want to be here. We want our releases. I think you are a man of your word, so give us our releases.' Bill Busch asked for a day to fix things and asked what we wanted. We told him that we just wanted someone other than Kevin Sullivan booking us."

Sullivan's idea for crushing the rebellion was to bribe Benoit with a heavyweight title reign, with the idea that the mark Benoit would be so blinded by the glory of winning the world title that he would betray his friends and withdraw his resistance to his booking regime. With Benoit onboard, Busch and Sullivan assumed that the rest of the mid-carders would fall into line. Though Benoit repeatedly stated backstage that he did not *want* the WCW title, he just wanted his release, Sullivan insisted that Benoit submit Sid Vicious in the main event title match. As an insurance policy, Sullivan told Vicious to keep his foot under the bottom rope, which technically nullified the submission and would allow management to claim if necessary that Benoit had never actually won the title.

"Between his meeting with Busch and his match with Sid," wrote the *Pro Wrestling Torch*, "Road agent Mike Graham approached Benoit. Graham would benefit from Sullivan's promotion. ...Benoit has told people that when Graham confronted him backstage, he asked him if the rumors were true that he and some other wrestlers demanded that he, Sullivan, and J.J. Dillon be fired. Benoit said the only name they brought up was Sullivan, and they didn't ask that anyone be fired; they asked for their releases, which is something Busch offered if wrestlers weren't happy. Benoit claims that Graham said something to the effect that it's a good thing Benoit didn't mess with his job...because he would have slit his throat in retaliation."

Though the match was as good as could be expected with a wrestler as bad as the Jheri-curled giant Vicious ("a helpless diaper-shitting baby" was one coworker's review), the world championship victory meant little to Benoit and the wrestling world at large. WCW titles had been so devalued by Nash and Russo that it did nothing for Benoit's credibility, and being the public face of a hapless company in terminal decline was hardly a great career move. After the match, Sullivan insisted on speaking with a reluctant Benoit face-to-face and told him that he had kept his word and made him champion. Sullivan claims that Benoit promised to have a "man-to-man" the next night to clear the air so that they could do business. "I never had that conversation yet," Sullivan said years later. With the benefit of his own experience and Nancy's peerless insight into the character of her former husband, Benoit knew that he could never trust Kevin Sullivan.

"I was drinking with Benoit at a bar right around when he asked for his release and got the title," Chad Damiani told me. "And Benoit wasn't a big talker. They were all talking about how they wondered what would happen if they didn't get the release they'd been promised, about how they all knew Sullivan was going to screw the hell out of Benoit and make a fool out of him. Benoit then said something with absolute finality that ended the conversation and all the speculation. He said, 'If they tell me to do something I don't want to do, I'm going to walk out on live TV and punch a ringpost and shatter my hand. Then I'm going to punch the ringpost with my other hand and shatter it too. Then I'm going to walk backstage, go to the hospital, and sit out while I recover.' Everyone just sat there watching him because they know he was dead serious; Benoit was a lot of things, but he wasn't a bullshitter. Everyone there believed him like he had just said the most natural thing in the world. It didn't even seem like an odd negotiation strategy to them at all.

"My question is," continued Damiani. "*Why the second fist?* He'd already be on the injured list for the first broken hand! Does he break the second one just for effect?"

The next afternoon, Busch met with the disgruntled wrestlers and promised to remove Sullivan from his job booking the two main WCW shows, *Nitro* and *Thunder*, which everyone agreed would be a fair compromise. Whether that was Busch's honest intention is impossible to know; some who have worked with him told me Busch was a "last guy he spoke to" decision-maker who caved into the demands of whoever was standing in his presence at that moment. Regardless, Busch soon afterwards approached Benoit's clique and announced that Sullivan was staying and that everyone besides Benoit was to be sent home immediately. When Benoit refused to be isolated and said that he would be going wherever his friends went, Busch promised him three title victories on that night's *Nitro* and a long run with the heavyweight title.

Though Benoit may have been a mark for the title, it was not enough to convince him to betray Eddy Guerrero, Dean Malenko, and his own long-term best interests. Benoit declined Busch's offer, although he did promise to protect the business by losing the title in the

ring on the first match on *Nitro*. Busch declined, and
Benoit left the title belt with a referee on the way out.
Even if granted a release, their contracts would not allow
them to work for another company for six months.

Luckily for Benoit and his friends, Mike Graham's
threat put WCW in a legal bind. If Benoit's group was not
given unconditional releases, then WCW was assured
that a lawsuit would be forthcoming; after all, it is
against the law for an employee's superior to threaten to
slit his throat if he complains about workplace conditions.
Benoit, Guerrero, Malenko, Saturn, Shane Douglas, and
Konnan (who chose to stay) were all given their
unconditional releases.

Benoit, Guerrero, Malenko, Saturn, and Douglas
had dinner that night and made a pact that they would
operate as a collective, negotiating and working only as
a group. This agreement was especially important to
Shane Douglas, who had bad blood from his previous
stint in WWE and probably required the assistance of
Benoit's bargaining power to get another chance there.
With a pregnant wife, Douglas needed the assurance of a
regular paycheck.

Five days later, Douglas received a phone call from
his friend Vince Russo, telling him that "his boys" were in
Connecticut negotiating with WWE. Douglas refused to
believe Russo and called Malenko to ask if he was in
Connecticut behind his back. When Malenko claimed to be
in Florida, Douglas asked him again, reminding his
longtime friend that his wife was pregnant and that it was
extremely important for him to know if he needed to keep
his options with WCW open. Malenko assured him, "How
long have you known me? Have I ever lied to you in that
time? I swear to you on my wife and my daughter that I'm
at my brother-in-law's house in Florida." When Douglas
called Russo back and staked his reputation that his
friends were not in Connecticut, Russo hinted that maybe
he should call the hotel near headquarters where WWE
talent stayed and ask if his friends had checked in. They

had. WWE wanted nothing to do with Douglas, so neither did Shane Douglas' friends. Business is business.

Douglas returned ignominiously to WCW, where Busch and Sullivan soon fell and were replaced by the nightmare tag team of Russo and Bischoff. On the way to WCW losing sixty-two million dollars in 2000, Russo would give himself and goofball actor David Arquette heavyweight title reigns. When WCW finally went under, wrestlers like Douglas who had bad blood with McMahon were ruined; today, former ECW heavyweight champion Shane works at a Target store.

Chapter XI
The Empire

"Personally, the most evil man in the world that I've ever met in my forty-two years is Vince McMahon. He is sheer, pure evil. I hope, and I will say this and you can document it, that I outlive him in life. Because, if I do, I'm going to drink a bunch of Schlitz Malt Liquor, take a flight to Connecticut, and do some *horrendous* things."

MICHAEL "ROAD WARRIOR HAWK" HEGSTRAND
Dead of a steroid-induced heart attack in 2003 at age forty-six.

THE PROFESSIONAL

UNLIKE MOST PRO WRESTLERS IN WCW, CHRIS BENOIT CONDUCTED HIMSELF IN A PROFESSIONAL MANNER. In comparison to his six-pack-smuggling colleagues in their tank tops and frayed denim shorts, Benoit arrived early at shows in freshly dry-cleaned or ironed casual-dress attire. He never missed a booking; he was never late. Before entering the locker room, Benoit was well known for happily signing autographs while Kevin Nash hurried past. Backstage, in a locker room overrun with drugs and booze-fueled revelry, Benoit quietly stretched, exercised, and went over matches with his friends. His interactions with his coworkers meticulously followed protocol: he was deferential with elders and stern with smart-mouthed rookies. He was obedient, loyal, and selfless with management past the point of reason, a border which WCW management reliably crossed without any assertive response from Benoit. When his wife's violent-junkie ex held his career hostage, Benoit quietly accepted the abuse and did not cause the office any trouble.

In the ring, Benoit went about his duties with a solemn blue-collar pride. Regardless of the laziness of his coworkers, Benoit owed it to *himself*—to his own honor, reputation, and legacy, to his teachers and the profession he loved—to always wrestle his ass off. He worked injured, and, even when his injuries dictated that he refrain from performing one of his trademark moves, Benoit performed them anyway: it was what the fans had paid good money to see, and he didn't want to hear that a Chris Benoit match let the fans down. Away from the ring, Benoit took pride in his body and, through hard work and expertly regimented drug consumption, constructed a majestic physique that could favorably compare with the Dynamite Kid's.

Benoit always put the business first, and this earned him the respect and admiration of his colleagues. If they worked with Benoit, they knew that they could count on him to make them look better than he did himself. Even with mortal enemy Kevin Sullivan, Benoit never once was selfish, uncooperative, or lazy in the ring; Sullivan never looked more formidable than when Benoit was selling his shitty offense and "carrying" him through his drug-addled fatigue. The veterans respected Benoit for enforcing locker room discipline and etiquette, and they knew that they could count on an unfailingly polite response if they ever asked for advice or a favor.

By the late 1990s, Benoit was the favorite of wrestling's hardcore Internet and newsletter fans. Benoit's fans dissected his work in longwinded, deeply researched reviews that could expend 5,000 words justifying why a fifteen-minute wrestling match deserved the sacred, perfect rating of five stars. From 1994-2007, this fanbase voted Benoit either Number One or Two in the *Wrestling Observer's* annual "Best Technical Wrestler" award in every year but 1998. A sizable number of these fans would treat Benoit's murder of his wife and child as a tragedy precisely because it would destroy any hopes of a future Benoit match. For many of them, it was hard to reconcile that Benoit was such a "good worker" but apparently such a bad person; it was far easier for some to assume that the murders were a conspiracy orchestrated by that "lazy choad" Kevin Sullivan than the saintly Canadian who gave his body for the fans' enjoyment.

To these fanatics, the five years of Benoit's wrestling prime that he had wasted in WCW were a tragedy for the art of pro wrestling. He should have been producing countless five-star matches in Japan with fellow demigod Jushin Liger or, at the very least, working for Vince McMahon, the canny businessman who gave every one of his wrestlers a chance to become popular and make him money.

"WOW, THIS GUY'S THE DEVIL."

Unprofessional in his personal behavior, McMahon was the ultimate professional when it came to making money. Unlike a "buddy system" boss like Bischoff, McMahon conducted himself with the impersonal ruthlessness of a businessman: if he thought you could make him money, he didn't give a damn about your talent, background, qualifications, personality, health, sanity, or backstage political acumen. Contrary to his ego-mad reputation, McMahon would even swallow his pride and ass-kiss former enemies, critics, and backstabbers if he felt it would be profitable—there have been at least a half-dozen times when Hogan or the Ultimate Warrior have screwed and publicly derided McMahon, only to be coddled into returning when there was money to be made.

Longtime New York boxing personality Stan Gordon told me a story about his first impression of Vince

McMahon, Jr. "I knew, loved, and respected Vince's father. When Vince Jr. bought the business, at first I didn't know much about him. Junior was having a hard time selling out a big card in the tri-state area. The ringside tickets were $100, $150—expensive, and they weren't selling. So Vince asked the arena's general manager, who was a friend of mine, how much the ringside chairs cost. He told Vince Jr. $20 a piece, so Vince said, 'Great, I'll buy 250.' Vince then had everyone in the locker room autograph the chairs and advertised that anyone who bought a ringside seat could take the autographed chairs home; the seats that wouldn't sell suddenly sold out overnight. That's when I knew that Vince Jr. was going to take the world by storm. He was a born hustler; he knows how to make money on a deal from twenty different angles while the average joe only knows the one or two."

Unlike a traditional promoter who view wrestlers as arena draws and T-shirt sellers, McMahon approaches each new wrestler as the basis for a trademarked multimedia entertainment product that, like a Homer Simpson or Mickey Mouse, can be sold through his company's highly developed merchandising, licensing, advertising, and programming platforms. "What people don't understand about Vince McMahon is his merchandising genius," one former WWE writer told me. "There are times when McMahon out-Disneys Disney when it comes to thinking, 'How can I turn this person or this idea into a T-shirt, a toy, a board game, a video game character, a movie, an album....' That's the first thing Vince thinks about with a new wrestler; the second thing is 'How can I change their name so I can trademark and own it?' It's very much big business."

Grossing in the ballpark of a quarter-billion dollars a year, in 2000 WWE boasted its own NYC nightclub, record label, publishing division, multiple branded magazines, and a nascent Las Vegas casino. Their stars wrote bestsellers and hosted *Saturday Night Live*. If

WCW could be considered a minor television production division in a huge diversified multimedia empire that happened to produce pro wrestling, WWE was a multimedia empire all of its own, built exclusively on the marketing, merchandising, packaging, production, and touring of its pro wrestling brand.

This business model came with incredible advantages for its employees over other wrestling companies. A pro wrestler never had a better chance of becoming a millionaire than with WWE's proven promotional machine behind his career. WWE stars were accompanied by the best entrance music and pyrotechnics, dressed by the best costume designers, filmed by the best camera crew, edited by the best production team, coached by the best wrestling minds, and pushed by the best and largest multimedia promotional network in wrestling. Best of all, ever since the departure of Hall and Nash and the retirement of their buddy Shawn Michaels, WWE was free of the most debilitating, career-ruining sort of backstage politics. A run with the WWE star-making machine was the best opportunity Chris Benoit, Eddy Guerrero, Dean Malenko, and Perry Saturn would ever have of achieving their dreams.

With the demise of ECW and WCW as viable entities (both would fold a little over a year after Benoit's WCW exit), Vince McMahon was the only man in an America with the power to make or break the career of an American pro wrestler. He exerted absolute power over the future of people who were professionally required to sacrifice their health, their future, and their families to their wild-eyed dreams of stardom. The greatest of the golden-age Hollywood studio moguls never held such sway over aspiring actors or actresses, and even porn producers do not deal with wannabes as desperate and ready to debase themselves. Vince McMahon's monopoly—earned, in all fairness, by superior business practices and programming—imbued him the power of an emperor for anyone who sought wrestling stardom in America. "If you complained, he'd fire you, so you'd better keep your mouth shut," said former WWE star Rick Steiner. "If he wants you to be the biggest star, he'll make you the biggest star. He has total control."

The broad-shouldered, 6'2" McMahon carried himself like a bodybuilder looking for a fight. Initiates in the WWE inner circle have asserted that the swaggering, imposing, over-the-top, temperamental, egomaniacal tycoon that Vince McMahon plays on television is inseparable from his actual personality and conduct as a boss. "Vince is absolutely, incredibly intimidating," former WWE producer and writer Domenic Cotter told me. "He's tremendously close to his on-screen character; he's just this big, tall guy with this big booming voice with huge balls; when you are in his presence, he *is* wrestling, the embodiment of the business."

"Vince is larger than life," former WWE writer Dr. Ranjan Chhibber told me. "These huge shoulders, these expensive suits, the giant hair, the enormous voice—he talks at people like he's cutting pro wrestling promos. We'd sit in creative meetings, and sometimes our job was just to listen to McMahon deliver these long-winded, passionate, growling pro wrestling interviews against whoever within the company was annoying him at the time. This could go on for an hour. He's one of those guys that's always on TV in his mind."

"He's the alpha of alpha dogs," ex-WWE television and film writer Dan Madigan has said. "He's the hardest worker I've met. You have to admire the guy because 'heavy is the brow that wears the crown.' If you took away every dime Vince had, he'd still promote. He lives the job, he loves the job, it's everything to him. We'd show up at a hotel at 2 a.m. and there'd be people waiting for autographs—he'd have been working for forty hours straight, and he'd jump to hug the fans, put on a show, be *on* at all times. He works seventy hours a week, lives and breathes wrestling, and that's why he is so demanding on his talent. What, they can work as hard as him? What, they're *tired* or *worn out* or *homesick*? Try telling that to your boss who works twice as hard as you." According to Hulk Hogan, "If Vince yawns, he does it in private."

With an obsessive workaholic like McMahon as boss, WWE employees are always driven as hard as can be humanly sustained. Former WWE writer Ed Ferrara recalled in an interview, "It was like a running joke. Every week at TV when we would be *stumbling* into the elevators to go up to our rooms at two in the morning when we checked in, and [McMahon] would look at us and say, 'Did I get it all? Did I get it all? Did I get all of it?'"

"I remember [heavily injured and drug addicted wrestler] Jeff Hardy was begging for time off," said former WWE diva Terri Runnels. "Begging for it. Finally he just started acting up and not showing up when they wouldn't give him time off [until he was fired]."

This callousness extended to a wrestler's family, as well. When Brian "Road Dogg" James' wife suffered a collapsed lung and was hospitalized in critical condition while he was on the road, he was denied permission to go home until he completed his tag title match that night. In response, James burst into the production meeting, lifted up his tag belt, dropped it on the ground like trash, and said, "Y'all can all fuck yourselves if you think your little 'angle' is more important than my wife's lung," before going home.

Writing team member Dan Madigan's wife suffered a miscarriage, had her beloved father die, and learned that her dog had cancer all within a matter of days. Madigan informed WWE of his family crisis and left the road to comfort her. At his father-in-law's gravesite, while he held his weeping wife over the loss of her father and their unborn child, Madigan's cell phone rang. "It was a call from Stephanie's secretary saying that she was disappointed that I missed the *Tough Enough* [WWE reality TV show] meeting. It was a fucking disgrace; that's when I knew I was done with the company," Madigan told me.

During his stint with McMahon in the 1980s, Billy Jack Haynes worked a tireless schedule including stretches as long as ninety-seven straight days away from home at a time. He was fired when he went home to be at the bedside of his blind, crippled father after he suffered a life-threatening stroke. "How could your dad not come before this business?" Haynes asked. McMahon's grudge against Haynes for "abandoning the business" was so well known that a crew of popular wrestlers engineered a rib on Haynes for McMahon's amusement years later. They told the washed-up, impoverished, desperate Haynes that he had a tryout match at a show in Amarillo, Texas. When Haynes arrived in his goofy ring gear after a "2,000-mile" drive, everyone snickered; there was no tryout. "I went to my car, broke down crying and the whole deal," Haynes recalled. "It demeaned me as a man. I'm going out there; I'm thirty-nine years old, I'm on my last leg, and they did this to me. So I went out to my car to get a gun; I was going to go in there and blow Vince's brains out." A close friend stopped Haynes, who worked extensively as a drug smuggler and gang enforcer, from changing wrestling history, perhaps for the better.

Scott Hall's first impression of McMahon was watching him tell wrestler Brian Knobbs to rely more heavily on booze and pills instead of complaining if he had a problem keeping up with the work schedule. "Knobbs got fined ten thousand dollars for being dirty for smoke [marijuana]. It was his fourth dirty piss test. So I'm standing behind Vince. He's got his suit on with the fuckin' shoulder pads in. He used to put pads in his shoulders of his suit. Knobbs is going, 'What the fuck! You fuckin' fine me ten thousand dollars. Why can't I relax in my room, you motherfucker! How the fuck am I supposed to calm down? I'm on the road 300 days a year. What the fuck?'

"Vince went, 'I guess you're just gonna have to drink more and take more pills,'" Hall remembers incredulously. "I was standing behind Vince and I'd just come to work for the company.... I remember going, 'Wow.' 'Cause, see, I wasn't in that drug culture then. I wasn't a pillhead then. I wasn't a hardcore drinker then. I remember going, 'Wow, this guy's the devil.' 'Cause that impacted me. Those are exactly the words he said. It's burned into my brain. I went, wow, this motherfucker don't give a fuck."

Whenever he's not under heavy federal or media pressure to test for drugs, Vince's permissiveness concerning narcotics use is legendary. "The first time that I went to the WWE, I won't say the names, but some guys were smoking pot in the showers. I was like, 'Wow,'" recalled Konnan. Anything that allowed a wrestler to make a booking or stay on the road was okay with him. In the 80s, it was common for McMahon to drink to incoherence with the boys, and, when a drug bust caused McMahon to institute testing in the late 80s, he responded by "having one more night out with the boys" during which he got so drunk and high that he dared the wrestlers to perform their finishing moves on him in a crowded bar. According to numerous sources, McMahon had a great love affair with cocaine that may or may not have ever subsided; he "liked to brag with apparent justification that 'I can snort as much of that stuff as anyone can put in front of me and never get hooked.'"

One WWE employee of recent years told me, "The boys and former office staff use euphemisms when they talk about Vince's 'energy.' You'll hear it in things like, 'I don't know where he gets all the energy.... He doesn't ever seem to sleep!' The inside joke about it is that sixty-something Vince most likely isn't that energetic over multi-day sleepless stretches without help. I've seen him so wired that his eyes looked like they were going to pop."

Though McMahon's cocaine use may be in dispute, there is no confusion over his longstanding love affair with steroids. In the 80s, Bret Hart recalls McMahon going to the office of a mark doctor who openly supplied the boys and leaving with "with grocery bags full of drugs." Obsessed with bodybuilding, McMahon trained with his most built stars and transformed his corporate headquarters into a personal gym. After McMahon hired a personal assistant specifically to ensure that he gorged on high-protein tuna throughout the day, the Stamford headquarters smelled so strongly of fish that even visiting Japanese dignitaries were overpowered by the stench and rushed through meetings at top speed. Some WWE writers told me stories of McMahon conducting meetings without a shirt while lifting weights or shaving his muscular arms and armpits. Bodybuilding is McMahon's passion; he candidly told an Australian interviewer in 2002 that his perfect day would consist exclusively of "good clean sex" and weight training.

Put on federal trial for distributing steroids to his employees in 1994, McMahon admitted his own steroid use on the way to getting acquitted. Though ostensibly clean since then, McMahon has probably been the most clearly chemically-enhanced star on WWE TV over the past decade. "You seen Schwarzenegger without his shirt lately?" one insider asked me. "He doesn't have that Schwarzenegger body anymore. If you see Vince McMahon without his shirt, he still has that ridiculous jacked-up Schwarzenegger physique, and he's *older* than Arnold. This isn't genetics; no sixty-three-year-old has twenty-four-inch guns and abs like God through hard work. A twenty-year-old doesn't have McMahon's body without roids. He looks grotesque. Stomach-turning. A freak." One former WWE writer told me, "I'm not exactly going out on a limb to say that some of McMahon's egotistical temper tantrums are chemically induced."

"It's no secret Vince has this mindset that you have to be a big, juiced-up steroid monster if you wanted to get pushed," Dominick Pagliaro told me. "It was strongly implied. You were either on it or you weren't a star. Looking at McMahon's physique and personal life, it's not hard to see where it comes from." Dan Madigan agrees, "It's like with everything else: McMahon doesn't ask anything of his talent that he doesn't do himself. But if *Vince* does it to himself—and this is a Medicare-age billionaire who never sleeps, throws himself off cages, and has a bodybuilder's body—then he damn expects you to do the same. In his mind, it's only fair."

"The culture of steroids is so pervasive in the WWE that even a few of their wrestling announcers are doing steroids," one WWE writer told me. "In fact, one of them was talking about it openly. At first, I had no idea what he was talking about. He was talking to another announcer about working out, and something called 'cycles,' and taking 'the juice.' When I came to discover what it was, I was shocked. At least two of them are on steroids, and neither of them are former wrestlers. They come from the world of broadcast journalism."

To succeed in WWE, Benoit, Guerrero, Saturn, and Malenko knew that they would be expected to unconditionally adopt McMahon's twisted lifestyle as their own. Outside of a few golden boys like Hulk Hogan and Shawn Michaels, McMahon brooked no complaint or opposition from his employees. It was a commonly told story how McMahon once berated Ric Flair and Randy Savage, two all-time legends, "like dogs" when they imprecisely followed his directions in the ring. Less accomplished stars were often humiliated on TV, hazed backstage, and eventually fired in retaliation for the slightest sign of independent thought. There is no loyalty; even the greatest WWE star of all time, Stone Cold Steve Austin, was unceremoniously dropped and badmouthed on TV after he balked at one idiotic, business-killing storyline. When Scott Hall made an appointment with Vince to ask for more money, he walked into McMahon's office and discovered that all of his posters had been replaced overnight with Undertaker posters.

"The WWE operates like a cult," Dan Madigan told me. "You're either an unquestioning, asskissing, belly-crawling, no-mind-of-your-own 'team player,' or you're not there. It's like Stalinism."

This obsequiousness extended to contract negotiations. The first words McMahon said to Benoit, Guerrero, and Saturn during their first meeting was "how much he admired" that they were "willing to give up all that money" on principle. Unlike WCW, McMahon did not offer guaranteed no-cut contracts or any allowances for road expenses; unlike in New Japan, there was no health coverage on tour, no perks, no free hotel rooms, no free bus transportation, no long-term promises. As the only game in town, McMahon held all the leverage. All three were given three-year "independent contractor" deals in which they were not even technically WWE employees, only freelance outsiders who were given no benefits and could be cut at any time. They were responsible for all of their own travel expenses and accommodations, and Benoit and Guerrero signed over considerable intellectual property rights to their own names. They would have no say in their character or storyline; if McMahon wanted to book the character of "Chris Benoit" as a Nazi pedophile, then that was his prerogative.

Their only security was a "downside" guarantee that they would make somewhere between $250,000 and $400,000 per year, which did not count the travel expenses that WWE star Randy Orton estimated at $100,000 a year. The pay was hardly generous for performers who, in addition to taking part in around a hundred touring events every year, would be playing a major televised role on both the top-rated program on cable television and the top-rated program on the UPN network. As Bad News Allen had warned Benoit about Vince McMahon, "If you shake hands with him, count your fingers afterwards."

Their salary could increase according to an impossible-to-audit, convoluted mathematical formula that supposedly pays according to a wrestler's spot on every card and how much it grosses. Many former WWE wrestlers believe the formula is a euphemism for "how much the office wants to give you." Some of these many wrestlers have reported severe pay irregularities that could not be produced by a constant, objective mathematical formula. Of course, Benoit and his friends

signed over many of their constitutional rights to contest
the terms of their contract and their pay in case of a
dispute. What rights they did not explicitly sign over they
effectively surrendered once they decided that they
wanted to be accepted by the WWE locker room.

If we judge by their own priorities, the sacrifice
was worth it for Benoit and Guerrero, who attained
greater stardom than any junior heavyweight in recent
American history.

THE BRIGHT LIGHTS

On the January 31, 2000 episode of WWE's
flagship show Raw is War, Benoit, Guerrero,
Malenko, and Saturn took seats in the front row of
the audience as common spectators. Announcer Jim
Ross seemed genuinely surprised to see them in
attendance. All four were dressed like sleazy middle-aged
men on the date-rape prowl at a disco, Benoit sporting
what appeared to be a sheer dress shirt with a smattering
of black velour inkblots. When Road Dogg, a wrestler in
the top heel stable D-Generation X, was whipped into the
guardrail in front of the "WCW Four," he chose to sucker
punch Benoit without apparent cause. All four wrestlers
then jumped the rail and beat up Road Dogg and his tag
partner in the ring; as the crowd cheered, Guerrero and
Benoit awkwardly climbed to the top rope in their street
clothes and performed their trademark maneuvers. As the
four wrestlers walked up the ramp to the backstage area,
announcer Jim Ross dubbed them "the Radicalz"—the
rebellious posse that had flouted their bosses in WCW and
escaped to WWE. Their debut WWE show drew a 6.59
rating to WCW's 2.79, which was seen in the industry as
a repudiation of WCW's dismissive attitude towards
their potential.

On the Smackdown episode taped for network TV
the next night, WWE world champion HHH offered the
Radicalz WWE contracts if they could beat his DX stable
in a best-of-three showdown. After Malenko lost his

match, Guerrero and Saturn were supposed to win a tag match to even the score and make Benoit's singles match with HHH decisive. Guerrero had returned prematurely from a surgery on his right elbow and, despite being told not to perform any high-risk moves, felt he needed to push himself as much as possible in his WWE debut. When Guerrero climbed to the top rope for his finish, the frogsplash, he unconsciously shied away from landing on his injured arm and instead crashed with his full weight onto his left arm, gruesomely popping his elbow out of its socket. Barely a month had passed since Guerrero's last near-fatal OD at a family Christmas party, and now he had yet another painful injury to rehabilitate. Knowing McMahon's feelings about employees who missed work, Guerrero was overcome with panic that he was going to squander his last opportunity to make it big in America. He apologized compulsively as he was taken to receive medical attention.

Since Guerrero could not finish his match as planned, the best-of-three series was already decided by the time Benoit faced HHH in the main event of *Smackdown*. Nonetheless, the WWE champion made the lowly WCW mid-carder look like a worthy contender, feverishly submitting to Benoit's finishing hold, the Crippler Crossface. After a cheap shot to the balls that would have made Bruce Hart proud, HHH scored the victory in what should have been the last Radicalz match in WWE. In reality, Benoit's hard work and solid, meat-and-potatoes performance had impressed both Vince McMahon and HHH, who was quickly becoming a backstage political powerhouse.

The February 7 *Raw* was the most successful television show of Chris Benoit's career. The Radicalz entered the ring during the episode's first segment to humbly say their goodbyes to the WWE fans and their benefactor Mick Foley. Shortly after giving Foley their heartfelt thanks, all four Radicalz (with Guerrero in a cast) ambushed him at the behest of HHH, revealing that they had "sold out" and turned heel in order to obtain

WWE contracts. In the main event of the show, the three healthy Radicalz teamed with HHH and stablemate X-Pac in a fantastic ten-man tag match that drew the highest television rating (an astronomical 8.1) and hottest crowd response of any match in Benoit's career. The *Pro Wrestling Torch* wrote "morale might be at an all-time high" after *Raw* since "everything clicked in the ten-man tag" in which "everybody was over, from top stars Rock [and] Triple H...to Chris Benoit, Dean Malenko, and Perry Saturn."

"Of all my years—I've been wrestling fourteen and a half years now," Benoit said shortly afterwards, "Of everywhere I've been: Mexico, Japan, Europe, the States, Canada—that was the most electrifying crowd for any match I've ever been in. It was just amazing. As loud as the people were and into it as they were, that's what we live for. A lot of people don't see the time on the road, getting to the gym, diets, and going to bed at a different time every night, that's the bad side of it. But we live for those moments. That makes up for all the other crap you have to put up with."

This tag match was a milestone in Benoit's career. He proved to management that, despite his lack of charisma and interview skills, if booked correctly his manifest wrestling talent would be enough to convince fans to take him seriously in the ring against megastars like The Rock. Unlike most wrestlers fresh from WCW, including his friend Chris Jericho, the versatile Benoit also showed that he could dumb his wrestling style down enough to fit in WWE's heavily simplified, kick-punch-finisher match format. Booked in the main event storyline for his first three shows, Benoit had held his own with the top WWE talents and gotten over with the audience using little besides his ruthless, aggressive wrestling style. Coveted by McMahon since at least 1995, when his New Japan commitments had prevented his hiring, Benoit's performance in the February 7, 2000 *Raw* main event seemed to settle any question of Benoit's job security as far as WWE was concerned. The next week, WWE would give him a crooked win over their biggest star, The Rock. Whether he knew it or not, Benoit was a WWE lifer.

"McMahon is a third-generation promoter, a kid who grew up wanting to be a wrestler," Dan Madigan told me. "For a guy like that, you can't help but admire Benoit—in the ring, there was no one better, no one who better embodied what a *real* wrestler was supposed to be, the guy who paid his dues. I think McMahon liked the prestige and credibility he brought to the locker room."

Benoit's crew thrived in the WWE locker room, though they were initially suspicious that the convivial atmosphere was just a ruse. "We were the ones that were, quiet," Guerrero said in an interview about the Radicalz' first few days in the WWE locker room. "We didn't know how to act around them. Guys used to come to us and say 'Loosen up, guys.' We didn't know, man; we had our guards up from [WCW], our guard was up all the time. We didn't know if a person was smiling at us because he was saying 'Yeah, I'm going to get ya' or if he was just like, 'Hi!'"

Enjoying all-time highs in attendance, ratings, and programming quality, the WWE roster was as ecstatic as WCW at the peak of the nWo's popularity—with one important difference. With the strong authority figure of Vince McMahon in charge, a reasonable degree of professionalism, decorum, and sobriety was maintained: there was order. "It's great to have a boss," Benoit said in an interview.

Wrestling for WWE had more in common with Benoit's tours with New Japan at its mid-90's peak than his last few years in WCW. In 2000, routine WWE shows in 15,000-seat arenas sold out within a couple days; major PPV events could sell 20,000 tickets in minutes. The fans in their expensive WWE T-shirts and replica belts were rowdy, deeply invested in the action, and ready to sing along with every catchphrase. The production values were incredible; Benoit was astounded at just how meticulously stage-managed every entrance, every camera angle, every match was. When Benoit wrestled in a WWE ring, there were dedicated film crews in expert sync with his every moment that always framed the action at the most dramatic and flattering angle.

One example of WWE's superior presentation was how they exploited one of Benoit's faults, his disfigured toothless smile; he supposedly lost a lateral incisor during playtime with his pet Rottweiler. The cameras zeroed in on it, using the handy visual to brand Benoit's character as a grizzled, battle-worn predator. Benoit was instructed to smile his toothless bully smile during interviews, which made him look far more disturbed and menacing than if he had clenched his brow and self-consciously tried to look tough. He growled and groaned while applying his Crippler Crossface finisher hold so that the camera could capture a close-up of his distorted, grotesque expression as his opponent tapped out. These little visual touches did more for Benoit's character than a million hours of Benoit's halting, unsure interviews, which WWE would improve as well; for the first time since ECW, Benoit was actually given specific talking points to cover in his interviews.

"Traveling with Dean, Eddie, and Perry really breaks the monotony," Benoit wrote on his webpage early in his WWE tenure. "We are like an extremely dysfunctional family all together. There is always something to laugh at or shake your head at. I consider them my family, my best brothers…. You see, I will sit in the front seat when Perry's driving in any of the 50 states, with the exception of New York. I swear, something happens to him, something or someone possesses him when he gets behind the wheel in that area. Dean, Eddie and I usually end up arguing 'Im [sic] not going to sit in the front, you sit in the front' while Perry is saying 'come on my driving's not that bad.' Well Perry from all of us to you—you're [sic] driving is UNACCEPTABLE in the state of New York."

This passage captures something of the flavor of Benoit's relationship with his fellow Radicalz, which was abnormally warm and brotherly even for longtime traveling partners on the road. Benoit took the ideal of the brotherhood of wrestlers seriously, and he would admit that his relationship with Eddy Guerrero in particular was as intimate and affectionate as any other in his life. It meant a great deal to Benoit that he escaped WCW and found professional success with his friends in tow; it would have been especially hard for him to leave Guerrero behind with his addictions and suicidal depression. Instead, Benoit and his friends had finally found professional fulfillment together—well, except for Target-bound Shane Douglas.

"I'm happy where I am now. I feel great about myself, I feel great about my career, my future," Benoit said in a February 18, 2000 audio interview on his Web site. A Web site commentary Benoit published shortly afterwards elaborated, "The last 36 days have been about the most pivotal in my career. I have this renewed passion I thought I lost for pro wrestling during my time in W.C.W. Actually I don't think I ever really lost it, I think I was very disorientated due to the extreme lack of direction as well as lack of leadership the company had. It was so hard to watch day in and day out so many talented people so many potential angles so much potential business go unnoticed or ignored because of blatant politics. ...I am so happy to see my close friends, Dean, Eddy and Perry having fun again, and not only wanting, but being encouraged to contribute to the business we all take so much pride in."

What may have been the happiest period of Benoit's life was crowned by the birth of his eagerly awaited son Daniel, his only child with Nancy. Benoit made running updates to his Web site, with a post on February 23, 2000, announcing that they were leaving for the hospital to induce labor and another on February 24 entitled, "Still no baby to announce." The next blog post read in full:

Nancy and I are very proud to announce the birth of Daniel Christopher on Friday February 25 at 3 A.M. He is a very healthy 9lbs, .09oz!

It's about 5:30 A.M now and I just came home to shower, eat and get back to the hospital. Nancy and I left for the hospital on Wednesday the 23rd to induce labour.

I want to say how tired I am, but after having witnessed what Nancy has gone through, I don't have a leg to stand on. I feel like waking up the whole neighborhood to tell them. So many emotions, I can't find the words to express them right now. I feel AWESOME! What a RUSH!"

Separated from his previous two children, Benoit greeted the birth of Daniel with what has been almost universally described as particularly deep joy and affection. Benoit spoke about Daniel's birth with uncommon giddiness on his website, posting photos of the baby and the new parents to his online gallery.

Another milestone followed shortly after Daniel's birth: Benoit's first *Wrestlemania,* the biggest event in pro wrestling's annual calendar. *Wrestlemania 2000* in Anaheim, California, was one of the most successful PPVs in WWE history. In the third-to-last match, Benoit faced his old friend Chris Jericho and Kurt Angle, an Olympic gold medalist in amateur wrestling, in a three-way, two-falls match with the WWE European and Intercontinental titles on the line. After a good match, Benoit would leave *Wrestlemania* with the IC title, his first of a dozen WWE title reigns. In a preview of WWE's creative downfall, *Wrestlemania* for the first time in history would not end with a heroic victory by a crowd favorite: instead, HHH and the entire McMahon family celebrated in the ring, united together in an evil alliance of self-indulgent airtime hogs.

Shortly after *Wrestlemania,* Guerrero's addictions and volatile emotional state had worn down Saturn and Malenko's patience. "I think Dean and Perry had grown tired of babysitting me," Guerrero wrote. Benoit wrote on his webpage that, "Now that it appears that the Radicals are drifting apart, Perry and Dean are arguing over custody of Eddie and I. Neither of them want us! If Eddie and I have to rely on each other on the road, we are screwed. Being on the road is very demanding, mentally, emotionally and physically." The road is especially unforgiving if your traveling partner is a frequently overdosed junkie and alcoholic with a pronounced suicidal streak. "Chris and I continued to ride together," Guerrero wrote in his book. "God bless him, he always looked out for me.... He would do pretty much all of the driving, mostly because he was afraid of me falling asleep at the wheel. I'd sit in the passenger seat, with a couple bottles of wine, while he stayed up all night getting us from one town to the next. On those rare occasions when I did drive, Chris wouldn't sleep so he could keep an eye on me."

While Guerrero continued his long emotional crisis, his wrestling career was enjoying a renaissance as he took on the comical Latin lover character, "Latino Heat." Guerrero was paired in a comedic romance with monstrous female bodybuilder Joanie "Chyna" Laurer, the most popular female wrestler in WWE history. Though Chyna was a star who received considerable airtime, she was also undergoing severe addiction problems, largely caused by the betrayal of her longtime real-life and on-screen lover, Paul "HHH" Levesque, who left her for an illicit affair with Vince McMahon's daughter, Stephanie. Unaware that her boyfriend's relationship with the boss' daughter was an open secret backstage, she called Vince. In a cold, uncharacteristic monotone, McMahon cut her off, "Ah, well, I hope you don't lose your job over this," and hung up. Instead, she lost her mind, entering a drug-fueled tailspin that would last for years; her company would do little to encourage Guerrero's sobriety.

Benoit's career would reach a new zenith in July, when WWE booked him to main-event the *Fully Loaded* PPV against the world champion, The Rock. Given Shane McMahon as a manager, The Crippler was sold as a sort of backwater sadist ("I love to see the Rock squeal! Squeal, Rock, squeal!"). "Chris Benoit is a man with deadly focus...Chris Benoit is a man that is coldhearted...Chris Benoit is a man that is absolutely ruthless!" intoned Shane McMahon in his distinctly stilted delivery.

Thanks to expert editing and a typically fantastic hype video, by the day of the PPV Benoit had been built into a credible contender for The Rock, whose charisma and popularity made it easy to for Benoit to get booed. There was some worry that Benoit would not be credible challenger standing next to the Rock, who was a half-foot taller and much more muscular.

Their PPV match contained a false ending in which Benoit was announced as champion and given a chance to celebrate with the belt; it was a sign of the WWE's success in cultivating Benoit's character that Benoit's victory was taken seriously by the fans in attendance. Benoit did not look remotely out of place holding the WWE championship belt, which he had taken from him within moments by an overruled referee decision. Despite there being little doubt that The Rock would win, the PPV drew a respectable buyrate in range with the previous year's July show. Benoit had proven himself to be, if nothing else, an acceptable main event opponent for an established draw like The Rock—and hence one of the top ten stars in WWE.

Benoit's role for the next three years would be stagnant; he was the respected, credible, moderately popular utility wrestler who could be cycled into the occasional PPV main event for a fresh match-up and a quality performance. In between main event programs, Benoit would be the roster's designated workhorse, providing depth to PPVs by putting on show-stopping "workrate" matches in the mid-card that attracted the hardcore fans and compensated for main events of varying wrestling quality. To most wrestling insiders, this second-tier role was the highest Benoit could ever aspire to fill in WWE.

In the months immediately after Benoit's match against The Rock, WWE's backstage culture underwent a political shift. This unwelcome change was publicly exposed during a love triangle storyline between HHH, his real life girlfriend Stephanie McMahon, and Kurt Angle. The storyline was a conventional daytime soap opera storyline, not a conventional pro wrestling soap opera storyline; it was rare for WWE to spend weeks drawing out the suspense on whether a kiss to the cheek between friends was innocent or not. Nonetheless, the storyline was popular with the live crowds, and their reaction made it clear that they desired for Stephanie McMahon to betray HHH and turn him into a vengeful babyface. Concerned only with selling tickets, McMahon usually adapted storylines to the fans' reaction so that they went home satisfied and wanted to buy more WWE merchandise.

However, this storyline was different. Despite the crowd's clear preference, HHH dominated Angle in successive PPV main events and Stephanie maintained her loyalties. At the time, this struck a jarring flat note more commonly associated with WCW's stubborn insistence on giving the fans what the top stars' egos desired instead of what they wanted. It came out shortly afterwards that Vince had crowned his buxom twenty-four-year-old daughter—who had zero writing or management experience and little apparent talent—as the new head of WWE Creative. This act of nepotism resulted in an overnight downturn in the writing quality of WWE programming and an immediately noticeable change in WWE backstage politics.

For the first time since the retirement of backstage terror Shawn Michaels, disproportionate backstage power devolved onto a single active wrestler: HHH, whose on-screen and off-screen relationship with booker Stephanie ensured that they were the dominating presence on WWE TV. On his first day in the company years earlier, Levesque had told one WWE talent, "I don't care what I have to do, but I'm going to run this place." Levesque, known as HHH in the ring, immediately ingratiated himself to the vindictive junkie clique then running the WWE locker room—Nash, Hall, and Michaels, much to the resentment of his fellow young wrestlers. "The only guy [in the business] that I don't think I would even say 'Hello' to is [HHH] because he's just a brown-noser," said former WWE wrestler Bam Bam Bigelow in a 1997 interview. "I mean I use to watch him carry Scott Hall, Shawn Michaels, and [Kevin Nash's] *bags*. He used to carry their *bags*; that's how a much of a pussy he is. He was up Kevin's ass. That big fucking nose of his was brown with little piles [of shit] on it."

The unprincipled, power-hungry Levesque's seduction of the boss' daughter—initiated, according to Stephanie, by sly on-screen groping—provoked widespread skepticism over the sincerity of his feelings and the honesty of his intentions. Even Kevin Nash hinted at what most everyone assumed. When asked if he was surprised by his former protégé's rise to power, he laughed. "Nah, why would I [be]? He was brought into the business by the masters. Why would I not think he would be smart? You can't determine who you fall in love with," Nash added with a sly smile. Levesque's behavior would soon prove that he had learned much from Nash; Levesque's former stablemate and friend Monty "Billy Gunn" Sopp described the boss' new son-in-law as, "A cocksucking, piece of fucking shit...a bad person; he stabs people in the back."

Though a talented and popular performer on his own merits, Levesque exploited his soon-to-be-wife's position within the company to ensure that his character enjoyed the type of narcissistic vanity-booking enjoyed by Hogan and Nash in WCW. Though even Vince McMahon made sure to humiliate and humble himself when playing against WWE's fan favorites, HHH became the one heel who always came out looking stronger, cooler, and more fearless than his opponents. WWE reliably denied the fans what they wanted and instead attempted to force-feed them the arbitrary booking decisions of the self-interested HHH and the clueless Stephanie.

Backstage politics skyrocketed as the boys humbled themselves before the royal couple—including Benoit, who was especially vocal in his support of their relationship, possibly thanks to his own experiences with Nancy. Ratings, attendance, and buyrates gradually declined; as WCW had proven, wrestling fans with their passionate loyalties will nevertheless abandon a product they perceive to be selfishly run. Since McMahon finally purchased hopeless WCW in March and ECW declared bankruptcy in April of 2001, those fans displeased with WWE's booking had no alternative and simply stopped watching wrestling. The wrestling boom was over; the amount of wrestling on TV was cut by more than half, and WWE's Monday night viewership in April 2001 was down nearly forty percent from the total Monday night wrestling viewership in April 2000.

Levesque's destructive influence can be seen in the booking of Stone Cold Steve Austin, the most popular and lucrative character in WWE history. In a blatantly crooked storyline, the incomparably beloved Austin was booked to turn heel against the crowd's wishes and become HHH's grim, humorless, unpleasant sidekick. The fans resisted at every step; yet no matter how much Austin berated the fans in interviews, they still loved him. In the old WWE, it was precisely this positive reaction to the vicious, heel dirtbag Austin that McMahon exploited to spark the greatest boom in wrestling history. With tone-deaf Stephanie in charge, WWE instead treated Austin's unplanned popularity like WCW would have: they systematically destroyed it for not being Stephanie's idea. Austin's signature theme music, which earned the largest crowd response every night, was changed specifically to deprive the fans of their Pavlovian rush. Since Austin was too fun on the microphone, Stephanie booked HHH to act as his mouthpiece. The ultimate wrestling tough guy was booked to be a sniveling wimp, which so flew in the face of Austin's established character that it came off as phony and preposterous.

The April and May 2001 PPVs where the Austin/HHH-heel tandem first headlined suffered a respective forty and twenty percent decrease in buyrates from the previous year's shows. Fresh the from the demise of ECW, longtime Benoit booster Paul Heyman had joined the creative team and launched a lobbying campaign to refocus WWE around ECW-style wrestling: long, hard-fought wrestling matches between talented in-ring performers with plenty of props and stunts thrown in to keep the viewers interested. Despite his own deep skepticism that wrestlers of their size could draw, a reluctant Vince was persuaded by the decline in business to give Benoit and Jericho—"Heyman's pair"—a chance to headline against Austin and HHH in a series of long, body-killing ECW-style matches.

On the May 21, 2001 *Raw*, Benoit and Jericho began their feud with Austin and HHH by defeating them in a tag-title match during which the immensely juiced-up HHH took a normal step that tore his left quadricep muscle so badly that it unraveled from the bone. Since Levesque sustained such a drastic muscle tear during the act of *walking*, the injury was commonly assumed to be caused by severe steroid abuse, which strains muscle tissue by stretching it far past its natural limits. The announcement that Levesque would miss almost a year of action was greeted with tickertape parade jubilation on the Internet.

For the next *Smackdown*, Heyman booked a four-way tag called "Tables, Ladders, and Chairs" as the main event of the show. This dangerous extravaganza of weapons shots and high-altitude falls was pitched as the perfect opportunity for Benoit to utilize his superior physical skills to perform a series of breathtaking Dynamite Kid-style stunts that would "wow" the crowd into getting behind him as a headliner. Instead, Benoit's own death-defying performance was lost in the shuffle of suicidal stunts, and he left the ring with a chilling numbness in his right arm and blinding pain in his neck. He knew he had a suffered a serious spinal injury.

With a PPV main event coming his way in a month, Benoit postponed visiting the doctor until after his big match. Despite the example of Tom Billington, Benoit was risking lifelong paralysis for a wrestling match.

The next week, Benoit faced Steve Austin in a singles match in the former Stampede Wrestling homebase of Calgary, where the crowd naturally adored him. A senile, debilitated Stu Hart sat in the front row with Bruce and Smith Hart, who were currying favor with McMahon by dragging their senile father to an event run by the mortal enemy of Bret Hart and Owen Hart's widow. "Tears came to my eyes as I watched the opening of the live show at home on TV," Bret wrote in his memoir. "There was a clearly tired, deflated and demoralized Stu sitting in the front row with...Bruce and Smith, who grinned as he held up a big sign that read, HA HA BRET."

What could have been an opportunity for Benoit to steal the show in front of his hometown fans and two of his trainers instead became a mean-spirited debacle. To humiliate the retired Bret, McMahon reenacted his betrayal of Bret for the title by announcing Austin "the winner" of the match by submission even though Benoit had never been submitted, forcing Bret's father to relive his son's humiliation in person. Bruce would repeat this stunt the next night in Benoit's hometown Edmonton, where an elderly Stu watched Benoit get screwed by McMahon in the main event *again*. In both matches, Benoit performed all of his signature moves, including the suplexes and dives that put incredible stress on his neck. The pain was becoming so bad that Benoit could not sleep or maintain a train of thought.

After the Austin matches in Stampede country, Benoit called Bret to apologize for McMahon's behavior and to ask if Stu was as unhealthy as he looked; Bret told him he was. Benoit was being used as a prop to demean his mentors, one brain-damaged and the other dying, in retaliation for their justifiable criticism of McMahon over his treatment of their family. In response to the family's disparagement after Owen's death, the billionaire

McMahon chose to mock two broken, harmless men on national television at every opportunity.

It was during this shabby episode that sources first indicate Benoit's unhappiness in WWE; his neck was in constant excruciating pain, he was beginning to lose the professional respect he had regained after leaving WCW, and—worst of all—his best friend was in serious trouble.

Eddy's drug addiction had gotten so dire that both Benoit and Malenko felt they had no choice but to turn him into management. Malenko tried to explain their decision to Guerrero by telling him, "I wouldn't be able to live with myself if I would've found you dead in a hotel room." After a stern lecture from management, Eddy arrived at the next show even more incapacitated than usual, which earned him a compulsory trip to rehab. Eddy's marriage was disintegrating, as well.

Heyman continued to book Benoit in extremely long, punishing matches on free television, which made hardcore wrestling fans ecstatic, but gravely increased the damage Benoit's body was accumulating without actually drawing any more money for WWE. The culminating blow would be a cage match against Benoit's old enemy Kurt Angle, the Olympian with the obsessive perfectionist streak and broken neck of his own. "Angle was a little off his rocker," Domenic Cotter has said. "Angle was [an] extremely intense guy to be around, more so than Benoit even. He didn't care at all about his own physical well-being; he had this mentality that he literally was the world's strongest man and the baddest man on the planet when, with all of his neck injuries, he could barely walk. You got the impression he literally wanted to die in the ring."

Standing in the ring with an athlete of Angle's quality made Benoit insecure and encouraged him to play a game of in-ring chicken with the Olympian, as if both men had a death wish. Like Benoit, Angle was a suplex specialist; these throws strained the neck of both the wrestler performing the move and the wrestler taking the move. Never one to be upstaged, Benoit insisted on topping Angle by performing a German suplex from the second rope followed by a ridiculously excessive nine consecutive German suplexes in a row, which not only killed any meaning the legitimately dangerous move could have but also put profound strain on Benoit's spine and numb arm.

When Angle back-flipped from the top of the cage all the way down to the mat, the audience knew that Benoit could never let such a daredevil feat go unanswered. Benoit prepared his tour de force: a diving headbutt from the top of the cage, or basically a glorified face-first belly flop onto hard canvas from around twelve or thirteen feet in the air. "I remember diving off the top of the cage and questioning myself right before I jumped," Benoit said. "I don't know if I should do this with my neck in this shape. But once you're out there, that adrenaline is flowing, and you the hear people screaming—the thought just went right through my mind." Benoit did his triumphant belly flop and immediately afterwards noticed that the entire right side of his body was numb. Like Tom Billington, Benoit's wrestling style had finally come to its obvious conclusion; the Crippler crippled himself.

Instead of sitting out immediately, Benoit kept wrestling until he finished his main event program with Austin for *King of the Ring*, which was a box-office flop. To the surprise of Heyman, giving away long, PPV-quality matches every night on free TV did not encourage the fans to spend thirty dollars extra to see the same characters wrestle the same match against each other again on PPV. Benoit had volunteered to play guinea pig for a patently stupid promotional strategy, and it was his reputation as "a main event draw" that would take the blame for the decline in business. In the coming years, HHH and Stephanie would point to the failure of this storyline as proof of Benoit's irrevocable second-tier status in the eyes of the fans. Benoit nearly paralyzed himself for dangerous television segments that would have drawn better ratings, increased PPV buys, and raised his value if they had been harmless Stone Cold interviews instead.

"The [WWE] locker room after the *King of the Ring* PPV ended looked like a scene in a ratings sweeps week for *E.R.* Blood everywhere, moaning and wincing, and body parts being iced and taped. Steve Austin suffered a hand injury, Kurt Angle suffered a potential broken tailbone and was knocked out briefly, Chris Jericho suffered a concussion, and Chris Benoit wrestled his last match before taking months off to recover from surgery this week," wrote the *Pro Wrestling Torch.*

Benoit's surgery was more serious than reported: a disc in his cervical spine had ruptured, applying pressure on his spinal cord and nerves. The corrective surgery came with the risk of stroke and paralysis, and in the best-case scenario a year of gradual rehabilitation would be required before he could be expected to even train normally. Benoit suffered a complete emotional breakdown in the doctor's office, screaming and crying. He told his friends and family that he was terrified, not by the surgical risks, but because he was so worried that, like the Dynamite Kid, he would never be able to wrestle up to the standards that he had before his neck injury. Benoit nervously asked WWE talent if they thought the company would remember him after a year's absence—would his career ever recover? Would he be able to perform all of his signature moves? Would he be able to keep up with the younger, faster wrestlers? Would WWE pass him by?

Should I continue my wrestling career even though it has destroyed my spine and almost resulted in my permanent paralysis? Should I continue to wrestle a style that crippled my idol and has shown that it will cripple me? Should I continue to work for a company that will only employ me if I destroy my body, use drugs, and work injured? These were the questions that apparently went unasked.

Chapter XII
Falling Upwards

"A few years ago, some people tried to destroy my family.... They tried to rip us apart, but all they did was make my family stronger...and that's exactly how America feels right now."

STEPHANIE MCMAHON ON 9/13/01
Comparing N.Y.C.'s 9/11 attacks to the 1993 federal indictment of Vince McMahon for distributing steroids to WWE talent.

SPINELESS

CHRIS BENOIT'S LIFE BEGAN TO DISINTEGRATE WHEN HE WAS REQUIRED TO ACTUALLY SPEND TIME AT HOME. After his brief professional and personal renaissance in 2000 passed, the symptoms of psychological illness Benoit began to display in WCW worsened at a literally breakneck pace.

On June 28, 2001, Benoit underwent an anterior cervical discectomy, in which ruptured spinal discs were removed from vertebrae at the base of his neck. To fill the gaps in his spine, a bone graft from his pelvic bone was inserted through the front of Benoit's neck and held in place by a titanium plate. Over time, this bone graft would fuse the two vertebrae together, creating a solid titanium-reinforced hunk of bone in Benoit's spinal column. A WWE film crew taped the three-hour procedure and highlights aired that weekend on television, along with an interview where Benoit lied that he sustained the injuries in his last WWE match to cover up that he had performed numerous high-impact stunts over the past two months at the risk of paralysis.

After the successful surgery, a hard cervical collar was fastened around Benoit's neck, and the surgeon advised him that it would be at least three months before he would be allowed to begin exercising. The very next day, Benoit, with a fresh incision in his pelvis and an unhealed mineshaft in his spinal column, started training by scaling flights of stairs. To overcome the pain, Benoit wolfed down pills.

It was characteristic of Benoit's behavior that he learned nothing from the downfall of Tom Billington, Brian Pillman, and Eddy Guerrero, all of which he personally witnessed and blindly stumbled in their wake as if he had no idea of the consequences.

Tracing the decline in Chris Benoit's mental health is complicated by the considerable evidence that he was always something of a crackpot. Benoit's adolescent infatuation with Tom Billington seems neurotic and pitiful in retrospect; why was an otherwise normal teenage boy so abjectly preoccupied with receiving the approval of a pro wrestler? This fixation became undeniably bizarre when Benoit carried it into adulthood, when most people eventually overcome their adolescent awe of their idols enough to stop compulsively alluding to them in conversation. Benoit never did. His childish idolization of Billington manifested itself in his stalkerish copycatting of the Kid's mannerisms and his blind insistence on performing Dynamite's diving headbutt, despite repeated warnings and daily reminders that it was pulping his brain and destroying his spine.

Benoit's obsessive personality and crippling insecurity were also manifested in his apocalyptic perfectionism in the ring. Only a disturbed person would take pro wrestling so seriously that he runs away, hides, and physically punishes himself after an imperfect performance or proposes to protest an unfair storyline by intentionally breaking his hands on a ringpost on live TV. The complete disregard Benoit's wrestling style displayed for his own body and his future similarly does not suggest that he ever enjoyed pristine emotional health.

By the 2000s, Benoit's existing psychological disorders were being exacerbated by a preposterous number of factors, including catastrophic brain damage, steroid abuse, addiction to amphetamines, alcoholism, persistent excruciating pain, unsupervised use of psychiatric and pain medication, and the daily grind of the road.

Benoit had been an extremely heavy steroid user, which has been tied to depression, mood swings, and all manners of aggressive behavior, since 1985 at the absolute latest and 1980-81 at the earliest. This means that Benoit had been living with highly elevated testosterone levels for many years, and, since there is no reliable scientific evidence for how this might have affected his brain, the exact effects of his habit present a currently irresolvable gap in our understanding of his mental health.

The cumulative stress of the road itself—the monotony, the pressure, the loneliness—was enough to drive many normal men insane by itself. According to Benoit's own father and friends, Benoit was abusing amphetamines to cope and to keep his worn-out body going on the road. A prolonged daily amphetamine user like Benoit might suffer from hallucinations, suicidal depression, violent rages, feelings of paranoia and persecution, and other symptoms resembling an acute case of schizophrenia. Like most steroid users, Benoit was also chasing his roid intake with psychiatric drugs like Valium to fight "the rush"; psychiatric drugs, taken haphazardly without a monitoring physician and mixed with other narcotics, can wreak havoc on even an otherwise healthy person's psychological state.

It is also important to consider the physical toll taken on Benoit's body over his two decades in the wrestling business. The attritional effect of constant pain on a normal psyche can be enough to provoke irritability, anxiety, and suicidal depression, and who knows how the pain pills Benoit was taking were interacting with all the other chemically active substances he was consuming. According to Benoit's father, both Chris and Nancy abused alcohol, which in itself is often fatal when mixed with steroids, psychiatric drugs, amphetamines, and pain pills.

Finally, there is the physical toll on Benoit's brain caused by his head-bump-intensive wrestling style: this includes the chairshots, the dives outside of the ring, the brainbusters and powerbombs and suplexes he took in Japan, and the thousands of diving headbutts he performed, some from the top of ladders and cages. A peer-reviewed medical study showed that a history of frequent concussions in football players has been shown to lead to a great risk of profound behavioral change, including cognitive impairment and suicidal depression. After Benoit's death, another peer-reviewed postmortem medical study of Benoit's brain showed damage so severe that many believe proves Benoit could not be considered responsible for his own actions. Benoit's brain damage was so extensive that, according to neuropathologists who performed the studies, his mind became "disconnected, no longer able to cope with normal life's events and stressors." Such catastrophic damage would likely have been well-advanced by 2001 and 2002, when Benoit's behavior took an extreme turn for the worse.

All of these factors likely played a part in Benoit's psychological and mental degeneration, and, as far as culpability is concerned, the degree to which they all contributed is irrelevant. Each of these negative influences was a direct result of Benoit's voluntary decision to live the lifestyle he did, and the ultimate responsibility for their effects belongs solely to him. Unlike so many in pro wrestling, Benoit's reputation and fame was such that he could have easily retired to take a job as backstage agent and trainer, much like his less-

heralded friend Dean Malenko did in 2001. There was no
compelling financial reason for Benoit to live the life he
did once it became clear it was endangering his long-term
mental and physical health.

Spinal surgery placed this disturbed, brain-
damaged addict at home with his wife and infant son for
an uninterrupted period of a year. During Chris and
Nancy's four-year relationship, both had become
accustomed to living separately for around half the year,
and the transition to full-time cohabitation was likely to
be stressful no matter what the circumstances. Benoit
described feelings of intense anxiety and insecurity
whenever he saw WWE programming and realized that
the pro wrestling business was continuing without him.
Nancy, who had become accustomed to her independence
as a stay-at-home mother, likely felt suffocated having
this intensely needy, unhappy, troubled man in her
presence at all times. Though Benoit was reputed to be
extremely gentle and doting to Daniel, one has to wonder
if Nancy ever worried for his safety in his increasingly
volatile father's presence.

According to coworkers and friends, Chris and
Nancy fought often during Benoit's year-long
rehabilitation. After thirteen years with Kevin Sullivan,
Nancy knew how to fight, both verbally and physically,
and her friends insist that she could hold her own and that
it would be wrong to portray her as a wilting victim of
abuse. "Nancy could fight," one friend told me. "She was a
tough bitch with a fiery temper, to be honest. She could
definitely hold her own." Though Nancy in 2003 would
accuse Benoit of destroying inanimate objects during their
arguments, there is no indication that she ever claimed
that he became physically violent with her until later—
though it hardly seems out of the question.

Though Benoit's rehabilitation from June of 2001
to May of 2002 put incredible stress on his marriage and
psyche, neither would improve when he finally returned to
WWE television. Heralded by a front-page photo in his

hometown newspaper, the *Edmonton Journal*, Chris Benoit returned to WWE in a flat segment with his best friend Eddy Guerrero at a *Raw* in Edmonton.

In his absence, Guerrero had graduated from rehab and was fired immediately afterward for drunkenly attempting to steamroll through the entrance of his gated community in his pickup truck. While fired, he had sobered up for good (from alcohol at least), impressed the wrestling community with tours of the indies and New Japan, won back his estranged wife, and sucked up to McMahon by doing an enormous amount of steroids. The grotesquely veiny, muscular, cobra-necked Guerrero had returned to WWE and was currently enjoying the biggest push of his career, in a feud with Steve Austin. For the segments, McMahon, no stranger to substance abuse, insisted the recovering alcoholic film vignettes in a bar with real beers in his hand. Benoit especially appreciated being able to spend time with Eddy again, who was the only person with whom he felt comfortable being completely honest and forthcoming about his problems. Guerrero was the moderating and calming influence in Benoit's life, an empathetic and warm friend who offered gentle, Gospel-quoting advice on how Benoit should aspire above all to be a loving, forgiving, and understanding person.

Besides Guerrero's return, Benoit had little to be excited about backstage in WWE. While Benoit was recuperating, WWE's fortunes and programming had taken a drastic fall. The McMahon family had let their passion for TV time derail the most potentially profitable angle in wrestling history, WCW and ECW's invasion of WWE. Instead of choosing charismatic, credible outsiders like the available Bischoff or Flair to lead WCW and Heyman to lead ECW, Stephanie nonsensically merged the two philosophically opposed promotions and cast herself—the absolute least credible leader of an anti-WWE faction—as the person supposedly trying to put the company she would inherit out of business. This had the effect of transforming the most compelling storyline in wrestling into the least: McMahon family feud, part 10,000. The angle tanked, losing WWE tens of millions of dollars and causing a panic in management now that the storyline that they had assumed would resuscitate business had only made things worse. WWE was desperate, and Benoit would suffer the consequences.

In a desperate bid for ratings, WWE sold out roster morale by dredging up all the most selfish and unlikable pricks of the 1990's wrestling boom: Hulk Hogan, Kevin Nash, Scott Hall, Eric Bischoff, and Shawn Michaels all joined the WWE locker room. Whatever pride Benoit felt in his workplace disappeared once Hulk Hogan was given yet another multimillion-dollar run on top while he and Eddy were booked to play the nerds who got bullied and zinged by the ever-witty high school bully Kevin Nash. While Eric Bischoff was getting paid six figures, Benoit's friend Perry Saturn suffered an injury and was unceremoniously fired.

WWE became increasingly known within the industry for its bloodthirsty backstage politics (centered around HHH and Michaels) and its repressive, tattling corporate atmosphere rather than its programming excellence. "Everybody's sitting there and they're depressed, they're worried about eyes in the back of their head so they're not getting stabbed in the back," says the Sandman about the WWE locker room.

One backstage source claims that Benoit took out his frustration with the politically inviolate veterans by hazing the younger wrestlers. On two occasions, Benoit supposedly publicly berated young wrestlers for minor transgressions and threw their bags into the hall, telling them they had to dress outside because they weren't worthy of changing with the men. He was also implicated in the frequent bouts of hazing on overseas tours.

Backstage descriptions of Benoit after his return from surgery bring to mind a quiet, distracted loner who strived to be a team player despite his own obvious displeasure. "I worked with Benoit all the time backstage," WWE production assistant and writer Dominick Pagliaro told me. "He was always so intense, like he had the weight of the world on his shoulders. Benoit looked like he was living in a world of shit. When I heard he committed suicide—that was anything but a surprise. He always seemed down, physically and emotionally."

"There was no bravado or bluster in Benoit," says ex-WWE writer Dan Madigan. "He seemed like a gentle guy in a rough business, and the business was eating him up. He seemed broken, insecure, like maybe he had lost something. I remember talking to Paul Heyman about how great Benoit was, and Paul said to me, 'Don't tell me, tell him.' As if the poor guy really needed to hear it. So I walked up to Benoit and said, 'I'm not blowing smoke up your ass, but you're great. I'm in awe every time I watch you.' He just looked at me with this meek look and says, 'Really?' He really didn't realize how good he was, or he never felt secure in it."

"It was Chris Benoit who gave me the advice that, had I followed it, would have let me last in WWE Creative forever," says Dr. Ranjan Chhibber. "I said, 'Hey Chris, as a fellow Canadian, can you give me some advice on how I can survive back here?' Benoit looked around in the corridors backstage in the arena we were at, and he pulled me aside where he knew no one could overhear us. I was expecting a long pep talk, but instead received only one line of advice: 'Just keep your mouth shut.' I said to him, 'That's it?!' He said, 'That's it. You wanna have a job here, just keep your thoughts and opinions to yourself, no matter how wrong the other guys are.'

"Benoit was quiet backstage, for the most part," continues Dr. Chhibber. "I was quite taken aback at how gentle and soft-spoken he was. It was almost as if he was speaking in whispers. He always had a toothpick in his mouth, reminding me of the TV persona of Scott Hall. He was not the kind of guy you would go up to and make small talk with. I remember on one of the rare charter flights that WWE would use to fly all the wrestlers from one city in the US to another, Benoit sat by himself on the plane. I could tell that he wanted to be alone. When Benoit got off the flight, I saw him walk alone, get his bags alone, and head off alone into the night."

"You tend to think there's a lot of camaraderie backstage—the boys are a tight fraternity, you'd figured they'd be *so* tight traveling so much together—but it's shocking how solitary a life it really is," says Dan Madigan. "Those guys are *lonely.* Benoit especially. He looked lost, troubled."

Less than a year after his return to the road, Chris and Nancy separated. On May 12, 2003, she filed for divorce and obtained a restraining order preventing Benoit from moving within 100 yards of Nancy or their three-year-old son, Daniel. In the suit, she alleged that Benoit threatened her, broke furniture in fits of rage, and was guilty of "cruel treatment." Her attorney requested Benoit sign over to Nancy their house in Peachtree, Georgia, a different eight acres of property they owned, their brand-new 2003 Hummer, her share in Wolverine Sports, Inc. (the company through which she managed Benoit's assets and wrestling career), and $8500 a month in child and spousal support. Very few of Benoit's coworkers knew of his marital trouble. Six months later, without any foreseeable explanation, Nancy withdrew the divorce paperwork and dropped the restraining order.

For some unknown reason, perhaps simply love, Nancy let Chris Benoit back into their home. Some of her friends from the wrestling business have speculated that she took Chris back for Daniel's sake. Daniel loved Benoit dearly, and Benoit as far as any outsider could tell was the ideal father.

POWER OF VINCE COMPELS YOU

CHRIS BENOIT: BRAIN-DAMAGED MELTDOWN ARTIST, SADOMASOCHIST, PILL-HEAD, ROID MONSTER, SPEED FREAK, SUICIDAL WRETCH, BLAND THIRTY-SEVEN-YEAR-OLD

CANADIAN TECHNICAL WRESTLER WITH A TITANIUM-PLATED BROKEN NECK AND DISPROPORTIONATELY SHORT T-REX ARMS—AND THE FACE OF A PUBLICLY TRADED MEGA-CORPORATION WITH $364 MILLION IN ANNUAL REVENUE. It's impossible to understand why WWE chose to give Chris Benoit the world heavyweight championship or their unbelievably self-defeating, disingenuous, and stupid response to his death without coming to terms with the madcap braintrust behind America's wrestling monopoly.

Vince McMahon still retains final say over storylines and match results in WWE, but over the years he has gradually lost touch with his audience and his own business. "You can't have an elderly billionaire deciding what the teenagers think is hip," says Dominick Pagliaro. "Vince lives in a 24/7 wrestling world and has no idea about mainstream culture—it's not quite Howard Hughes, but it's not healthy."

"Vince has become the evil character he is on TV," says one former WWE writer. "He's lost it—he's completely consumed in this dream world. As an initiation for all new writers, we are told to ride in the McMahon family limo the first few times on the road. Vince, Stephanie, and HHH were each having their own cell phone calls, and not one person in the family was talking to each other.... Vince was barking into his phone, yelling at his lawyer, Jerry McDevitt: 'Fuck him Jerry! Take him to the cleaners. I want him to know he can't fuck with me!' Stephanie was yelling at someone on her cell phone about making sure her vacation plans with HHH were booked First Class, and that she would not settle for less than the best suite in the hotel. At times, it sounded like she was trying to out-yell Vince. HHH was on his phone, but it was hard to make out a word he was saying, as he would talk in a low mumble a lot of the time. He was the only one smiling and laughing during his phone call.

"All of a sudden, a hand touched my shoulder and said in a comforting voice, 'How are you doing?' It was Linda McMahon. It was like your Mom comforting you in second grade after a bully beat you up at school. Linda could tell I was stressed out, and asked me, 'Have you ever been to this state before?' I believe we were in Nebraska, so I told her I had never been there. Then she began telling me a very interesting story: 'I remember the first time that Vince and I came out here. This was back in the 1980s and we were driving a van to the shows. Vince kept getting lost and everytime I tried to tell him the directions, he wouldn't listen and [would] insist he was going the right way....'

"All of a sudden Vince screams, tossing his cell phone to his side: 'What are you telling him? WHAT THE HELL ARE YOU TELLING HIM?' Even Stephanie and HHH paused their cell phone calls and had the same look of fear that I did. Vince's wrath was directed towards his own wife, and I couldn't believe he would talk to her that way in front of a stranger like myself. Stephanie and HHH started laughing. Stephanie said to her Mom, 'Are you getting senile, Mom? You know not to piss off Dad like that.' And then HHH replied, 'I hope this isn't an early sign of Alzheimer's, Linda!' It really opened my eyes to how Vince is. ...He'd sit in creative meetings and just stare at the wall forever, and then suddenly wake up and go off on a tirade about some irrelevant wrestler for no reason, and then go back into hibernation."

"Vince is fucking nuts," says Dan Madigan. "This guy would unfurl these incredibly awesome storyline ideas, these wonderful insightful monologues, these Shakespearean plotlines that were just *perfect*...and then he'd end it with a fart joke. He's lost his mind.

"I remember when I was working with Carlito [Puerto Rican wrestler Carlos Colon] when he just started. Vince wanted to talk to him to get to know him, and I was asked to attend the meeting to help work out a character. So we're there, Carlito's talking to him, just a normal conversation; Carlito comes from a good background, has money. He speaks well. Vince interrupts Carlito mid-sentence and says to him, 'Hey, can you *spic* it up some?

Y'know, spic it up when you talk?' I look at Vince, this billionaire who just asked some Puerto Rican employee to 'spic it up' right to his face, and I just look at Carlito and say, 'Yeah, spic it up' like it was a joke," says Madigan, laughing. "Vince's image of a Puerto Rican was a Puerto Rican pimp. How out of touch do you have to be to not realize you could get in trouble for that?"

McMahon is not the only member of management to be accused of flouting workplace discrimination laws. According to three former members of the WWE creative team, the writing staff's trio of wrestling veterans— Michael Hayes, Bruce "Brother Love" Pritchard, and Dusty Rhodes—all regularly indulge in racist banter on WWE corporate premises. Hayes is said to have openly referred to Indian writer Dr. Ranjan Chhibber as "the sand nigger" and supposedly regularly drops the word "nigger" in reference to black people during the long, uncomfortable stretches of minstrel humor at the office. "It's such a disgrace to have Pritchard in the front office of a major corporation," said one WWE writer. "This is a guy that walks around shaking violently, looking ill, asking for pain medication, and inexplicably busts out crying during writing meetings. He frequently disappears to deal with 'personal issues.' This is a guy that shouldn't be in management; if this guy is leadership, what does that say about the company?" Considering that Vince McMahon is the CEO, it shouldn't be surprising that chemical dependencies would exist in the upper echelons of WWE.

"Vince is pretty whacked out," says Dominick Pagliaro. "He's in his own little place. I remember I once asked him in his limo how he made it so big, and he just told me, 'I've eaten shit from everybody every day of my life. That's all I do: I *eat shit*.'"

With Vince "increasingly detached from his brain" as one WWE writer put it, day-to-day responsibility fell on Stephanie McMahon, who was promoted to the head of the WWE creative team. Perhaps because of her essential unsuitability for the job, Stephanie defensively conducts herself, according to one pithy observer, "As if she went to college and majored in Everything."

"She tries to impersonate Vince," says Dominick Pagliaro, by far the most sympathetic former coworker of Stephanie's. "She was born into it, trying to ape that Vince swagger. It's a defense mechanism."

"Stephanie liked to think she was Vince Jr.," says Dan Madigan. "Everyone gets bobbleheaded around Vince, won't look at him in the eye when he challenges them. I'm a man, though, and I'd talk to him like him a man, and Stephanie would get all offended. 'You can't talk to Vince that way!' she'd say as if I were insulting her by speaking to him as a normal human. So I told her, 'Stephanie, in all honesty, he's not the pontiff. And even if he were, I still wouldn't keep my mouth shut.' I felt like she was about to scream 'Power of Vince compels you!' as if I was possessed to be speaking of Vince in such a way. She buys into that TV, emperor of the world bullshit. It's reality to her."

"Stephanie's not as smart as she thinks she is," says one former WWE writer. "You can't tell her a damn thing; she was confrontational about her stupidity, like coming up to you and saying 'I know you don't think I deserve this job!' To be honest, put fake tits on a rattlesnake and that's Stephanie. She's a conniving little cunt who I personally saw bury her brother Shane relentlessly to people in the industry, I mean just shit all over her own brother. She's disgusting; she's got that Lady Macbeth ego on her."

Stephanie staffed the WWE writing team with a volatile mixture of spineless toadies with an all-consuming nerd passion for wrestling and outsiders from the conventional entertainment world whom she periodically recruits to "mainstream" WWE. It is the last group, composed of outsiders such as MTV producer Domenic Cotter, film writer and lucha libre historian Dan Madigan, and award-winning academic Dr. Ranjan Chhibber, that enjoys the highest turnover.

"WWE Creative feeds off the insular, batten-down-the-hatches, us-against-the-world, circle-the-wagon attitude," says Dan Madigan. "Everyone's worried about their job, and they screw anyone who shows the talent to get ahead. The only people that survive are the completely talentless hacks and eunuchs willing to tell Stephanie her dumb fucking ideas make sense."

"The way they operate is very, very, unbelievably paranoid," says Domenic Cotter. "You really are made to feel like you had to sell your soul to the whole program or you're suspect. They lived, breathed, sweated, *everything* wrestling. To these guys, the only reason they have to live is to work in WWE, and that makes them kiss unbelievable amounts of ass. They fuck you harder, and more behind your back, than anywhere else I've been. The problem with the WWE is that the people who make it there—the people they rely on to make decisions and guide the company—are completely consumed by wrestling. The guys in creative only talked about wrestling; I mean, they have no conception of the outside world in the least. They really needed to get laid; they needed to get a life. Wrestling 24/7 warps your mind and screws your judgment. I would describe it as a cult-like atmosphere, with these marathon phone calls and unending meetings and endless conversations, all about wrestling."

"They work eighty hours a week and don't pay attention to anything besides the WWE," says Dominick Pagliaro. "That's why they seem so strange, defensive, and out-of-touch when there's a press scandal. That's why you can have guys that, to the outside world, are obviously falling apart, like Benoit or Eddy, and no one there notices it. They live, eat, breathe wrestling and all the dysfunction that comes with it."

For the last few years of Benoit's career in WWE, the two most powerful and notorious of these "comic book guy" writers were *Raw* head writer Brian Gewirtz and eventual *Smackdown* head writer Dave Lagana. "Ah, Lagana and Gewirtz," recalls Dan Madigan. "They live in comic books and wrestling and don't even *visit* the real world."

Dominick Pagliaro speaks for many sources when he says, "Brian Gewirtz will never know the love of a woman, and it was apparent in his writing. Gewirtz is twisted; he could never write a storyline with a three-dimensional female character because he's not aware they exist. He's not the person to rely on for having a tight grasp of reality or human society, and he's the head writer!"

Unfortunately for WWE talent, Dave Lagana was all too aware of all three dimensions of the female (and male) talent. "Lagana was quirky—John Wayne Gacy quirky," says Cotter. "Lagana was without a doubt one of the biggest pieces of shit I have ever come upon, and I have come upon many in my life," says Dan Madigan. "He is a liar, a coward, and a sneak. He is everything that is wrong with wrestling. He is a whore. He would get a business phone call from a wrestler in public and answer it very loudly like, 'Oh, HELLO Stone Cold Steve Austin!' so everyone could hear. He brought Stephanie flowers and gifts and told her that her stupid fucking ideas were good."

"Dave Lagana was a fucking pervert who leveraged his power for sexual favors—guys or girls," says Dominick Pagliaro. "I always knew he was a weirdo. He was always in touch with the women in [the] developmental [territories], like 'What's up baby?' when he saw them. You could tell something was very wrong."

"I heard Human Resources was compiling a strong case against Lagana when they received numerous complaints from young women who were trying to break into the business," Madigan says regarding Lagana's 2008 firing. "It seems that Lagana would answer their queries with demands for sexual favors in return for getting them into the business. I was told the company knew about it for a year, but he was Stephanie's boy so he got a pass. How fucked up is that?

"It finally blew up in his face when he came on to a male wrestler in a bathroom, a wrestler I know and respect very much and will not mention his name in order not to further embarrass him [according to my other sources, Kevin "Thorn" Fertig]. When my friend realized that Lagana's proposition for oral favors was not a joke [reportedly some variation of "How would you like to fuck my face?"] and after he 'flicked his nipples,' the harassed wrestler reported this incident to a very well-respected veteran backstage [reportedly the Undertaker], who marched into Talent Relations and used his cred to finally get something done. That is when it came out in the locker room that Lagana had done the same thing to *several* other male wrestlers. And that's just the ones that admitted it! How many did he do it to that have since left the company or don't want to talk about it? This hadn't just started; it had to be going on for years. I got all of this from several highly respectable and irrefutable sources, all of whom independently confirmed it when all this came out."

With unconditional lackeys Gewirtz and Lagana as her two top lieutenants, Stephanie pushed a hackneyed, heavily scripted, phony product on WWE viewers that had none of the spontaneity and excitement of WWE's golden years. Wrestlers are bad actors, so handing them long, wordy scripts to memorize and then regurgitate on live TV with little rehearsal time made WWE unbearably boring and awkward. "They should call it *Monday Night Contrived*," says Kevin Nash. Thanks to both Stephanie and Vince's fetish for jacked-up physiques, WWE TV was also overrun with "cookie cutter bodybuilders" who, since Stephanie had no appreciation for wrestling skill, were often rushed onto TV with little training. Benoit was "Very upset about [WWE] developmental," according to friend Bryan Alvarez, "Very upset about big musclehead guys coming in with no talent and guys with passion being left out."

"Vince once told me, in a moment of lucidity," says Madigan, "'All I wanted to do was be the biggest wrestling promoter in the world. And I am. But I fucked myself. There's nowhere for my young guys to come up and get seasoned; I've got nothing but green boys who had no idea what to do in the ring. It's embarrassing.'" The immobile bodybuilders who had to overcome their own inexperience and Stephanie's belabored scripts and cheesy gimmicks naturally found it nearly impossible to compete with the popularity level of the already established stars, especially those who were too respected to ever be forced to read from a script.

The primary beneficiaries of the overly rigid show structure were HHH and his mentor Shawn Michaels. Together, they have dominated the main event scene of the WWE *Raw* brand for years with their stale acts by relying on their freedom to do what they please on the microphone and their influence on the booking committee through Levesque's marriage to Stephanie. "There's a certain individual who's in the family now," says Dan Madigan. "And when he says something at an agent or creative meeting, that man's career's over. It's said like a joke, always—but it's dripping with venom, and it gets results. It's called 'ribbing on the square': saying something with a wink and a nod, but letting everyone know it's serious."

"After a *Raw*, Stephanie said she wanted to talk to me," Dr. Chhibber told me. "The other writers had all left, and I knew I was in for some trouble. By then I was known to be an ally of Paul Heyman, who was Stephanie's enemy backstage. I was told to wait in the Writer's Room. Thirty minutes had elapsed, and no sign of Stephanie. Now nearly midnight, I decided to grab some Red Bull to give me some energy....

"Moments later, HHH walked into the room. And for the next thirty minutes, he proceeded to tell me how to be a good writer, and why I was failing as one. Last I looked at the company corporate chart, HHH was not an official member of WWE Creative. But the way he was talking to me, it sounding like a manager reprimanding me. First and foremost, he said that I had picked the wrong people to work with, and that by associating oneself with a failing team, I would go down with that team. He said, 'Paul E and his friends couldn't care less about you.

They're just using you, Ranjan. They want to see you fail.
They're setting you up to fail. You should hear what they
say about you behind your back. If I was you, I would say,
'Fuck those guys.' You should help Brian [Gewirtz] and
Stephanie whenever you can. They really want to see you
succeed, as do I.'

"He continued to give me advice so that I 'would be
with the company as long as [Bruce] Pritchard has been
there.' Being compared to Pritchard was not something I
liked, and I realized that to stay in this company would
mean being the lowest form of vermin on earth," says Dr.
Chhibber, who would go on to serve as an officer in the
Canadian Navy. "While he was talking, VP of Talent
Relations, Johnny Ace, walked in. Apparently, I was
booked to ride on his limo to the airport, so that we could
fly to the next town where *Smackdown* was to be taped the
next day. And he had no idea why I wasn't on the limo. He
looked at me, and then saw HHH. HHH gave him this
nasty stare, and Johnny Ace's lip almost trembled.
Clearly, I could see that HHH was the one in charge here.
HHH then said, 'We're busy Johnny. Just wait in your
limo.' By the time I got to the limo, Johnny was treating
me like I was HHH's son. He was asking me about shows,
about some women wrestlers who had tryouts, and many
other things which no one had cared to ask me before."

"The one thing I wonder about HHH is: how could
you love Steph?" says Madigan. "It's a work, man. Lemme
tell you a story. I was riding in the McMahon family limo.
Stephanie was sleeping in Vince's arms in that creepy way
that starts all those rumors about them. I caught HHH
watching Stephanie nuzzled into her father like a baby,
and, lemme tell you, the look I saw wasn't a look of love.
It was this contemptuous, objectifying look, like: yeah, I
got it, I got the world in my hands, I got the prize ham at
the fair. It was an ugly look. Our eyes met for a second,
and he laughed and shrugged, like he dropped the act for
a second and he didn't give a shit that I noticed."

In addition to the prospect of inheriting WWE in the future, HHH along with a few choice veterans enjoys more humble perks, like the right to receive medical treatment for his injuries and time off to rehabilitate whenever he needs it. "Aaron Aguilera was a young wrestler that was well-liked backstage; even Stephanie and HHH liked him," says one ex-writer. "But then he ran afoul of Michael Hayes. Hayes saw Aguilera using the WWE's chiropractor backstage one night. Hayes immediately reported this to Vince McMahon and poisoned McMahon's mind that this young guy was using these free services meant for only established WWE stars (there was no written rule about this but rather some old carny philosophy that only the big names deserved medical treatment). Hayes ordered agents to spy on Aguilera, and one day, when Aguilera had a very minor injury, he went to the WWE's full-time trainer on *Smackdown*.

"At a subsequent creative meeting to discuss future *Smackdown*, a storyline concerning Aguilera came up. Vince immediately said, 'It's time to end our association with that asshole. I've had reports that he's already made good friends with our trainers and chiropractors. We don't have time to invest in pussies like that.' The story reached other WWE wrestlers, and they all kept their injuries and pain to themselves from then on. I saw only untouchable stars like The Undertaker and HHH using the chiropractors and trainers after that. No one else dared to. Wrestlers who had busted their lips in matches were even treating those minor cuts themselves. They were afraid that Hayes would rat them out. Hayes was the same guy who always suggested that Benoit and the other wrestlers get hit in the heads with chairs; he used to say, 'C'mon, it's not like he can't take it!' and 'Boom! RIGHT IN THE HEAD!'"

"The worst thing I ever witnessed in the WWE was at *Wrestlemania XIX* [in 2003] when Kurt Angle faced Brock Lesnar in the main event," says Pagliaro. "Angle was suffering from really severe neck and spinal problems—he needed surgery immediately. His doctor told him that if he wrestled that match against Lesnar, he probably wouldn't be able to stand up and walk out of the ring; he'd be paralyzed. So Kurt goes to McMahon and tells him this, and I watch Vince. Vince just looks at him and is like, 'Yes, you could *not* wrestle the match, or you could wrestle the match,' in this way that was Vince very subtly letting him know that, even knowing that he might be paralyzed, he expected him to wrestle that match. It was implied, 'Unless you are dead, you're wrestling.' I watched Kurt after that match, and he was laid out on the floor spasming out of control and foaming at the mouth and just in unimaginable pain and fear for his life. They had to call in the medics—you can watch, and you'll see Kurt was never the same after." In the aftermath of that match, Angle's arms developed the localized atrophy associated with severe spinal damage, and he allegedly developed an addiction to pain pills so severe that WWE released him so as not to be held responsible in case he dropped dead.

When it came time to decide the next year's *Wrestlemania* main event, the lucky wrestler who would receive the biggest payday of the year was largely chosen because of his own history of displaying the sort of "courage" that permanently ruined Angle's body and quality of life the year before. Though there was little debate that HHH and Michaels would somehow end up in the main event together, their singles feud was extremely stale. There needed to be a variable inserted into their familiar match to make it a viable main event. Since there were no obvious choices, McMahon threw the question to both the creative team and road agents, the veteran wrestlers who helped plan each match and coach the young stars backstage.

Paul Heyman and Michael Hayes championed Benoit on the creative team, but the decisive response was from the road agents, who unanimously supported Chris

Benoit as a "lifetime achievement award" pick, a wrestler who should finally receive his reward for all that he had done in the business. There is some dispute whether HHH and Stephanie opposed Benoit's main event spot; Dominick Pagliaro insists to me that they did, and Paul Heyman insists that they didn't. Furthermore, Pagliaro claims that Heyman took disproportionate credit for pushing Benoit in WWE and calls Heyman "one of these pieces of shit who only cares about himself...one of those vengeful mean guys who would fuck you if you stepped in his way." To this appraisal, Heyman replies, "Was the janitor unavailable? I think you, as a reporter, know to consider the source. You can't possibly expect me to take his statement with any credibility, can you? You would shock me if you put any faith into that bonehead."

Regardless, the main event was decided when Vince McMahon, to the surprise of many, fully endorsed Benoit as the headliner: it would be "Benoit's medal" for long service, for working injured countless times, for always being a loyal, hardworking, and obedient employee. Perhaps more importantly, it would be a wonderful labor management tool: wrestlers would learn that if keep your mouth shut, juice up your body, work through the most dangerous injuries, and accept whatever treatment is given to you then maybe, one day, you might receive the ultimate prize. This effect was only compounded by Eddy Guerrero's successful defense of *Smackdown*'s top title in the semi-main event. Benoit and Guerrero had finally proven their detractors wrong, and all it cost was their lives.

NOW THAT'S A CHAMPION

CHRIS BENOIT'S LAST GREAT RUN IN THE WRESTLING BUSINESS BEGAN IN THE CITY WHERE THE CRIPPLER WAS BORN A DECADE BEFORE: PHILADELPHIA. The January 25, 2004 *Royal Rumble* PPV hosted the seventeenth annual thirty-man battle royal which awarded the winner a world title shot at *Wrestlemania* two months later. Chris Benoit was the first wrestler to enter the ring, and, sixty-one minutes later, he would be the last man standing, winning the prestigious Royal Rumble match by using a guillotine chokehold, one of the first shoot submission holds taught to him by the Harts, to drag the seven-foot, 500-pound Paul "Big Show" Wight over the top rope. Benoit's victory set the record for the longest performance in Royal Rumble history, a sign of WWE's faith in his ability to keep himself interesting for an uninterrupted hour of action. As Benoit fell to his knees and shook his fists at the ceiling, Benoit's hardcore wrestling fanbase on the Internet celebrated; a babyface winner of the *Rumble* never loses at *Wrestlemania*. Benoit would get his long-deserved world title run.

The storyline leading up to *Wrestlemania* itself was underwhelming. Instead of building a coherent storyline with depth between Benoit and the champion, HHH, most of the TV shows concentrated on tortured attempts to find a compelling reason to shoehorn middle-aged Shawn Michaels into the match despite the crowd's disinterest. Though Benoit was the fresh face who had just won the biggest match of his career at the *Rumble*, *Raw* still revolved entirely around the HHH and Shawn show. "The 'diminishing' of Benoit's importance was a total con by HHH and Shawn in the agent meetings," says a then-major player in the WWE writing team. "HHH and Shawn made sure Benoit never got accepted as a main eventer by the audience, by the agents, and therefore by Vince."

On March 14, 2004, a capacity crowd filled Madison Square Garden for the twentieth anniversary of *Wrestlemania*. The Chris Benoit vs. Shawn Michaels vs. HHH main event was a noticeably low-anticipation main event, with little of the "electricity" in the crowd that normally distinguishes the biggest PPV match of the year. Before the match, Eddy visited Benoit in the locker room in what was meant to be one of Stephanie's poignant soap opera moments, two best friends and underdogs reassuring each other that, even if no one else believes in them, they believe in each other. It is a monument to Eddy Guerrero's talent that he makes the segment believable despite Benoit's limited acting ability and Stephanie's typically contrived writing.

Benoit paces back and forth, his slicked-back hair accentuating what seems to be an enlarged skull, a side effect of human growth hormone abuse. Benoit's face looks prematurely old, flat, and sharklike, and his arms are so swollen even for him that it's clear he upped his dosage for his big night. As Benoit paces, Guerrero applies the pressure, "All the years that you put into it, working out, the time away from your family, working through the injuries...." reminding him of everything real he had sacrificed to earn this fictional match with its real payday and prestige.

The crowd response to all three wrestlers' entrance was noticeably lukewarm, a sign of how hard it is to properly build a convoluted three-way feud instead of a traditional *mano a mano* storyline. The match began with a prolonged period of clichéd three-way-dance tropes, in which one wrestler is taken out of the action so the other two can wrestle, only for the injured wrestler to ambush whoever has the advantage at the opportune, just-in-the-nick-of-time moment to prevent a pinfall. As the match progressed, it became clear the crowd didn't want to see Michaels in the match, booing him every time he asked for their support. Twenty-three minutes into the match, Benoit locked his Crippler Crossface submission hold on HHH and, after a particularly long and courageous fight for a supposed heel, HHH tapped out, making Benoit the champion. Tame for much of the show, the hardcore New York City crowd exploded when Chris Benoit, the ultimate everyman, the nicest guy in wrestling, the man many believed to be the most underrated and underappreciated wrestler in WWE, finally got his due.

"Chris Benoit's eighteen-year odyssey has culminated in winning the world's heavyweight title at *Wrestlemania XX!*" screamed Jim Ross with a voice that sounded like he was gargling fire, as Benoit cried into his bloody hands and hugged the heavyweight championship belt. As confetti cascaded from the ceiling, Benoit was joined by his best friend, Eddy Guerrero, who successfully defended the other version of the world title at *Wrestlemania*. Together, the two men who fans believed typified everything good about pro wrestling shared their miraculous moment together, the breach in wrestling convention that allowed a 5'9" Canadian who couldn't talk and a 5'6" Mexican-American with a homely face to follow in the footsteps of Hulk Hogan and become WWE world champions.

Eddy quickly left the ring so Benoit could have his moment alone in the spotlight, and Nancy, tiny Daniel (dressed in a vest and tie), his father Michael, and his eldest son David joined him in the ring. Benoit hugged Daniel with his bloody hand, clutching him to his sweaty chest as the confetti continued to fall. Backstage, after the celebration, Eddy and Chris kneeled together in deference to Eddy's faith and prayed. Standing up, Eddy kissed Chris on the cheek and told him, "I love you man. I'm so happy for you. Nobody deserves it more."

"That was a defining moment in my career," Benoit said in an interview shortly afterwards. "I had all these thoughts going through my mind. Visions of training with Stu Hart, my first matches in Calgary and Edmonton, those years working on the road, going to Japan, Mexico, Europe, WCW, ECW, WWE.... A hundred years from now, at *Wrestlemania 120*, they'll look back and see Chris Benoit made Triple H tap out at Madison Square Garden. It was such a huge event that carried so much meaning, it's hard to find the accurate words to describe it."

After Benoit's victory, Stephanie McMahon made a disgusted face and told Dan Madigan, "This isn't going to last. He isn't like Shawn: the guys don't wanna be him, and the girls don't wanna fuck him. He's just drab and bland." After a five-month title reign distinguished largely by how minimal a role he played on television and how little respect his championship was given, Benoit lost the title cleanly to HHH's protégé Randy Orton, a bodybuilder with a gay porn-star look and an infamous record for sexually harassing WWE employees who rejected his advances.

Shortly afterwards, Dr. Ranjan Chhibber left WWE. He remembers Benoit as a kind and gentle man who treated him with respect. "When I first approached Benoit to introduce myself backstage, he interrupted me and said, 'Were you at an autograph signing at *Wrestlemania* in Toronto a few years ago?' I was flabbergasted. I couldn't believe he remembered me. I was just some fan, and years later he recognized me and remembered our conversation. That really defined Chris Benoit to me, the Chris Benoit I knew: a man who was a hero and legend to so many who carried himself with uncommon gentleness and humility."

Chapter XIII
The Call

"In wrestling, the term is known as 'the call.'
For those who have been around for decades,
it's someone you know, their voice cracking.
Usually they start rambling before they say
anything, and you immediately know it's
'the call.' Somebody well known in the
profession, and usually somebody you know
personally, has just died."

DAVE MELTZER
Wrestling Observer *newsletter, May 9, 2005*

"HEAVEN NEEDED A LOWRIDER"

IN THE SIX YEARS SINCE OWEN HART'S DEATH, over
two dozen of Chris Benoit's former colleagues and
traveling partners had died prematurely due to
complications from their longtime consumption of the
"wrestler's cocktail" of steroids and drugs. Even if we limit
that number to just "name" wrestlers who worked for
major national promotions, a by-no-means comprehensive
review leaves fourteen *famous* victims of the wrestling
lifestyle: Gary Albright (age 37), Bobby Duncum, Jr. (34),
Terry Gordy (40), Russ Haas (27), Big Dick Dudley (36),
Davey Boy Smith (39), Rocco Rock (49), Curt Hennig (44),
Pitbull #2 (38), Road Warrior Hawk (46), Crash Holly (32),
The Wall (37), Hercules Hernandez (46), and Big Bossman

(41). This fatality list does *not* include the wrestlers Benoit knew who died from 1985 to May of 1999 or those left crippled; these are just fourteen major coworkers and friends who died within that six year period. It shouldn't be a surprise that Benoit, in addition to being a profoundly brain-damaged speed addict and alcoholic, felt increasingly paranoid and depressed because his professional brotherhood was suffering from a wartime attrition rate.

In the months leading up to his death, Eddy Guerrero was depressed, likely for many of the same reasons as Benoit. His first run had stalled because of an emotional flameout; after years of striving to succeed, the sensitive and insecure Guerrero had found the pressure of "carrying the strap" too heavy to bear. Without the title, Guerrero doggedly refocused himself on perfecting his act, improving his body, and building up his strength so that he could succeed if he was given another chance at the top. Two WWE insiders report allegedly seeing Dean Malenko, his close friend, giving the recovering drug addict Eddy painkillers to keep him going despite his body breaking down.

A third WWE source finds this chilling story plausible. "It was always a big joke by the Malenkos that Joe Malenko was a great hookup for the Japanese bookers who wanted Vicodin and Xanax. Joe is a pharmacist in Tampa. Dean used to joke about it when he talked about why the Japanese liked his brother more than him. I would not be surprised if the story you heard is true." Dominick Pagliaro, who worked often with Eddy, believes that only wrestling people could have missed Eddy's advanced degenerative state. "Eddy looked dead on his feet some days, just fuckin' awful looking and ill and broken. You could tell he was not in a good way, that he was just beat to shit."

By late 2005, Guerrero's charisma, comedic talent, and inherent likeability had made him arguably WWE's top ratings and attendance draw, a "Latino Stone Cold" whose humor subverted a stereotypical sneaky Mexican character. Despite his track record for unreliability, on November 12, the writing team decided to give Eddy the belt once again. This time, Guerrero would crown his long career with a title reign that would go down as one of the most entertaining and fulfilling of all time.

The next morning, Eddy's nephew Chavo called hotel security after Eddy failed to respond to repeated phone calls or knocks on his door. It had always been said that they'd find Eddy dead in a hotel room one day. When security opened the door, they found Eddy gently slumped over in the hotel bathroom, fresh toothpaste on his toothbrush. The first person Chavo called was Benoit, who came up to see the corpse, which he embraced and tenderly kissed as paramedics were taking it away.

As always, Eddy Guerrero greatly exceeded expectations: instead of dying of a drug overdose in his early thirties as everyone assumed, Eddy died of steroid-induced heart disease at the comparatively ancient age of thirty-eight. In the words of his wife Vickie, "The blood vessels were very worn and narrow, and that just showed all the abuse from the scheduling of work and his past. And Eddie just worked out like crazy all the time. It made his heart grow bigger and work harder, and the vessels were getting smaller, and that's what caused the heart failure." Bench presses and curls don't jack up the heart to elephantine proportions but heavy steroid abuse does. Damaged by steroids and overtaxed from supporting a gigantic artificial buildup of muscles, Eddy's heart simply quit one morning while he brushed his teeth.

"Eddy literally was the nicest person on the fucking planet," says Dan Madigan. "He was one of the amazing people I've had the honor to work with. When I was really down when my wife lost her baby and her father, he walks up to me, a casual acquaintance, and says, 'Dan, Jesus loves you and so do I. If you need me, just tell me.' For weeks after that, he kept checking on me, telling with sincerity and empathy how concerned he was for me. I've heard stories: he would've done anything for me, for anyone. He was everyone's best friend.

"Unfortunately, I was not surprised by his death. These guys who wrestle on the juice stay on the juice; they don't cycle. They're just *on* until they retire—it destroys their heart. It's never a surprise when they drop dead, unfortunately."

In the aftermath of the Eddy's death, *Wrestling Observer* editor Dave Meltzer was speaking with a former WWE world champion. "We expected it to be huge news the next day, and it wasn't news at all. I mean, nobody even picked up on it. And here you had a guy that died. It was steroids and growth hormone right across the board. Eddie was on those Latino TV commercials and was really at his peak as a personality. It was like a nonstory. My thought was, 'Okay, now I know. I don't care if there's two hundred people that died—this will never become a story. You will never have a bigger star than Eddie Guerrero die with steroids right on his death certificate. It will never happen again."

In his review of the Eddy Guerrero memorial episode of WWE's Friday Night *Smackdown*, Dave Meltzer stated that the "last memory" of "the most emotional and arguably the most memorable pro wrestling television show in history" was "seeing Chris Benoit break down over the loss of his best friend of 15 years. In a world of fantasy, there was nothing any more real than that."

In fact, Chris Benoit had two emotional breakdowns on WWE broadcasts, both of which were the main focus of their respective shows. The November 15, 2005 *Raw* began with a ten-bell salute witnessed by the entire WWE roster standing on the stage, the WWE cameras lingering on Chris Benoit's tears. Later in the show, Benoit delivered his personal tribute to Eddy Guerrero seated in front of a blank, photography studio background, his face in close-up staring directly at the camera.

Eddy Guerrero is my best friend. I'm sure there's a lot of people that he knew that would be able to say the same thing about him. He was such a beautiful person. He was such a kindhearted person. I couldn't find the right words—words couldn't describe what kind of human being Eddy truly was. I've known Eddy for fifteen years and spent a good portion of those fifteen years together. ...He was the one friend that I had that I could go to and pour my heart out to, if I was going through something, if I had a personal issue or a personal problem. He was the one guy that I could call and talk to and know that he'd understand and know that he would *talk me out of it.* We never left each other without telling each other that we loved each other, and I truly can say that I love Eddy Guerrero. He's a man that I can say that I love, and I love his family. And my thoughts, and my hearts, and my prayers go out to his family...I can't imagine the sorrow they're going through right now.... And Eddy, I know that you're in a better place, and I know that you're looking down on me right now, and know that I love you. And I miss you.

At this point, Chris Benoit the most stoic, tough, poker-faced wrestler in WWE history finally cracks and explodes into deep, wailing, literally boo-hooing sobs. He continues, choking through the tears:

"Eddy you *made*, you made such a great impression on my life, and I want to thank you for everything you've ever given me, and I want to thank you from my heart and tell you that I love and I'll never forgot you. And that *we'll see each other again*, and I love you Eddy." Benoit's face swings downward, literally falling off screen.

"Ladies and gentlemen, the word love is often overused, but not in this case," *Smackdown*'s Michael Cole announced grandly as he introduced Benoit for the main event of the November 18 episode. "Chris Benoit *loved* Eddy Guerrero. Chris Benoit was Eddy Guerrero's very best friend. He was with Eddy through all of his highs and all of his lows. No one knew Eddy Guerrero better than that man, Chris Benoit." Cole's co-announcer Peter "Tazz" Senerchia added, "Both of these men have been up and down the ropes together, have trained and dieted and stayed in hotels and rented rent-a-cars and been on airplanes—throughout the world, Benoit and Guerrero have traveled together.

"I tried earlier tonight to speak with Chris Benoit," Tazz continues in a tone that gives the impression that talking to Benoit was a difficult and awkward task, "In this empty arena earlier in the day, Chris Benoit...was training—he was doing Hindu squats and running the steps. That's how Chris Benoit channels his frustrations, anger, and emotions."

The difference between Chris Benoit's stoic, businesslike demeanor in the Owen Hart tribute match and his full-throttled emotional breakdown in his match for Eddy Guerrero six years later is apparent immediately upon Benoit's entrance. The close-up camera angle as Benoit breaks through the entrance curtain reveals raw, eviscerating, uncomfortably "in your face" agony. The Chris Benoit of 2005 looks roughly fifteen years older and a few steps backwards on the human evolutionary ladder than the Chris Benoit of 1999: His face is rawboned and worn, his eyes crimson-webbed and sore, his wet hair thinning over his human-growth-hormone-enlarged mutant brow, his mouth erratically gasping for air that he hopes will let him keep his emotions under control. From the neck up, Benoit with his unhealthy pallor, half-ass beard, and blotchy skin resembles a cirrhotic drunk on a barstool, but somehow this sickly head is welded onto the oiled, muscular, absurdly thick body of a pro wrestler who knows his livelihood depends on it.

Paired against HHH in the show's main event, Benoit turns in a technically fine but pointedly unrestrained performance. His trademarked "Canadian chops" to the chest, already notoriously stiff, were delivered in a wild, flailing, exhaust-pipe bursts, as if this is the only release Benoit had been able to find for his emotions. When Benoit screams in pain from a HHH move, his voice is a distinctly haggard howl. The only words the audience hears Benoit say that night are short, angry barks of in-ring banter: wails of "NO-O! NO-O!" when he's in pain, ferocious screams of "TAP! TA-AP!" when he wants his opponent to "tap out," the heaving growls and grunts of battle as Benoit throws strikes and executes moves.

After Benoit wins the match with a fluke rollup, his self-control immediately collapses, as if by winning the match Benoit has dispensed with the one thing important enough to distract him from his anguish. Benoit rolls onto his knees, throws his fists to cover his spontaneously weeping eyes, and in a strikingly visceral image of authentic horror, removes his fists to expose inflamed, raving mad eyes that look up to heaven with helpless desolation and fear. Benoit stands up and begins to throttle his sweaty, jiggling, huge left pectoral muscle in hysterical grief, punching his heart with visually palpable force, beating out a quick rhythm and turning to the crowd to let them know he wants them to chant "Ed-dy! Ed-dy! Ed-dy!" to the beat. His face contorted into a pinched, crimson scowl, Benoit collapses onto the sweaty chest of the far taller Levesque, openly weeping, as Levesque takes a sudden nurturing turn: cradling Benoit's head as if he were a child, hugging him tightly, and lowering his own head to rest consolingly against Benoit's wet brow. The camera pans to the crowd, to fans waving homemade signs that read "Latino Heaven" and "Heaven needed a lowrider—*vaya con dios*, Eddie."

"How fuckin' tacky was the Eddie Guerrero tribute? Are you fuckin' ribbin' me?" raged Scott Hall in an interview. "I've worked for Vince long enough to know that when the broadcasters are out there, [Jim] Ross and [Jerry] Lawler are sitting out there, it's people in the back telling them in their earpiece what to say. Mention this, mention this, say this, say that. So they'd have some matches and Lawler would go, 'I'm tellin' ya, that's one match Eddie Guerrero would have really liked.' And I'm goin', oh my god! Are you fuckin' ribbin' me? Eddie Guerrero would have rather been sitting at home with his daughters on his lap. What the fuck are you talking about, he would have liked this match? Just fuckin' brutal."

For a tribute to a man who died thanks to his career-necessitated abuse of steroids and illicit drugs, there was a great deal of unintentionally ironic praise for Eddy's obsessive devotion to the pro wrestling industry. Dave Batista crowed like a hyperactive televangelist: "Eddy Guerrero *loved* this business...he ate, he breathed, he slept, he *bled* this business! And no matter how much pain he was in, when he stepped through that curtain all that pain went away and he found peace in the ring." The more knowledgeable wrestling fans watching at home thought to themselves, *Exactly*. That was the entire problem; wrestling was a lifestyle that methodically killed off those who loved it and bought into it the most.

And Vince McMahon—the man who had fired Eddy in 2002 after he repeatedly failed at kicking his addictions, who put Eddy back on the road despite Eddy's outrageous steroid abuse, who put Eddy back on the road knowing his longstanding inability to live a stable life while wrestling, who had decided to give Eddy the world title a second time despite his obvious physical degeneration and the psychiatric problems caused by his first title reign—was less than credible when he shed arduously dredged-up tears for the camera. The entire industry knew that, if he was at all concerned about the deaths of his employees, McMahon had the power to instantly fix pro wrestling's deadly dysfunctional culture with four easy steps that would entail a financially negligible sacrifice for the hugely profitable WWE:

1. Breaks in the schedule so that wrestlers could physically recuperate, and recognition from management that maintaining long-term physical viability is more important than working through injuries.

2. Comprehensive drug and steroid testing without any loopholes.

3. A decision by management to no longer hire and promote only wrestlers with clearly unnatural, chemically enhanced physiques.

4. Comprehensive pension and healthcare plans so
that aging workers released by WWE would not be forced
to wrestle for decades past their physical prime in
increasingly abysmal conditions simply to survive.

These four easy changes have been suggested by
countless experts, respected veterans, and pro wrestling
legends for decades, but McMahon has always ignored
their advice. He has in effect neglected to save dozens of
lives and alleviate the suffering of the incomprehensible
number of former WWE/WCW wrestlers who will make it
to crippled, enfeebled, impoverished old age—all in
exchange for slightly larger billion-dollar fortune and
slightly more extortionate control over his employees.

Instead, after the death of Eddy Guerrero, a man
who had made the McMahon family tens of millions of
dollars, the publicly grieving Vince McMahon essentially
trivialized Eddy's death.

McMahon instituted a program of compulsory drug
tests to prevent a similar tragedy, a program that is now
notorious for its ineffectivenes and glaring loopholes that
allow "prescription" drugs obtained through a mark doctor.

McMahon also hired Eddy's cash-strapped widow,
the beloved Vickie, for an on-camera role as a WWE
manager, putting her in storylines where she was asked to
portray herself as a greedy, dishonest, melodramatic
shrew who exploited her grief over Eddy as an excuse to
betray and verbally abuse Eddy's friends. In addition, it
was insinuated on WWE television that Vickie had
venally bilked Eddy's estate.

Of course, Vince McMahon was right to provide
financial help for Eddy Guerrero's family. At Eddy's
funeral, one of his brothers allegedly lobbied for a job by
loudly apologizing to Vince for any inconvenience or
embarrassment caused to him by the death of his baby
brother. Still, McMahon, whose family fortune is at least
eight zeroes deep, could have supported Eddy's children in
a way that did not require the bereaved mother to make a
globally broadcast mockery of his death and her own

integrity. How could Vickie turn him down? One can only imagine the inner-turmoil felt by Benoit when WWE booked him in a feud against Chavo and Vickie, during which Benoit was told in front of millions that Eddy did not love him as much as he thought and that Benoit's continued grief over Eddy was preventing Vickie from moving on with her life. Benoit did complain to WWE Creative when they booked Randy Orton to tell Vickie that "Eddy's in hell."

FOOTSTEPS

ON JANUARY 28, 2006, CHRIS BENOIT'S BEST FRIEND LEFT IN THE WRESTLING BUSINESS, VICTOR "BLACK CAT" MAR, DIED OF A MASSIVE HEART ATTACK. The New Japan office knew that Mar and Benoit were like brothers, and they reached out to Scott Norton, once his best friend on the tour bus, to tell him. Norton initially demurred due to Benoit's bizarre behavior over the past eight years, but he eventually agreed. A close friend of Mar himself, Norton knew how badly Benoit would be hurt by the death of the universally admired Cat, whose reputation as a wonderful man was on par with Eddy Guerrero's.

"I called him and he was so messed up I couldn't believe it," Norton wearily told me. "He was worse than I had ever heard before. He told me he was having such a hard time with Eddy and with Black Cat. He said, 'Scott, I really need to talk to you about this. I have to work tonight, but after that, please wait up. I need to talk.' So I waited up all night, and he never called. That was it for me; I was done with him for good."

Less than three weeks later, Benoit's *next* best friend in wrestling, Mike "Johnny Grunge" Durham, who also happened to be his neighbor and primary hometown social partner, died of a heart attack. Dave Meltzer referred him to as "the stereotype of a wrestler who lives to be loaded" in his orbituary. Sadly, Durham left two small children fatherless.

Mourning the premature death of almost his entire social circle and support system, Benoit was experiencing the bitter loneliness that most healthy men normally experience in their seventies or eighties. Benoit became anxious and paranoid, intensely aware of his own mortality. As he became more withdrawn, his fear festered in the cold, dark pit of his increasingly twisted and alienated-from-reality mind.

Benoit's grief over Eddy's death had been so excessive that Nancy bought him a devotional journal as a way for him to work out his feelings. It had the Christian poem *Footsteps* on the cover and quotes from Scripture on the bottom of the pages—an allusion to Eddy's faith, which Benoit had taken up during his grief. Inside this journal are letters to Eddy handwritten over a period of eleven days after his death. "Oh Eddie, I forgot to tell you about my dream last night. I dreamt that both my parents were taken, perished. And Nancy and I were trying to get to her parents in Daytona to save them, because we felt that they were being taken next. And these people after them were very powerful people, high-ranking people. When we got to Daytona, it was too late; her parents were gone too, perished."

Benoit told Eddy about how he feared his lurking, unnamed enemies and how he felt strong premonitions of his own death. "I will be with you soon," Benoit promised Eddy. Peppering his letters with biblical quotes, Benoit compared Eddy to Job, the Bible's most grievously mistreated victim, whose suffering, unlike Eddy's, was inflicted by God—not himself.

"Chris was totally paranoid," said his father Michael in a TV interview. "They said that the chauffeur that actually used to drive him home from the airport at times said Chris would tell him, 'Take a different route. I don't want anyone to follow me home.' They had their son in a locked-down school so no one would kidnap him. They moved into this new house with large fencing all around and went out and got trained German Shepherds to protect the house because people were after them."

In his letters to Eddy, the only subjects that broke Benoit's paranoid schizophrenic spell were Nancy and

Daniel, both of whom he wrote about tenderly. Nancy was "his best friend," and by now we all know what happens to Benoit's best friends. "Chris loved Daniel," said Benoit's father. "He didn't love him, he *adored* him, absolutely adored him. Chris would be on the road; he'd be dragging his rear-end. You'd talk to him; he'd seem down, depressed. You'd say, 'Boy, this life is sure taking it out of him. I don't know why he doesn't get out.' And you'd say 'How's Daniel doing?' And his whole demeanor would change. It'd just light up. He just loved that kid so much."

Benoit's friends and coworkers from WWE all remember him as an especially warm, attentive, and doting father. "I remember a specific incident when he had his son on the road and he was so loving with him," says Domenic Cotter. "He seemed like a very happy, sweet dad, picking up his kid and giving him a kiss." Dan Madigan recalls the celebration backstage at *Wrestlemania XX*. "I remember watching Benoit with his son backstage, and I never saw such a strong, tough, gruff-looking guy look so gentle and loving." Even Dominick Pagliaro, whose memories of Benoit are of a wretched man, asserts that "Only when his family was around did he seem happy, like he was light on his feet and an extremely proud of them."

Contrary to unsubstantiated rumors dishonestly advanced by Linda McMahon on *Good Morning America* and other WWE representatives in the aftermath of his murder, there is no evidence to suggest Daniel suffered from the learning disability Fragile X or any other form of mental retardation. By claiming inside knowledge of stress within the Benoit family over Daniel's fabricated mental disabilities, WWE sullied the memory of Daniel Benoit in a desperate attempt to shield the wrestling culture from taking any blame for Benoit's mental breakdown.

Daniel was a small but extremely energetic and happy child who had been raised to be very polite around strangers. Whenever he attended WWE events, he was always in a suit; idolizing his father, Daniel mimicked his father's pre-match warm-up exercises backstage in his formal attire. Otherwise, he stayed close to Nancy, to whom Daniel was so attached that family members joked he would one day ask his mom to the prom. Wrestling legend "Superstar" Billy Graham remembers meeting Nancy and Daniel backstage at a WWE event. While he talked with Nancy about how much she enjoyed being "a boring old housewife" and making gift baskets as a hobby, Daniel became hyperactive, running around the room, away from the boring old people. Benoit walked in the room, saw Daniel, and fixed a harrowing, dark stare on Nancy. "You better keep an eye on *my* kid," he barked at her in a gruff voice. "In no uncertain terms, he put the eyeball on Nancy," says Graham.

The Benoits' marriage collapsed in the aftermath of Eddy's death due to a decline in the sobriety and psychological stability of both Chris and Nancy. During the last few months of their lives, steroids were the most contentious issue in the Benoit household. Nancy blamed Benoit's sudden sexual impotence and erratic behavior almost entirely on his "bee stinging"—her pet term for steroids and other injected drugs. Fearing for her life, Nancy argued with Chris to stop using steroids and even went as far as to hide or throw away his drugs when he went on the road, which precipitated extremely violent fights.

Friends report that Nancy was frequently beaten and bruised, something they had never noticed before, and on occasion Benoit would lock her in their fortress of a house against her will. "Are you trying to say this is how you grew up, watching your dad call your mom names and making her cry? No. Then what gives you the right," Nancy wrote Benoit in a text message from her cellular phone. Benoit emotionally tortured Nancy with hints that he was having an affair with a certain WWE diva (which my WWE sources have denied). When Benoit supposedly took phone calls from this diva in Nancy's presence, he made ostentatious gestures of secrecy to make her jealous.

"I will not accept this steroid induced roller coaster ride of emotional abuse," wrote Nancy in a text message to

Benoit on May 9, 2007. "Ignoring the problem or running away isn't going to help you face it. You need professional [help] and only if you're fully honest about all of it." Later that day, she wrote to Benoit that it was obvious to everyone that he was abusing steroids and that "we both know the [WWE drug testing] wellness program is a joke." Nancy even blamed Benoit's drug abuse for her own alcohol and pharmaceutical pill addiction, which had become serious.

Throughout the last twenty months of her life, Nancy had ample reason to fear for the safety of herself and her child. Whether she stayed out of fear or love for her troubled husband will never be known. In April of 2007, Chris Benoit passed his final WWE "Wellness Program" drug test with flying colors and invited Nancy to accompany him on a WWE tour of the United Kingdom, perhaps in a last-ditch attempt to salvage their relationship. Whatever loyalty she was showing to Chris by staying with him seemed to have been trumped by her responsibility for her son's safety.

In early June of 2007, Nancy Benoit bought Chris a silver cross necklace to commemorate his newfound faith.

Benoit knew that he needed help, but his warped mind only sought it in the wrestling industry that he had destroyed himself for. Numerous veteran wrestlers such as Billy Graham have come forward in the aftermath of the murders to claim that Benoit was avidly seeking them out, telling them he was lonely and asking to go out to dinner. Among the numerous veterans he contacted was drug-addled Howard Stern sideshow Khosrow "The Iron Sheik" Vaziri. "That's a sad state of affairs when you need serious mental help, and the person you go to is the goddamn Iron Sheik," says one ex-WWE writer. "You have to be a real nut to think that a crack-smoking Persian wrestler will be more helpful to you than a psychiatrist."

Shortly before his suicide, Benoit spoke to Robert "Rob Van Dam" Szatkowski, who had recently retired from WWE in the prime of his career to spend time with

his family and live a normal life. "[Benoit] kept saying how
much he loved watching me wrestle, and he said, 'I have
so much respect for you for leaving.' Then he says, 'A lot of
us don't know when to walk away from this business.' It
seemed like he was saying, 'Damn, I wish I could walk
away right now.'"

While Benoit impotently dreamed of leaving, the
pro wrestling mortality conveyor belt kept chugging along:
his "Megadoses" tag partner Shayne "Biff Wellington"
Bower from a predictable steroid-induced heart attack;
WCW colleagues Scott "Bam Bam" Bigelow and
"Sensational" Sherri Martel from drug overdoses; and
Michael "Mike Awesome" Alfonso from suicide by
hanging, whose last days were eerily similar to Benoit's.

His mentor Bad News Allen also died, after publicly
disowning the man whose career he launched and who he
once called his "adopted son." Like Scott Norton, Bad News
Allen took offense that his phone calls were not returned.

MY PHYSICAL ADDRESS IS....

ON JUNE 11, 2007, ONE OF WRESTLING'S BIGGEST
SUPERSTARS DIED ON LIVE TELEVISION: VINCE MCMAHON.
McMahon had made a creative decision more self-
destructive and foolhardy than any of his numerous other
mistakes; an act of such flagrant hubris that it was
immediately recognized as not only tempting fate but as
practically *begging* for a tragedy. McMahon, who as WWE
boss had presided over the premature deaths of scores of
current and former employees, had decided to air a multi-
week storyline about his fictional assassination that
would parody, mock, and undercut every single facet of
pro wrestling's response to death.

Intentionally acting brain-damaged and senile,
Vince McMahon wobbled and tottered through *Raw* as a
parody of the stereotypical wrestling casualty: a broken-
down, decrepit, and mentally deranged old fool. Laughing
at the reaper, McMahon read off a statement that
included the prescient lines, "There has been some

speculation [that] the ECW World Title has had an adverse affect on my psyche; I assure you I am in complete control of my faculties." He would prove not to be. In a nod to the last episode of *The Sopranos*, which was dominating the pop cultural press that month, McMahon ended the show by slowly leaving the arena and entering a white limousine; the cheers of the audience promptly exploded.

On orders from Vince McMahon, WWE put a great deal of effort into making sure that the televised assassination was treated as seriously as possible. The flags at WWE headquarters flew at half-mast; the WWE Web site ran non-stop updates, written tributes from wrestlers, and interviews with explosives and law enforcement experts; press releases were issued that treated the crime as a homicide and stated the FBI was investigating; and actual WWE house counsel Jerry McDevitt held a press conference asking for the press to respect the McMahon family's privacy in their time of bereavement. Despite being a publicly traded, multibillion-dollar company, WWE even violated rule 10b5 of the Securities Exchange Act by falsifying their business records in support of the charade, which drew the ridicule of the *Wall Street Journal*:

> In a news release put out on Business Wire and fed into the company-research pages on Web sites including Yahoo, TheStreet.com and WSJ.com, wrestling promoter WWE reported that.... Chairman Vince McMahon's limousine suddenly exploded after Mr. McMahon got into the vehicle. The release adds: "Although full details have not been disclosed, initial reports indicate that Mr. McMahon is presumed dead. An official investigation into Monday night's events is currently underway."

WWE received the response they wanted: the local Wilkes-Barre police were swamped by calls reporting the murder, and there were reports of candlelight vigils at WWE headquarters in Stamford, Connecticut. When CNBC business reporter Darren Rovell criticized the stupidity and recklessness of the storyline, WWE released a press release stating that he was a suspect in the murder.

Of course, there were those who saw the humor in McMahon's ludicrous decision to do a fictional storyline about wrestling deaths. One letter from "Andrew J. Wallace, PhD" to the *Wrestling Observer* read, "I have never seen anything so singularly fucking incredibly awesome in my entire goddamn life. Tonight, wrestling transcended itself; I'm not even sure what I just saw. It was art. Tonight's episode of *Raw* contained multitudes." On countless Internet wrestling message boards, including the ubiquitous "Wrestler Death Pool," savvy wrestling fans bet each other how long it would take for a WWE wrestler to actually die and thus humiliate WWE by forcing them to abandon the fictional death in order to refrain from belittling the real death.

Four days later, former WWE star Sherri Martel died of a drug overdose at the age of forty-nine, but she wasn't famous enough to sabotage the angle. Her death was reported on the WWE Web site beneath headline stories about the murder of Vince McMahon.

On the June 12 *ECW* and June 15 *Smackdown* episodes, Vince McMahon dug both his figurative and fictional grave even deeper. Both shows were spectacularly tasteless, note-for-note parodies of the Pillman, Hart, and Guerrero memorial tributes. Both shows began with an announcer asking for the audience to stand for a moment of silence and ten-bell salute in Vince McMahon's memory; the *Smackdown* show even had the gumption to ask the wrestlers to stand onstage during the ten-bell salute and impersonate the grief they displayed during Owen and Eddy's tributes. When the live audience members booed at having their intelligence and the memories of other wrestlers insulted, grimacing announcer John Bradshaw Layfield grumbled, "This is pathetic. This man is the father of two children and the grandfather of three...the people who are catcalling and booing are...embarrassing to the city of Philadelphia."

For the rest of the two shows, the announcers spoke exclusively in what is known as "The Owen Voice," the somber, pointedly restrained, monotone speaking style made famous by Jim Ross in the aftermath of Owen's death. From that night on, whenever WWE announcers were confronted with a real-life tragedy, they would mimic the Owen Voice as a handy rhetorical trick to break the fourth wall and let fans know that whatever was being said was explicitly outside of the fictional realm of pro wrestling and should be taken seriously. The Owen Voice became a sort of unspoken ceasefire agreement between wrestling promoter and wrestling fan; under it, promoters would suspend all attempts to manipulate or bullshit the fans in return for the fans' willingness to turn off their bullshit detectors and take the words spoken in that one tone of voice at face value. Fans were appalled that the Owen Voice was being used for McMahon's ridiculous storyline.

The crowd's negative reaction to the exploitative angle was one reason why the arena microphones were turned off while the taped, out-of-character "tributes" to Mr. McMahon were aired. These were delivered in a manner and before a background identical to those given to Eddy Guerrero twenty months before, a fact that made it all the more uncomfortable and inappropriate when Eddy's nephew Chavo was trotted out to deliver the passive-aggressive eulogy that: "[McMahon] built this business by being a jerk at times, and, if he wasn't a jerk, this business wouldn't be what it is today. If you love this business like I do, you should thank Mr. McMahon for being the jerk that he was." One can only imagine the Philly crowd's response to Teddy Long, the black general manager of *Smackdown*, as he was comparing Vince McMahon to Martin Luther King. "In my *Smackdown* general manager's office, there are two pictures on the back of the wall. They mean something to me.... There is a picture of Dr. Martin Luther King, and there is a picture of Mr. McMahon. My theory for those two pictures are that Mr. McMahon made it happen, and Dr. King made it all possible."

The Internet fanbase's response to these mock memorial shows was unsurprisingly naïve, as there were thousands of longtime wrestling fans who only at this point realized that wrestling was a crass, callous, and stupid form of entertainment. Many critiques from hardcore fans, however, were cynical and scathing in the extreme, like Deathvalleydriver.com-poster KCook's comment that, "You'd have to be without the faintest scintilla of compassion or decency to actually ask these people, especially Vickie Guerrero, to assume the solemn and sacred 'we are shook because our friend died' pose.... The idea that Vince McMahon and his colorful troupe of performers are burnt out husks who are incapable of human emotion doesn't shock me.... [The original, serious tribute shows] were far more offensive than the exploitation of their nauseating fake emotion is—people pretending to cry, pretending that fake fights are a good way to honor someone who died because of fake fighting, pretending they still have their capacity to feel pain."

But no one provided more piercing insight into how McMahon's death storyline painted WWE into a tragicomic corner than Tom Karro-Gassner of wrestling blog Segunda Caida:

> The tributes to Owen, Eddie, and Pillman aren't geniune [sic] moments. They're works. They're effective works. Moments where wrestling fans might question the object of their affection and are distracted. Instead of going "Wow this sleazy profession [sic] killed Owen, Pillman or Eddie." Audience goes "Wow look at all the love...they really care for each other and worry about peoples families." Tributes are a hustle to avoid questions of to what degree the WWE is complicit in a wrestlers death.... This angle has exposed the buisness [sic] by showing everyone how obvious the "work" in a "tribute" is. Maybe they really believe in the effectiveness of the wellness policy. But my guess is that there will be deaths of active stars in the future. Maybe [Mark "The Undertaker"] Calloway will take too many painkillers while riding his motorcycle. Maybe [bodybuilder Dave] Batista's heart will

explode.... The tribute hustle is a work that they
will need to have available to them in the future.
Exposing the work may not be a good long term
decision.

In the week prior to the murders, Nancy
discovered that Chris had purchased a new life insurance
policy with his ex-wife and their children as beneficiaries.
When Nancy insisted that Chris make Daniel and herself
the beneficiaries instead, Chris refused, leading to an
extremely violent fight. Afterwards, Nancy told her friend
Pam Clark, Brian Hildebrand's widow, that she kept
meticulous records of how Benoit has mistreated her in a
safety deposit box in preparation for a flight and divorce.
Nancy made Clark promise that, if anything happened to
her, she would inform police that Benoit was responsible.
When police opened Nancy's safe deposit box, they only
found photos showing physical abuse from *before* her
relationship with Benoit.

On Thursday, June 21, Benoit called a friend to
reserve a secluded spot on his property so that the Benoit
family could watch the Peachtree City fireworks on July 4.
On that same day, Nancy called one of her friends in a
panic and said, "If anything happens to me, look at Chris."
On Friday, June 22, Benoit visited the family doctor, Phil
Astin, who was prescribing Benoit a ten-month dosage of
anabolic steroids every month in addition to copious
amounts of painkillers for both Nancy and Chris.
According to the Drug Enforcement Agency, Astin had
written prescriptions for one million dosages of controlled
substances in the past two years, which means that the
patients of one smalltime doctor in Carrollton, GA, were
consuming on-average 1,370 prescribed doses a day. In
other words, the last person Chris Benoit visited before
killing his family was his drug dealer.

From May 30 to June 19, Astin prescribed Nancy
Benoit 360 pills of the addictive painkiller Hydrocodone
(marketed as Lorcet and Vicodin). Over the last twenty-
four days of her life, 278 of those 360 Lorcet pills were

consumed, an average of over eleven extremely strong painkillers per day for a slender suburban housewife. In the two weeks prior to his meltdown, Chris Benoit polished off his own prescription of 120 Lorcets, and, over the bloody last two days of his life, Benoit consumed thirty-five more Lorcets from his June 22 prescription. When combined with Chris' brain damage and competing drug addictions and Nancy's own reputed alcoholism, this massive painkiller habit suggests that the final hours of both Chris and Nancy Benoit's lives were spent in a bewildering, heavily sedated haze.

After returning from his appointment with Dr. Astin on June 22, Chris Benoit was seen barbecuing outside with Daniel at his side. That evening, in addition to her normal diet of alcohol and Lorcets, Nancy also consumed Hydromorphone pain pills and Alprazolam (Xanax) anti-anxiety pills. We have no way of knowing whether she did so under duress; Benoit himself had Xanax and Lorcet in his system. At 9:25 p.m., someone police assume to be Nancy called information to ask for the phone number for the police department; at 9:32 and 9:33 she left two apparently normal messages on her neighbor's answering machine.

Shortly afterwards, Chris Benoit duct-taped her hands and feet in an upstairs family room on the opposite side of the house from Daniel's room. We are unsure how violently she resisted Chris Benoit—if she had, could she have won the fight? The ambiguity has lead some to indulge in the asinine speculation that given her kinky S&M wrestling character, she may have agreed to be tied up. Unable to move, Nancy was pinned to the floor with a knee to her spine and strangled with a TV cable. When she feebly struggled to get free, Benoit most likely slammed her head into the floor. Wrapped in a towel, she was left there to decompose with a Bible at her side.

According to some reports, Benoit went swimming the next day with Daniel Benoit while his mother's corpse rotted in the upstairs bedroom. Though the precise moment of death is impossible to pinpoint, some time from the early morning to the afternoon of Saturday, June 23, Benoit crept into his son's room, doped Daniel with Xanax, and suffocated him. Daniel's corpse exhibited bruising across the face and one arm, with no apparent harm done to his throat. Judging by this distinctive wound pattern, Benoit likely killed his own child using his wrestling finishing move, the Crippler Crossface, in a room covered with photos and posters of him performing that very move. Like most of his opponents who took the Crippler Crossface, Chris Benoit's son had needle marks on his body and a history of bodybuilding drug use. According to the police, Benoit had been injecting his normally sized son with human growth hormone. A Bible was placed at his side. Daniel was seven years old.

Afterwards, Chris Benoit conducted an Internet search looking for information on the Old Testament prophet Elijah. One of Elijah's greatest feats was persuading God to resurrect the body of a dead boy.

Hours later, Benoit was still alive: why? He had a WWE booking to make! It's not surprising that a man so disoriented and fixated on wrestling, who murdered his own child with his character's wrestling move, would seriously consider returning to the one place where felt happy: in the ring. While Daniel died, did Benoit hear Jim Ross announcing in the background? Was he screaming, "TAP! TAP!"? Was the crowd booing or cheering? There's no reason to believe Benoit was above working through this tragedy like he had so many others—the question is how long would he have been able to keep up the charade? Until Nancy's parents got suspicious around the holiday season?

According to police, Benoit rescheduled his flight so that he could make the next WWE show in Beaumont, Texas, as planned on Saturday. Since the later flight time meant Benoit would be unable to meet up with friend Chavo Guerrero as usual before that night's show, Benoit left a message for Guerrero to let him know that he'd be late for the show but would make the booking.

When Guerrero called him back, a strained Benoit repeated his story, which supports that it was a premeditated lie. In a "forced" tone, Benoit told Chavo he loved him before hanging up. Sensing that Benoit was hiding something, Eddy's nephew called Benoit again to ask if anything was wrong. Benoit told him Nancy and Daniel were sick with food poisoning, but that "Everything's fine. I'll still make tonight's show."

Afterwards, a discombobulated Benoit wandered outside, which once again supports the notion that he had not settled on killing himself. His family had been dead for twelve hours or more. Had he slept afterwards? Was he considering making a run for it, fulfilling his wrestling dates until he was discovered, or getting one more match in? There's no way of knowing, and even the most outlandish speculation is feasible considering Benoit's extremely disturbed mental state. A female neighbor saw Benoit puttering about outside and was told in an "extremely odd" conversation about Nancy and Chris' sickness. Benoit was apparently not crying or in any other way ostentatiously displaying his grief. Spooked by human contact, Benoit went back inside. When a neighbor Nancy called the previous night returned her call, Benoit embarked on an unending description of the spectacular *Exorcist*-like case of food poisoning that Nancy and Daniel were afflicted with.

Canadian wrestling journalist and friend Greg Oliver e-mailed Benoit that day to ask his feelings about the steroid-induced death of his former tag partner Biff Wellington. Since wrestling news moves quickly, he also gave his "best wishes" since he had heard that a family member was ill. He received no response. Benoit was hemmed in by death.

At 3:53 a.m. on Sunday, June 24, Chavo received a text message on his phone: "My physical address is 130 Green Meadow Lane, Fayetteville, Georgia 30215." Two minutes later, he received another: "The dogs are in the enclosed pool area. Garage side door is open." He then received the first message from Nancy's number three more times. Satisfied that someone would come and investigate, Benoit went down to his in-house gym with a half-empty bottle of wine. Placing the wine next to his lat-pulldown weight machine, he removed the machine's handlebar and sat down as if he were going to exercise. With a towel wrapped around his throat, Benoit tied the weight machine's steel cord around the towel, adjusted the weight to the comparatively light weight of 240 pounds, and released the pressure. With his legendarily strong neck muscles and the moderate pressure applied, his death was likely slow, yet there was no sign of resistance.

When Benoit's father was informed of the deaths of his son, daughter-in-law, and grandson, he never considered that Chris could be responsible. Chris murdering Nancy was "very plausible" in his words, but it was completely inconceivable that he could harm Daniel.

On the day of his death, Benoit—like Eddy Guerrero before him—was scheduled to win one of the WWE world titles. Instead, he missed his second straight show. Fourteen hours before the police discovered her body, a prankster on the online encyclopedia Wikipedia made an edit claiming that Benoit missed that night's show because of "the death of his wife Nancy." It was just a lucky guess, though Dave Meltzer later said that once you heard Benoit had missed *two* shows, you knew most likely someone had died.

WWE was in Corpus Christi, Texas, on the afternoon of Monday, January 25, preparing for that night's *Raw*. The production staff was decorating the backstage area with funeral bouquets; a hearse was waiting for a test run; writer Ed Koskey was preparing a eulogy. *Raw* was to be headlined by a live, on-air funeral for Vince McMahon, which is why most WWE staff members that afternoon learned of the slaying of the Benoit family while surrounded by funeral arrangements. Some were even dressed for a wake.

Chris Benoit was no Sherri Martel; his death, let alone the death of his wife and child, was more than enough to derail the RIP Vince storyline. Having utterly discredited their tribute show format and implied that WWE fans who had bought into them were naïve buffoons, there was no way the resurrected Vince and his crew could deliver a live tribute show to one of WWE's biggest and most beloved stars immediately after they spent two weeks pissing all over the very idea. The crowd response could be embarrassing; Vince had no choice but to cancel the live in-ring portion of *Raw*.

Early in the afternoon, Vince decided to air a pre-taped, canned tribute show to the Benoit family, which would be accompanied by live arena appearances by himself and the announcers. There was already suspicion backstage about Benoit's guilt: who the hell is going to be tough enough to break into *Chris Benoit*'s house and kill him? When, according to numerous sources, later that afternoon the news was leaked to WWE that Benoit was officially the primary suspect in the murders, Vince was hamstrung by his own ego.

Addressing the Benoit family tragedy directly would leave WWE with two choices: airing a tribute show that risked being seen as a lavish three-hour tribute to a child-murderer; or producing a neutral, news-report style program that acknowledged Benoit as a suspect in the murders, which risked being seen as a desecration of his memory if he was later exonerated. The only sane option was to run a disclaimer at the beginning of the timeslot that said *WWE Raw* was cancelled in the wake of the slaying of the Benoit family, take the financial hit and let the network fill the time or air *any* rerun in its place.

Unfortunately, Vince McMahon doesn't cancel shows, no matter what the circumstances. After the Owen Hart debacle and his self-righteous defense of his decision, he had bricked himself into that corner for life. To cancel a show now would appear to be admitting that he was wrong, both about the "show must always go on" Owen

Hart decision and about dismissing criticism that his death storyline would make it impossible to air future tribute shows. That was simply unacceptable; McMahon was willing to preside over a company whose business practices killed off its employees at an incredible rate, but he drew the line at admitting he was wrong.

McMahon decided to go forward with the tribute show to the baby-murdering junkie, making an already juicy news story—the O.J. of pro wrestling, driven mad by *Incredible Hulk*-esque "roid rage"—into a guaranteed feeding frenzy for merchants of mock indignation and manufactured outrage like Bill O'Reilly, Glenn Beck, and Nancy Grace. The media carnival would lead to a federal probe into steroids and dubious online pharmacies, eventually catching dozens of WWE stars in the dragnet and exposing the WWE's drug policy as a sham.

Interspersed between clips from Benoit's *Hard Knocks* retrospective DVD, the WWE talent paid tribute to Chris Benoit's life. Adam "Edge" Copeland admitted that Benoit "would be hot at me for crying" over the death of his own *family*, bringing to mind the weeping New Japan referee Benoit supposedly consoled with "What a gay bitch!" Paul Levesque expressed his admiration through a touching story about how Benoit had disciplined a rookie by forcing him to do 1,000 Hindu squats in front of the locker room and then 500 more the next day on his sore, immobile legs. It was John Cena, however, who at least captured half the story: "He truly lived for the business."

Chris Benoit truly died for the business. He did fatal damage to himself in a multitude of ways to fulfill his childhood dream, even though he knew that the fulfillment of that dream for a man of his size and personality would require unimaginable physical and mental sacrifices. It is exclusively Chris Benoit's fault that he bought into that dream, the Wrestling Con, and made those suicidal sacrifices.

"The world [of wrestling] doesn't push you to the depths of darkness. *You* do." Chris Benoit was right, but that doesn't exonerate the men like Vince McMahon whose business practices ensured that the road to pro wrestling success must pass right through the Depths of Darkness. Vince McMahon never made anyone walk down that road, but he did pave the way and reward those who made the journey with fame, wealth, and a chance to fulfill their dreams. To claim that he has no culpability when he rewards odious and suicidal behavior—using the free will of his victims as his scapegoat—is to suggest that the person who pays a hitman to kill has committed no sin.

The devil doesn't make anyone sell his soul. He simply makes such a compelling offer that the desperate, the dumb, and the dysfunctional agree to do so of their own volition. To my knowledge Vince McMahon has never killed anyone, but he has unapologetically tempted hundreds who don't know any better to pursue their own destruction and death for his financial profit.

Thanks

First of all, I'd like to thank my agent, Andrew Lownie, for brokering the deal for this book and Henrietta Tiefenthaler at Phoenix Books for her belief in the project and her incomparable assistance along the way. The patience she displayed with me was incredible. I am deeply indebted to my gifted editor, Julie McCarron, who convinced me to rethink my original plan to commit many gratuitous and ghastly crimes against the English language. The faults in this book likely lie wherever I ignored her counsel. Also at Phoenix, I'd like to thank Alina Poniewaz and Sonia Fiore for their tireless hard work in preparing the final manuscript.

I'd next like to thank my mother, Jeannie Morris, and my wife, Melissa, for their bottomless patience with my behavior and their assistance preparing and editing this book.

To all the wrestling personalities around the world who risked their jobs and reputations to speak with me anonymously, thank you for trusting that I'd keep your identity a secret.

For the American sections of the book, I thank my friend Dr. Ranjan Chhibber, who went through immense trouble to secure exclusive information and sources. David Bixenspan and Zach Arnold (puroresupower.com) also provided numerous favors, large and small, during the course of this project.

Punctual Paul Heyman: thanks for being deposed.

I'd also like to thank Mike Pontarelli, Kenny Gallo (whose memoir about his life in the Mafia you can find out about at MatthewRandazzo.com), Dan Madigan (author of *Mondo Lucha a Go-Go*), Domenic Cotter (President of Sound Off Productions, Inc.), Chad Damiani, Scott Norton, Sheldon Goldberg (necwwrestling.com), David Marquez, Howard Brody, Corey Morgan, Osamu Nishimura, Simon Inoki (igf.jp), Kurt "Vandal Drummond" Brown, Eddie Edwards, Steve Sims, Jose Fernandez, Bob Barnett (BobBarnett.com), Stan Gordon, Daniel Lyttelton, Stuart Max (puroresufan.com), Glenn Tsunekawa, and anyone I've forgotten who assisted the writing of this book in any way.

It would have been impossible to write the history of the pro wrestling industry without the work done by Dave Meltzer at the *Wrestling Observer* newsletter (Wrestlingobserver.com) and Bryan Alvarez at the *Figure Four Weekly* (Figurefourweekly.com). Their work together on the *Wrestling Observer Live* radio show was invaluable, as well, and I'd also like to thank Dave and Bryan for their help in answering various questions I had during the course of the project.

Wade Keller and Bruce Mitchell at the *Pro Wrestling Torch* (pwtorch.com) provided great insight into the wrestling business over the past twenty years, as did the various people behind the shoot video series at RF Video (RFVideo.com), Highspots (Highspots.com), and Ring of Honor (ROHWrestling.com). The historical research done by Paul MacArthur and David Skolnick of the *Wrestling Perspective* newsletter (wrestlingperspective.com) was also a priceless resource.

Lastly, I would like to thank the photographers who made their work available for the book: Dave Layne, Bob Leonard, Adrian Guy Crook (www.adriancrook.com), Colin Williamson, Terence Kelly, and Danilo S. Nuestro.

Bibliography

BOOKS

Assael, Shaun and Mooneyham, Mike. *Sex, Lies, and Headlocks: The Real Story of Vince McMahon and the World Wrestling Federation.* New York: Crown Publishers, 2002.

Billington, Tom and Coleman, Alison. *Pure Dynamite: The Price You Pay for Wrestling Stardom.* Etobicoke, Ontario: Winding Stair Press, 2001.

Bischoff, Eric with Roberts, Jeremy. *Controversy Creates Cash.* New York: World Wrestling Entertainment, 2006.

Blassie, Classy Freddie with Greenberg, Keith Elliot. *The Legends of Wrestling: Classy Freddie Blassie—Listen, You Pencil Necked Geeks.* New York: World Wrestling Entertainment, 2003.

Flair, Ric with Greenberg, Keith Elliot. *Ric Flair: To Be the Man.* New York: World Wrestling Entertainment, 2005.

Foley, Mick. *Have a Nice Day: A Tale of Blood and Sweatsocks.* New York: Regan Books, 1999.

Foley, Mick. *Foley is Good: And The Real World Is Faker Than Pro Wrestling*. New York: HarperCollins, 2001.

Foley, Mick. *The Hardcore Diaries*. New York: Pocket Books, 2007.

Funk, Terry with Williams, Scott. *Terry Funk: More Than Just Hardcore*. Champaign, IL: Sports Publishing, L.L.C., 2005.

Guerrero, Eddie and Krugman, Michael. *Cheating Death, Stealing Life: The Eddie Guerrero Story*. New York: Pocket Books, 2005.

Hart, Bret. *Hitman: My Real Life in the Cartoon World of Wrestling*. New York: Random House Canada, 2007.

Hogan, Hollywood Hulk. *Hollywood Hulk Hogan*. New York: World Wrestling Entertainment, 2003.

Hyatt, Missy with Salzburg, Charles & Goldblatt, Mark. *Missy Hyatt: First Lady of Wrestling*. Toronto, Canada: ECW Press, 2001.

Jericho, Chris with Fornatale, Peter Thomas. *A Lion's Tale: Around the World in Spandex*. New York: Grand Central Publishing, 2007.

Johnson, Steven et al. *Benoit: Wrestling with the Horror that Destroyed a Family and Crippled a Sport*. Toronto, Canada: ECW Press, 2007.

Kaplan, David E. and Dubro, Alec. *Yakuza: Japan's Criminal Underworld*. Berkeley, California: University of California Press, 2003.

McCoy, Heath. *Pain and Passion: The History of Stampede Wrestling*. Toronto, Canada: ECW Press, 2007.
Meltzer, Dave. *Tributes II: Remembering More of the*

World's Greatest Professional Wrestlers. Champaign, IL: Sports Publishing, L.L.C., 2004.

Reynolds, R.D. and Alvarez, Bryan. *Wrestlecrap and Figure Four Weekly Present: The Death of WCW.* Toronto: ECW Press, 2004.

Rhodes, Dusty with Brody, Howard. *Dusty Rhodes: Reflections of an American Dream.* Champaign, IL: Sports Publishing L.L.C., 2005.

Watts, Bill with Williams, Scott. *The Cowboy and The Cross: The Bill Watts Story.* Toronto, Canada: ECW Press, 2006.

Williams, Scott E. *Hardcore History: The Extremely Unauthorized Story of ECW.* Champaign, IL: Sports Publishing L.L.C., 2006.

NEWSLETTERS

Keller, Wade et al. *Pro Wrestling Torch*: 6/21/93-12/7/02.

Meltzer, Dave. *Wrestling Observer* Newsletter: 2/19/90-3/17/08.

RADIO

Wrestling Observer Live. Dave Meltzer and Brian Alvarez. Episodes: 7/8/07, 9/2/07, 10/28/07, 11/4/07.

WEBSITES

Butikas, Jake & Hansbrough, Brian. "Interview with Maxx Payne." *Pinfalls.com.* 12/8/02. <http://www.pinfalls.com/maxx.html> (Accessed January 19, 2008).

Clevett, Jason. "Wrestlers open up about Benoit tragedy" *Slam! Wrestling*. 6/28/07. <*http*://slam.canoe.ca/Slam/Wrestling/Benoit/2007/06/28/4 299036.html> (Accessed November 30, 2007).

Curatolo, Fred. "20 Questions with Chris Benoit: The Crippler just a family guy." *Slam! Wrestling / Edmonton Sun*. <http://slam.canoe.ca/SlamWrestlingBenoit/benoit_00ma y28.html> (Accessed December 30, 2000).

East Coast J (Internet username). "Wrestling Observer Newsletter Back Issue Quotes." 9/14/05. < http://board.deathvalleydriver.com/index.php?showtopic= 294> (Accessed November 30, 2007).

Hanrahan, Tim. "News Flash: Pro Wrestling Is Fake." *Wall Street Journal Online*. 6/6/07. <http://online.wsj.com/article_email/SB118196318952337 549-1MyQjAxMDE3ODExNzkxNjczWj.html> (Accessed November 2, 2007).

Kobayashi, Takanori. "Pro Wrestlers Uncommon Sense." *Japan Today*. 8/9/02. <http://www.japantoday.com/jp/book/128/all> (Accessed January 2, 2008).

Laible, Don. "Nancy Benoit—The lady I knew ... and liked" *The Keeler Show*. 9/16/07. <http://www.keelerradio.com/blog/blog.php?bid=90> (Accessed November 30, 2007).

Lewis, Michael. "The Last Days of Chris Benoit." *Maxim Online*. <http://www.maximonline.com/Thelastdaysofchrisbenoit/ articles/1/9733.aspx> (Accessed November 24, 2007).

MacArthur, Paul and Skolnick, David. "Fake...Working Through Wrestling's Past: The Wrestling Perspective

Newspaper Archive Project." *The Wrestling Perspective.*
<http://wrestlingperspective.com/working.html>
(Accessed December 23, 2007).

Oliver, Greg. "Trevor Murdoch 'confused' by Benoit
tragedy." *Slam! Wrestling.* 7/30/07.
<http://slam.canoe.ca/Slam/Wrestling/Benoit/2007/07/26/4
370048.html> (Accessed November 30, 2007).

Oliver, Greg. "The revealing Benoit emails." *Slam!
Wrestling.* 6/30/07.
<http://slam.canoe.ca/Slam/Wrestling/Benoit/2007/06/29/4
301351-ca.html> (Accessed November 30, 2007).

Pro Wrestling Torch VIP
<http://www.pwtorch.com/members> 1987-2007.

Storm, Lance. "Otto Wanz: CWA-Catch." *Storm Wrestling.*
8/20/07.
< http://www.stormwrestling.com/082007.html> (Accessed
12/13/07).

Tate, Rich & Brawler, Mick N. "Aftermath of a Tragedy."
Georgia Wrestling History. 2007. Georgia Wrestling
History, Inc.
<http://www.georgiawrestlinghistory.com/benoit-astin-
steroids-wwe/home.html > (Accessed November 24, 2007).

Zerr, Scott. "Fans give Benoit a day to remember." *Slam!
Wrestling.* 4/16/04.
<http://slam.canoe.ca/Slam/Wrestling/2004/04/16/423389.
html> (Accessed january 24, 2008).

"Heavy Petting: A gruesome death hits Japan's already
ailing national sport." *The Economist—Asia.* 10/11/07.
<http://www.economist.com/world/asia/displaystory.cfm?s
tory_id=9963190> (Accessed November 30, 2007).

TELEVISION, VIDEOS, DVD

Billy Jack Haynes: Shoot Interview. RF Video.

Bad News Allen: Shoot Interview. RF Video, 2005.

Bam Bam Bigelow: Shoot Interview. RF Video, 1997.

Bobby Heenan: Shoot Interview. Highspots, 2004.

Cryme Tyme: Shoot Interview. RF Video, 2007.

Diamond Dallas Page. RF Video, 2007.

Eddy Guerrero: Shoot Interview. RF Video.

David Schultz: Shoot Interview. RF Video, 2006.

Forever Hardcore. Big Vision, 2005.

Face Off With Honky Tonk Man & Raven. RF Video, 2007.

Face Off Volume 2—When Worlds Collide. RF Video, 2007.

The Fifth Estate. Canadian Broadcasting Corporation. "Fight to the Death." February 5, 2008.

Full Case of Tales. Highspots.

Gaea Girls. British Broadcasting Corporation and Vixen Films. 2000.

Kevin Nash: Shoot Interview. RF Video, 2007.

Kevin Sullivan: Shoot Interview. RF Video, 2001.

Marty Jannetty: Shoot Interview. RF Video, 2004.

The Nasty Boys: Shoot Interview. RF Video.

Off the Record with Michael Landsberg. The Sports Network, 2004.

Ole Anderson: Shoot Interview. Highspots.

The Outlaws: Shoot Video. RF Video, 2006.

The Outsiders: Shoot Interview. RF Video, 2007.

Pro Wrestling's Ultimate Insiders Volume 1: Inside the WWE. Big Vision.

The Road Warriors: Shoot Interview. RF Video, 2000.

Ron Simmons Shoot Interview. Highspots.

Scott Hall: Shoot Interview. RF Video, 2007.

Scott Norton: Shoot Interview. RF Video.

Shane Douglas: Shoot Interview. RF Video, 2003.

Straight Shootin' with Jim Mitchell. Ring of Honor Video, 2005.

Straight Shootin'with Raven & Sandman: Volume 1. Ring of Honor Video, 2005.

Straight Shootin'with Raven & Sandman: Volume 2. Ring of Honor Video, 2006.

Straight Shootin' with Jim Cornette & Bill Watts: Volume 1. Ring of Honor Video, 2005.

Straight Shootin' with Jim Cornette & Bobby "The Brain" Heenan. Ring of Honor Video, 2005.

Sabu: Shoot Interview. RF Video.

Straight Shootin' with Jim Cornette & Bill Watts: Volume 2. Ring of Honor Video, 2005.

Tammy Sytch: Shoot Interview. RF Video, 2006.

Team 3D: Shoot Interview. RF Video and Highspots.

Ultimate Warrior: Shoot Interview. Ringside Collectibles.